THE POLITICS OF

REPRESENTATION

Lying Down Together: Law, Metaphor, and Theology
Milner S. Ball

Politics and Ambiguity
William E. Connolly

Machiavelli and the History of Prudence
Eugene Garver

The Rhetoric of Economics
Donald N. McCloskey

Therapeutic Discourse and Socratic Dialogue: A Cultural Critique
Tullio Maranhão

The Rhetoric of the Human Sciences: Language and Argument
in Public Affairs
John S. Nelson, Allan Megill, and Donald N. McCloskey, eds.

The Politics of Representation: Writing Practices in Biography,
Photography, and Policy Analysis
Michael J. Shapiro

The Unspeakable: Discourse, Dialogue, and Rhetoric in the
Postmodern World
Stephen A. Tyler

Heracles' Bow: Essays on the Rhetoric and Poetics of the Law
James Boyd White

The Politics of Representation

WRITING PRACTICES IN BIOGRAPHY,

PHOTOGRAPHY, AND POLICY ANALYSIS

MICHAEL J. SHAPIRO

THE UNIVERSITY OF WISCONSIN PRESS

Published 1988

The University of Wisconsin Press
114 North Murray Street
Madison, Wisconsin 53715

The University of Wisconsin Press, Ltd.
1 Gower Street
London WC1E 6HA, England

P95.8
·554
1988

First printing

Printed in the United States of America

For LC CIP information see the colophon

ISBN 0-299-11630-1

To my mother,
Adelaide Lopiansky Shapiro,
a teacher

CONTENTS

ILLUSTRATIONS

Illustrations

PREFACE

When Flaubert's characters Bouvard and Pécuchet team up and begin to move in social domains they had not previously known, they find many of their experiences unintelligible ("We don't know," said Bouvard, "what is happening in our own household").[1] Rather than withdrawing to their previous terra cognita, however, they confront their ignorance with various kinds of contemporary knowledge. Finding that the "facts" do not adequately speak for themselves, they turn to imaginative genres. For example, deciding that "without imagination history is defective,"[2] they turn to the historical novel, beginning with Sir Walter Scott. Nevertheless, the "real" remains for them illusory despite their stubborn attempts to find departments in the institutionalized system of worldly knowledge that will finally coincide with an immediate (empirical) reality. While the folly of their investigations, based on the assumption that the "real" awaits a particular mode of knowing, supplies the humor of the novel, it supplies, as well, a disclosure about representation that is pertinent to *my* investigations in the chapters that follow. It is disclosed that representations do not imitate reality but are the practices through which things take on meaning and value; to the extent that a representation is regarded as realistic, it is because it is so familiar it operates transparently.

For example, photography, the subject of Chapter 4, is one of the representational practices that has become so naturalized that, as I put it, "The grammar of discussions of photographs tends to approximate the grammar of face-to-face encounters; 'this is John' is an intelligible and appropriate utterance whether one is introducing someone to John or showing them a picture of John." It is a simple matter, of course, to impeach the representational verisimilitude of the photograph, for among other things, it is a two-dimensional rendering of something we experience in three dimensions when photographic mediation is absent, and we are tempted to say, simply, that the photograph is, for some purposes, an imperfect substitute for having a person actually "present" to us. This is seemingly just a case of a difference between a copy and the "real," which the grammar of the statement fails to register. However, could we not make more problematic the so-called real and ask whether or not another person is ever actually present (i.e., not represented) to us? There is the case, for example, when we know a person, "John," during his earlier years and encounter him again in his older ones and sense the inadequacy of a grammar that suggests that the contemporary embodiment is a stand-in for the John who existed before. We remain steadfast in identifying the older version of John as the same person only insofar as we bracket temporality in our identification of persons.

Thus, to the extent that seeing a photograph of John tends to produce the grammar of face-to-face interactions, it is because of a similar way of treating *two representations*, of rendering two practices as compatible, not of recognizing a copy of the "real." In simple terms, then, representation is the absence of presence, but because the real is never wholly present to us — how it is real for us is always mediated through some representational practice — we lose something when we think of representation as mimetic.[3] What we lose, in general, is insight into the institutions, actions, and episodes through which the real has been fashioned, a fashioning that has not been so much a matter of immediate acts of consciousness by persons in everyday life as it has been a historically developing kind of imposition, now largely institutionalized in the prevailing kinds of meanings deeply inscribed on things, persons, and structures. Therefore, to read the "real" as a text that has been produced (written) is to disclose an aspect of human conduct that is fugitive in approaches that collapse the *process* of inscription into a static reality.

More specifically, committed to the view that the world of meaningful entities and aggregates should be treated as texts whose productions are hidden within the familiar modes of speaking/writing, both in everyday life and the language of inquiry of the social sciences, my analyses are directed to the dimensions of power and authority, in short, to the politics implicit in these texts. Accordingly, my discussions seek to render politically relevant the rhetoric or writing practices through which we have tended to naturalize the objects of representation in the practices of inquiry or the writing genres that give us public policy, accounts of lives, foreign policy, and visual images. And I attempt to discern the more radical and distancing modes of writing practice that have a politicizing effect by making the objects of representation problematic and ambiguous, thereby making possible the recognition that what we have regarded as political realities could be rendered otherwise.

Thus, in each chapter, my discussion contrasts what I regard as pious versus impious modes of representation, the former having the effect of reproducing or reinforcing the prevailing modes of power and authority and the latter tending to challenge them. Because I want to extend political analysis and I assume that there is a radical entanglement between textual and political practices, my discussions privilege the latter mode. Conceptually and, to some extent, stylistically this book issues a plea for treating the language of inquiry less as an occasion for clarity and precision than as an opportunity for disruption and transgression, for writing peculiarly in order to disclose that what has made for intelligibility and coherence in our analyses is not the intelligible world but our intelligibility-producing practices.

However, one cannot be wholly unintelligible while exposing the practices of intelligibility; analysis and criticism of this kind must push off from shore but keep the land in sight. But my off-shore position may make one wonder at the rapidly shifting views and different land masses (domains of discourse) on which I focus. I would like to be able to claim that my concern with representation as a political practice provides a tight coherence both within and among the four studies in this book, but I am aware that many readers will not be able easily to domesticate my wanderings within this general theme. Much of what directs my writing is the dialogic element of my text. I address diverse readers, attempting at different times to confront the interpretive codes of different modes of political analysis. As my prose thinks out loud, it is acknowledging diverse reading styles — at times that of the committed phenomenologist who emphasizes the meaning production of immediate consciousness, at times the empiricist who privileges the meaning-delegating power of things, and at times it is a particular ideational commitment responsible for naturalizing and making a fixed set of objects out of what I want to treat as a polyguous text.

While I hope my implied readers and the dialogics of my statements are marked, I recognize that the variety of contexts I address threatens those aspects of intelligibility I am trying to preserve. For example, in Chapter 2 I treat Freud's analysis of Leonardo da Vinci's life and work and analyses by more empirically oriented psychohistorians together. I do this to draw attention to the problem of writing, not as some social scientists would, to accumulate propositions or assertions about lives in order to make another deposit in the knowledge fund. Freud's sensitivity to representation, his deep and theoretically guided suspicion about what stands for what in the scripting practices of others, was nevertheless mystified in some of his own writing, which he treated as a set of unproblematic assertions whose value related to the science of psychoanalysis. So much the worse, then, for writers less sensitive to the problem of representation, e.g., some of those known as psycho-historians.

Ultimately, of course, although I am responsible for my text's inadequacies, I cannot control and therefore be responsible for the various ways it will be read. I shall simply hope that those who go beyond this preface will find an approach that will help them discover a world of at least potential political contention where many find an unproblematic, pacified world of things. What remains is to thank some of those who bear the major responsibility for helping me to appreciate the pertinence of regarding social theorists and analysts as writers.

For the past several years I have participated in a study group on the relationship between literary and political theory comprised primarily of colleagues and students in English and Political Science departments of the University of Hawaii. My special thanks to the group's earliest and continuing participants: Christina Baccalega, Joe Chadwick, Craig Howes, Folke Lindahl, Allan McGregor, John Rieder, Brook Thomas, and Phyllis Turnbull, and to many others, too numerous to mention, who have participated subsequently. In addition, many friends and colleagues have offered support and criticism during the preparation of this book. I am grateful to Bill Carroll, Bill Connolly, Fred Dallmayr, Tom Dumm, Fred Fortin, Ed Friedman, Peter Manicas, John McDermott, Deane Neubauer, Vince Rafael, and Tracy Strong.

THE POLITICS OF
REPRESENTATION

1

THE PROBLEM OF IDEOLOGY

LOCATING THE POLITICAL

ANALYST/WRITER

Introduction: Politicizing Styles

Between the third and fifth centuries there occurred a radical shift in the way Mediterranean people construed human agency. Associated with the rise of the Christian church was the idea that " 'divine power' did not only manifest itself directly to the average individual or through perennially established institutions: rather 'divine power' was represented on earth by a limited number of exceptional human agents, who had been empowered to bring it to bear among their fellows by reason of a relationship with the supernatural that was personal to them, stable, and clearly perceptible to fellow believers."[1] Not surprisingly, this development led first of all to a kind of interpersonal scrutiny wherein "men watched each other closely for those signs of intimacy with the supernatural that would validate their claim [of divine power]."[2] It also led both to some important genres of writing, e.g., pious biographies and autobiographies, which emphasized the relationship of certain persons to the divine, and, more significantly, led to an important identity distinction, that between sorcerers and saints. While both sorcerers and saints were thought to have special powers based on a relationship with the divine, the former were those who used that power selfishly while the latter used it for the general well-being. And this was in an age in which there existed a close relationship between relationships to the divine and (to use a modern construction) public goods.

Accordingly, the subsequent discipline that developed — the study of holy men, demons, and sorcerers — was not merely academic (another metaphor that postdates the epoch of which I speak), for it touched people's daily lives and inserted itself within the sociopolitical fabric. At a lower

This chapter is a revision of a paper prepared for presentation at the annual convention of the International Communication Association, Honolulu, Hawaii, 24–29 May 1985.

level of social organization, allegations of sorcery were both an important form of social control and a tactic of interpersonal conflict over resources and influence. At a higher level, the piety or intimacy of the emperor with the divine continued to be an important part of state legitimation (as it had been in what are called "pagan" periods).

Living as we do in a world that has been largely desacralized, we regard these human identities (saints and sorcerers) and their associated models of agency (the divine speaking through selected humans) as exotic, unbelievable constructions. As a result, when we speak of such former ages, our style of discourse differs from that of the age's contemporary believers in these identities and models of agency. While they, in a descriptive style, spoke familiarly and acceptingly of "holy men," and "divine will," I imply that what for them was considered fact — the great "is," as it were — can be better understood in terms of how their age constituted the "is." My substitution of a verb for a noun — referring not to the sacred but to a world that had been sacralized — has the similar import of turning their fact about the world into something imposed, into the making of a world.

It is more difficult to achieve this kind of distance from our own age because our identities and models of agency are part of the linguistic currency of present institutional realities and everyday life. For example, the now-intimate connection between psychiatric concepts and approaches to crime resides in our speech practices largely in the form of simple descriptive utterances. We refer to persons as being "criminally insane," and the existence of this "reality" is closely connected with a process of scrutiny every bit as intense as that evidenced in late antiquity, when people were searching for those thought to be intimate with the divine. This modern form of scrutiny is part of our way of dealing with criminal danger, our way of constituting identities for persons and competencies for agents of knowledge, given our prevailing understanding of public safety.

To gain a distance from this modern identity and model of agency — persons who are dangerous on the one hand but not responsible for their actions on the other — we must again become resistant, but this time to our current discursive practices, not to antiquated ones. Among the ways to do this is to historicize the contemporary practices, to view as remarkable the current, institutionalized conversations between psychiatrists and jurists. When we do this, we learn, as Michel Foucault has shown, that in a particular historical period, the early nineteenth century, there occurred the beginning of this "psychiatrization of criminal danger."[3] This way of speaking, referring not to things but to how they have been made, has a demystifying effect on our current self-understanding. Rather than seeing ourselves as functioning in a world of "criminally insane" persons — a view that helps animate and reinforce the legitimacy of various social-control agencies and their institutionalized approaches to crime — we can appreciate the processes through which our world has been imposed.

But we do not have to select extraordinary types of persons to illustrate the ideational force of some linguistic practices and the demystifying effects of others. The modern political self is susceptible to the same kind of demystifying. Who and what we are as citizens can be seen as a production or imposition rather than an expression of a perennial essence when placed in historical perspective. For example, whereas in medieval society the individual had a value or worth based on a place within a universal hierarchy with God at the apex, the modern person has "an 'individuality' which likes to regard itself as completely autonomous and imagines itself as having sovereign rights vis-à-vis a society."[4]

There is no reason to believe that this modern aspect of the person has any more resistance to interpretive practice than the medieval counterpart, for as A. J. Gurevich, a scholar who has contrasted medieval and modern construals of the self, has been able to perceive, "It is not the only possible hypostasis of the human personality."[5] However, to help us to recognize that what we view as a political person is a historical imposition of one among countless possibilities, we need a discourse that marks that historical process; we need to distance ourselves, as Gurevich does, by placing "individuality" in quotes and by speaking not descriptively of persons as autonomous but of the process of autonomizing the person.

A politicized form of writing, therefore, can show that the things we have in general and the kinds of persons and modes of agency we have in particular represent policy, not some form of disembodied reality. This level of policy, which is built into our representational practices, is unavailable to us unless we become linguistically self-conscious and evasive and show thereby how a form of ideological scripting masks the limitations, exclusions, and silences connected with the dominant forms of the recognized public-policy discourse. Within a linguistically self-reflective posture, the analysis of public policy deploys itself on a broader terrain to include not only what a society tends to regard explicitly as its policy problems but also the policy immanent in the ideas of the self and the order within which what is commonly thought of as public policy is executed. In what follows then I construe the problem of ideology as a form of naturalizing what is actually human practice and do so within a linguistic framework in general and as a problem of writing in particular.

The Ideological Mode: Some Initial Formulations

Despite the somewhat unorthodox beginning, which juxtaposes ideological and self-conscious/evasive modes of writing, my approach will evoke both conventional and unconventional standpoints. The conventional one, which I share with almost anyone involved in the production of academic discourse, is the commitment to avoid simply reinforcing existing forms of ideological thinking. Theodor Adorno's statement on what constitutes nonideological thinking supplies a point of departure. For him "the unideological thought is that which does not permit itself to be reduced to 'operational terms' and instead strives solely to help the things themselves to that articulation to which they are otherwise cut off by the prevailing language."[6] Here Adorno was speaking of a form of articulation that does not pander to particular partisan interests (those which benefit from what he called "operational terms"). In referring to the "things themselves" Adorno is not adopting the view that reality speaks to us as if it were a kind of object with meaning independent of the structure of our apprehension or of how we live. For Adorno the thing has to be understood not as an object immediately given to one's experience or perception but as something reflecting the social totality of which it is a part. To understand the thing unideologically is to recover the historically developing way of life it reflects. For example, to think of a diamond ring as both a sign of marital commitment and a status symbol is to think unideologically, whereas to think of it, after the DeBeers advertisements, as "forever" is to think ideologically (i.e., in the diamond merchant DeBeers's operational terms).

The approach here intersects with Adorno's statement at several points, not the least of which is his focus on the mystifying effects of the "prevailing language." However, it is important to distance ourselves from the seeming implication that ideology is a matter of specific terms. Language practices are inserted in a field of more general practices. To the extent that a statement is to be intelligible, it must accommodate to some degree to what is authoritative and must thus contain whatever mystifications are institutionalized in the realities that societies construct and administer. As I elaborate this theme, I will be treating ideology within the metaphorical terrain of reading and writing. Accordingly, ideological production will be characterized as a kind of writing and ideological thinking as a kind of reading, an enforced dyslexia wherein the reader is disenabled by being encouraged to adopt a politically insensitive view of the surrounding social formation and the objects, relationships, and events it contains. Much of the ideological production that will be my concern is an ideological reproduction generated in the writings of social and political analysts, a group that generally sees itself as nonideological (or even antiideological). But to the extent that it is not linguistically self-conscious, modern social science is part of society's legitimating and disciplinary mechanisms. In reproducing prevailing discursive practices, it helps to fix persons, objects, and relations in such a way that the authority of institutionalized social-control mechanisms is maintained.

While ideological production is not the goal or intention informing the field of social and political analysis, it is a consequence of the practices that shape a field, that is, of the prevailing boundary commitments that separate one domain of knowledge/practice and its objects of attention from another. An unreflecting acceptance of that field, especially of the boundaries that give legitimacy to analysis itself, amounts to a failure of the analysts to recognize that they are part of the social formation that is the object of investigation. The fact of belonging to that social formation is reflected in the ready-to-hand language, which imposes form on the social reality within which the analyst functions and reinscribes that social form unless the analyst undertakes linguistically evasive moves.

In social theory and analysis, then, the formulation of strategies of linguistic evasion requires a change in the self-understanding that constitutes the field of social and political analysis. Part of what must be rejected is that aspect of the terrain predicated on a radical distinction between what is thought of as fictional and scientific genres of writing. In the history of thought the distinction has been supported by the notion that the fictional text, e.g., the story, play, or novel, manufactures its own objects and events in acts of imagination, while the epistemologically respectable genres, such as the scientific text, have "real" objects and events, which provide a warrant for the knowledge-value of those of the text's statements purporting to be about the objects and events.

Without rehearsing all of the philosophical developments that have impeached this view of the value of statements, here I shall simply refer to the now familiar dilemma of epistemology: any claim to absolute knowledge about the external world of objects and events produces statements which cannot be proven and attempts to achieve objectivity result in dilemmas of circularity or an infinite regress. What is increasingly recognized is that objects and events are inseparable from the process of apprehension (indeed the imaginative processes) within which they are formed. To analyze how things in the world take on meanings, it is necessary to analyze the structure of our imaginative processes. The imaginative enactments that produce meanings are not simply acts of a pure, disembodied consciousness; they are historically developed practices that reside in the very style in which statements are made, of the grammatical, rhetorical, and narrative structures that compose even the discourses of the sciences.

In recognition of the irreducibly rhetorical nature of all discourses, literary theorists have called our attention to how valuation is to be discerned in the subtle, meaning creating "rhetorical motions" of texts which purport to merely describe and analyze. Paul de Man, emphasizing the

The Problem of Ideology

literariness of even philosophical discourses, has demonstrated how the philosophers Locke, Condillac, and Kant inadvertently prove the pervasiveness of the rhetorical mechanisms of language, for they rely upon metaphor in their arguments that knowledge-related discourses must eschew figuration.[7] For example, Locke's claim that figurative language interrupts the knowledge channel between an idea of a thing and the thing itself is undercut by de Man's demonstration that because "idea" comes from the Greek, *eide* meaning light, Locke's figuration was already there in the very epistemological discourse he wished to protect from metaphorical language.[8]

Attunement to the literariness of all discourses shows us that objects and events cannot be construed outside of the grammar, figuration, and plots which animate and connect them one to another. Thus, when one undertakes the familiar empiricist task of attempting to pin down the real by focusing on the link between knowledge systems and a nondiscursive domain of evidence, one must end by recognizing Wittgenstein's discovery that the pursuit of facticity seems only to lead us to "a sharpened awareness of the grammar of our language."[9]

A recognition that the real, or the what of our knowing, is inseparable from how it resides in our modes of representation must lead us to questions of style and to appreciation that attunement to style is not preoccupation with how best to communicate but a posture that liberates reflection on how reality is constituted. What we accept as the real amounts to our use of various interpretive codes, which we use so unreflectingly, we tend to regard them as simple acts of perception. Traditionally those styles of writing in disciplines regarded as primarily knowledge related are thus not seen as styles at all. Insofar as an interrogation of style is an interrogation of the way that form is imposed on an otherwise unruly world and meaning and value are created, we see that disciplines such as biological science, history, and the various genres of social analysis have been delusional to the extent that they have failed to heed their literariness and imagined that the meanings upon which their understandings are constructed have a wholly extralinguistic origin. The *what* of any knowledge system is radically entangled with the *how* of its writing/speaking. For this reason, the literary text which is self-conscious about its own rhetorical structure is the exemplar of the nondelusional mode of writing.[10]

The recognition that meaning and value are delivered in the writing of the texts of social and political analyses produces two relevant conclusions. The first is that there is a level of production in the text which operates outside of the author's explicit awareness. Even those texts that explicitly disavow particular ideational commitments end up reinscribing them in the linguistic mechanisms of their writing. The second is closely related to the first and occupies much of the argumentation of this chapter. Because meaning and value are immanent features of the written text, within whatever discourse we are referring to, the traditional notion that ethical thinking is an autonomous form of reasoning is called into question. In another place, I have made the argument that the difference between the style of descriptive or analytic discourse and the style of normative or ethical discourse, which explicitly invokes evaluation and resorts to imperatives or ought-type statements, is based on a recognition that in normative or ethical discourse the norms and values referenced are controversial. In discourses in which the style is more descriptive or analytic, the normative force they contain is implicit, existing in their deployment of categories, their figuration, and grammatical and narrative structures. An explicitly ethical discourse, therefore, differs from a descriptive one not because it is valuational but because it foregrounds its valuational content in its grammar (the imperatives) or its rhetoric (the terms and context of the utterances which reference a society's concern with evaluating conduct).[11]

Traditional ethical thinking—thinking that regards valuational discourse as wholly autonomous—is therefore ideological inasmuch as it encourages us to misread the source of value production. Fredric Jameson has described this ideological feature by noting that "ethical thought projects as permanent features of human 'experience,' and thus as a kind of 'wisdom' about personal life and interpersonal relations what are in reality the historical and institutional specifics of a determinant type of group solidarity or class cohesion."[12]

There are numerous examples of the pervasiveness of ethical thinking. A title of an address, "Can Medical Ethics Keep Pace with Technology," delivered at a recent conference, is exemplary. If we historicize "ethics" and recognize that the ethical discourse of a society is closely tied to its developing social, political, and administrative practices, we need have no worries about ethics keeping pace. It is created by such things as technological change. Because technology is an intrinsic part of a society's practices, it must necessarily contribute to conceptions of agency and therefore to what are regarded as value problems (this is the explicitly ethical part of a society's practices) and to what are taken as simply natural practices, unrelated to the problem of human decision. To see ethical problems as a form of practice rather than the reflection of something perennial, it is necessary to develop a historical perspective on how things come into discourse, whether as ethical problems or referents of a more descriptive discursive mode. Michel Foucault has provided this kind of perspective on a variety of practices that have been naturalized. Here he discloses the valuational practices involved in constituting what we now refer to unproblematically as a "population."

The Problem of Ideology

> One of the great innovations in the techniques of power in the eighteenth century was the emergence of "population" as an economic and political problem: population as wealth, population as manpower or labor capacity, population balanced between its own growth and the resources it commanded. Governments perceived that they were not dealing simply with subjects, or even with a "people," but with a "population," with its specific phenomena and its peculiar variables: birth and death rates, life expectancy, fertility, state of health, frequency of illness, patterns of diet and habitation.[13]

Thus, a "population" is not simply a referent of descriptive discourse; it represents a practice, a way of treating collectivities which is connected to modernity's commitments to how collective and individual compartments are to be organized and regulated. This kind of analysis gives us some critical distance from the above-mentioned address about ethics keeping pace with medical technology. The speaker was doubtless concerned with such issues as the implantation of artificial organs, but the query about ethics keeping pace with such developments presumes that medical discourse is a neutral medium that can only be evaluated when brought in contact with an autonomous, ethical code. It can be demonstrated, however, that medical discourse has had a historical role in creating what the human body is and, moreover, that these creations have been complicit with social-control mechanisms linked to power and authority. For example, speaking of another kind of attribute imposed on the body, Foucault has construed the medically produced code of "sexual perversions" as a "perverse implantation," showing how this medical constitution of the human body was linked to a social formation that was increasingly interested in having conduct measured, overseen, and regulated. As he put it, "The implantation of perversions is an instrument-effect; it is through the isolation, intensification, and consolidation of peripheral sexualities that the relation of power to sex and pleasure branched out and multiplied, measured the body, and penetrated modes of conduct."[14]

Medicine has thus been involved in a form of implantation all along, and the political implications of this can only be appreciated when we avoid treating various kinds of discourse as naturally separate. The domains of the ethical and the political take on their meanings in connection with discourses that purport to merely describe and analyze phenomena. These interrelationships are overlooked when one operates within a disabling view of language: the view that language is a transparent medium of communication. Within this view, it would be impossible, for example, to recover the value or ideational force functioning within the seemingly cognitive statement, "We now know more about sexual perversions than ever before."

Such a statement functions at two levels. As simple communication, what it means is easily intelligible to us (and to all those who have lived within the era in which medicine took an interest in sexuality). The statement implies that there are such things (or kinds of actions) called "sexual perversions." By focusing on the knowledge problem in a conventional way, the statement points us toward a consideration of the evidence that links the things and actions known as perversions to our agreed-upon procedures for what produces knowledge. For example, because there are probably more case histories of persons who have engaged in "sexual perversions," we have been told about what is thought to lead to such actions. But there is much that remains silent and unthought when we treat the statement as simply a form of communication. What we fail to appreciate within such a perspective is the process by which "sexual perversions" are constituted and incorporated into a form of authority and control. To view this process, we have to treat language as a discourse, not as transparent communication between subjects about things. Treating language as discourse involves regarding language as a kind of practice. In so doing, we view statements not on the basis of their truth-value in communication about things but on the basis of their capacity for value creation in human relations. This kind of treatment becomes possible within a notion of the relationship between the discursive and the nondiscursive that differs from traditional empiricism. For example, traditional empiricism construes the nondiscursive as the field of referents of language. By contrast, when we focus on discourse as practice, the nondiscursive is the field not of referents but of other possible practices. With this understanding of the intimate connection between language and practice, we are encouraged to view statements not on the basis of their truth but on the basis of their value. Why, we might ask, does one set of statements command a field of attention? In asking this kind of question, Foucault has developed an approach to discourse that provides a politicized alternative to the traditional preoccupation with the truth-value of individual statements and discursive formations as a whole.

> To analyze a discursive formation is to weigh the "value" of statements, a value that is not defined by their truth, that is not gauged by a secret content but which characterizes their place, their capacity for circulation and exchange, their possibility of transformation, not only in the economy of discourse, but more generally in the administration of scarce resources.[15]

This view of discourse alerts us to the political content sequestered in the subjects (kinds of persons), objects, and relationships about which we speak. It shows that statements can be evaluated as political resources. Discourse is, in Foucault's terms, an "asset," not an innocent mode of communication. Thus, the creation of the phenomenon of the "sexual perversion," understood by Foucault as a "perverse implantation," represents not a more precise understanding of a preexisting phenomenon but a step in the process whereby medicine took charge of explaining the increasing number of kinds of sexual abnormalities constituted and administered by a society whose exigencies required that persons become more and more calculable.

The role that medicine has played in the development of more elaborate modes of social control is especially evident in the history of the medicalization of perversities. For example, "The nineteenth century homosexual became a personage, a past, a case history, and a childhood, in addition to being a type of life, a life form, a morphology, with a discrete anatomy and possibly a mysterious physiology."[16] In this description, Foucault demonstrates how the "homosexual" was constituted as an object of medical knowledge. To the extent that we merely communicate about such things, we engage in a discourse that simply reproduces an existing structure of authority and an interconnected system of knowledge and social control. An alternative approach to discourse, one that stresses its constitutive rather than its communicative dimension, alerts us to the process wherein things come into speech and to the mechanisms and elements of a discourse in which things reside. For this purpose, we need a focus that is almost wholly unfamiliar to contemporary political science, which predicates its approaches to inquiry on the view that language is transparent and thus on the apprehension of phenomena that have already made their way into speech.

The idea of phenomena making their way into speech is another conception of language and meaning, that introduced by Ferdinand de Saussure, who bases meaning not on the relationship between word and object but on the relational structure of signifiers. For those influenced by the Saussurean linguistic tradition, in which meaning is based on the structure of difference among signifiers rather than the word-object relationship, the signifier precedes the signified. This implies that those phenomena (signifieds) about which we have understandings take on meaning in the context of signifying practices. Christian Metz has represented this precedence of the signifying practice in the knowledge process with a remark on how the love experienced by some men is predicated on a mental projection about its endurance. He states, "Far from the strength of their love guaranteeing it a real future, the psychical representation of that future is the prior condition for the full amorous potency in the present."[17]

Whatever credence one might give to this particular view — that it is the network of signifiers in which love and an imagined future participate that produces the phenomenon we identify as "love" — the epistemological implication is clear: an understanding of the phenomena about which we speak is not to be gained by formulating precise, technical rules to translate ideas into observations or to translate observations into the conscious intentions of actors. What is to be recovered is a nonconscious set of linguistic practices, which operate not as determined underlying structures (the position of traditional structuralists), but as concealed acts of exclusion and repression, responsible for the recognized authoritative discursive practices. Once we are alerted to this intimate relationship between language and practice, our attention is turned more toward the operation of discursive economies, and we are in a position to regard the things in the world — the unities, equivalences, and coherences represented by prevailing speech practices — as the imposition of a form on an otherwise chaotic experience, as a reality contrived and produced in intimate association with human practices, not as something natural or transcendental.

The Contention between the Hermeneutic and Genealogical Modes of Interpretation

The consideration of style and language above prepares the way for a further refinement in our approach to the problem of ideology, one which must confront two dominant modes of interpretation that resist traditional ideological thinking. The most important implication of the foregoing discussion, in which language was presented as seriously implicated in the constitution of that which is called "real," is that it puts pressure on some construals of ideological discourse which contrast ideology with nonideological forms of discourse. Which construals becomes clear when we inquire more carefully into approaches to the relationship between linguistic practices or discourse and the realm of the non- or prediscursive. What has been discredited, at a minimum, is the traditional approach of empiricists who saw themselves involved in closing the gap between word and object. A variety of different philosophical traditions have shown how the object cannot be construed outside of the practices within which human subjects apprehend them. For the English linguistic tradition of Austin and Wittgenstein, the force of utterances as well as their referential dimension are inseparable from the authority relations that sustain any judgment about what is. As Wittgenstein puts it, "I must recognize certain authorities in order to make judgments at all."[18]

Similarly, the Continental tradition in philosophy has introduced a

The Problem of Ideology

human subject into the language-reality relationship, and this complicates judgments about what is, rendering them arbitrary and uncertain (in the more radical positions represented by Derrida and de Man) or connecting them to the historical development of ways of life (in the neo-Heideggerian or hermeneutic positions). The tension worth considering with respect to how to construe the relationship of the nondiscursive to the discursive, then, is that between the interpretive or hermeneutic approaches and genealogical (or antiinterpretive) approaches. While what follows does not examine this relationship fully or propose a resolution of the positions, the depth in which it is treated relates to the problem at hand, isolating the ideological mode of discourse.

Foucault's approach, as exemplified in the brief review of his treatment of the medical production of perversions, is genealogical. This approach, drawn primarily from Nietzsche, assumes an ontology of disorder. For Nietzsche every discursive form, every concept, definition, or statement is a form of false arrest of experience, and all attempts to vindicate the arrest, e.g., by resort to a transcendental telos or some version of human nature, is a form of theology. For Foucault, then, there is no order or form to be discovered in the pre- or nondiscursive realm.

> We must not resolve discourse into a play of pre-existing significations: we must not imagine that the world turns toward us a legible face which we would have only to decipher; the world is not the accomplice of our knowledge; there is no pre-discursive providence which disposes the world in our favor. We must conceive discourse as a violence which we do to things, or in any case as a practice which we impose on them.[19]

Foucault, after Nietzsche, endeavors to apply genealogy to dissolve the coherences and unities that one takes as the real, to show how that which is taken to be timeless and universally valid is the arbitrary imposition of a form of order. There is, nevertheless, a hermeneutic dimension in Foucault's analysis (which I elaborate below).

Heidegger, a major influence on hermeneutic approaches, saw the interpretive enterprise as one of disclosure. Our discourse, if attuned to the nondiscursive, would allow things to emerge or be revealed. Heidegger's position on interpretation comes close to what I suggested above in presenting Adorno's concept of nonideological thought. Heidegger is not arguing for a view of the object as a thing that presents itself to thought. Language for him is not simply aimed at objects. As he puts it, "The saying of language is not necessarily an expressing of propositions about objects."[20] Emphasizing recovery rather than correspondence, Heidegger thought that genuine thinking would reveal the way that being or human existence is intertwined with what is taken to be a thing. It is not just a matter of disclosing the what of things but of coming to understand the how of things — how things are for us.

For Heidegger, to understand a thing merely as a thing involves a self-forgetting, a failure to recover how things are for us; it is forgetting that we are in part what we have been, and only the exercising of the capacity of correct thought will disclose things as they are. The contrast of the Heideggerian and Nietzschean ontologies is nowhere more apparent than in Heidegger's lectures on Nietzsche. At one point, for example, Heidegger construes our ability to understand Nietzsche as a kind of attunement. Speaking of how to construe one of Nietzsche's ideas, he says, "Waxing in confrontation with the matter itself, we must become capable of the capable word."[21] Genealogy is never a reconciliation with the self in any form, for the self is always generated as part of the perspective in any interpretation. Interpretation is for Nietzsche, as for Heidegger, a kind of action (Foucault called it a "violence"). Nietzsche would not, in any case, think of it in terms of capability.

Hermeneutic analysts are not all necessarily directly influenced by Heidegger, but the attunement or reconciliation dimension of Heideggerian thought is in evidence in various interpretive projects. For example, even though he rejects a hermeneutic that seeks to recover tradition or the bygone in the present, the structure of Jurgen Habermas's approach is hermeneutic in a Heideggerian sense. What Habermas seeks is also an attunement. His attunement, however, is future oriented; it is a movement toward a telos of understanding immanent in language.[22]

The more directly Heideggerian model of hermeneutics is manifested in the writings of Hans-Georg Gadamer. Like Heidegger, Gadamer sees the subject of thinking as one embedded in language. For Heidegger one who speaks is caught up in the flow of language, which has a built-in way of conceiving the world. Gadamer sees a structure of prejudice, an inherited world deposited in language and forming an unavoidable constituent of ongoing events of understanding. Gadamer's hermeneutics is clearly not genealogy. The task is one of overcoming alienation in order to achieve understanding. It is not empiricism's overcoming of a gap between word and object but between one speech practice and another. In every interpretation, one's initial understanding is up for grabs, but the outcome is an attunement of both the person/interpreter with himself/herself and with the other in a "fusion of horizons."[23]

In practice, the hermeneutic enterprise is an attempt to disclose the meanings of various cultural practices in a way that makes us (those who share the culture of the interpreter) reflect on the meanings of our own practices. For example, functioning primarily within a textual metaphor,

The Problem of Ideology

Clifford Geertz has applied the synecdochic logic typical of interpretive analyses, showing how various individual parts of a culture, e.g., the Balinese cockfight or the ancient Balinese water irrigation system, can be read in a way that reveals the cultural text as a whole.[24] From this step Geertz moves to a phenomenological way of construing ethnographic investigation, showing how the understanding of seemingly exotic practices and the coherences they contain in their own contexts can help us deal with incoherences in our own self-understandings. In his most recent study of Bali, he ends up telling us that we should recognize how in our political theory in general we have misconceived the connections between "the dignified parts of government and the efficient ones."[25]

This overcoming of a delusion in our political understanding, which orients Geertz's analysis of nineteenth-century Bali, provides a good contrast with the political delusion toward which Foucault's genealogical analyses are aimed. For Geertz we fail to grasp political processes because we operate with a disabling metaphorization of politics — the old engine, machine, and plumbing metaphors which lead us to ask how political systems function.[26] Geertz substitutes a literary metaphor with which he construes institutional forms and actions on the basis of how they speak. Culture is to be read because it can be regarded more as a semiological system than an efficient, goal-oriented, need-fulfilling system. Thus, the understanding of the Balinese cockfight emerges when we appreciate that the pattern of betting, which cannot be made intelligible as an attempt to maximize winnings, represents a Balinese way of saying where each person belongs in the pattern of ritual obligations. Similarly, with the same figuration, Geertz presents the nineteenth-century Balinese state as a system of governance directed "toward the public dramatization of the ruling obsession of the Balinese culture: social inequality and status pride."[27] Accordingly, state functions like treaty making and water irrigation become intelligible when it is shown how they conform to the pattern of ritual obligation.

What, then, is the structure of the delusion of traditional political analysis? According to Geertz the delusion is the result of our aggressiveness. We are too "impressed with command." We look so hard for direct relations of power that "we see little else."[28] Bali makes visible, by virtue of its display orientation, what our conceptual orientation makes invisible. "What our concept of public power obscures, that of the Balinese exposes; and vice versa."[29] Of course, here Geertz is being a bit too modest. What is revealed about the Balinese polity has a lot to do with Geertz's reconceptualization or, better, refiguration of our understanding of the political.

The burden of Geertz's implication is that the Balinese are their own authors, that the figuration is literally produced by Balinese practices.

Inasmuch as the configuration of the palaces, funeral processions, etc., are supposed to represent a timeless authority, Geertz sees the Balinese state as a "metaphorical polity." Although this seems to ascribe the figuration to Bali rather than his own writing, a good part of Geertz's creation of the text is dialogical. He constructs the text of Balinese culture, merging his self-understanding with that of the Balinese, and, in what is a medley of hermeneutic gestures (after the theories of Ricoeur and Gadamer), he adjusts his self-understanding, particularly his notion of the effective political analysis, as a result of his encounter with the exotic text.[30] The delusion Geertz overcomes is a poverty of meaning, a failure of analysts to figure politics in a way that will yield coherent interpretations. The delusion has been a failure, in short, to pay attention to culture, an attention that must be paid within a capable metaphorics. As Geertz has noted, "A country's politics reflects the design of its culture."[31]

Foucault's analyses are addressed to a similar delusion, our inability to see the functioning of power as a result of our impoverished construal of the political domain. The prevailing construction of the political discourse, the ways of putting controversy over power and authority into language, is monopolized by a narrow notion of what is considered the political, for the idea of power operating in the West has been tied for centuries to the sovereignty discourse. To the extent that the history of political discourse has concerned itself with the limits of sovereign power and the other face of sovereign power, the exercise of individual rights, what have remained silent are other forms of power.[32] Just as one is misled by writing a history of sexuality as the history of prohibited speech, one is misled by treating the history of the political as the history of the limitation of sovereign power. Again, emphasizing how the creation of a particular discourse is an imposition of a form of order, Foucault refers to how a prevailing discourse, in this case, the constitution of the "political," creates an economy which has the effect of silencing alternative economies, other ways of constituting political problems.

> In a society such as ours, but basically in any society, there are manifold relations of power which permeate, characterise and constitute the social body, and these relations of power cannot themselves be established, consolidated nor implemented without the production, accumulation, circulation and functioning of a discourse. There can be no possible exercise of power without a certain economy of discourses of truth which operates through and on the basis of this association.[33]

Within the confines of the political discourse, which emphasizes sovereignty and rights, what has been silent are the controls and potential chal-

The Problem of Ideology

lenges and refusals immanent in the creation of the human subject as we "know" it. This is the human subject scripted, not only by recognized disciplinary agencies such as medicine, social work, education, and the recognized carceral institution, the prison, but also by knowledge disciplines themselves — political science, sociology, psychology, biology, etc. The creation of identities by knowledge agents is, according to Foucault, disciplinary in a sense similar to the discipline emanating from what are recognized as social-control agents. Knowledge agents, the human sciences in particular, act as relays for power by both monopolizing the discourse controlling what can be said and by whom and by helping to script the kind of identity or self-understanding that is docile in the face of demands from controlling social, political, and administrative institutions. In the absence of alternative discursive possibilities for constituting the self, one cannot oppose power because, to the extent that power is only thought within the confines of the narrow sovereignty/rights political discourse, it is represented as something else; it is masked in the guise of caring, curing, educating, evaluating, motivating, and resolving disputes. Without interrogating the power implications of discourses that produce the modern subject, one cannot question power because power is continually reinscribed, even within forms of knowledge that seek not only to disclose it but, ironically, to disavow it or at least escape its worst excesses.

Thus while Foucault, like Geertz, refigures — with such rhetorical gestures as identifying education and social work as carceral functions — the domain of the political, his approach departs radically from the interpretive methods of Geertz and others of the hermeneutic persuasion. Foucault is not seeking a frame of analysis that shows how the behavior of various actors can be recovered if we know their cultures or background fields of meaning and use a more informed view of culture. To interpret according to Foucault is to unreflectingly accept the "rarity" of sets of statements; it is to seek to find their hidden meaning rather than to undertake a more politicized inquiry into the discursive economies they represent. Accordingly, Foucault has produced an archeological analysis in which he demonstrates how control over discourse, the various linguistic practices which give us objects, subjects, and the understandings within which they function, produces the economies of meaning and value in given historical periods. He also offers a genealogical analysis with which he seeks to recover the process wherein the modern individual has become a subject of disciplinary power — a sexual, medical, psychiatric, and potentially criminal self, whose body has become a site for an intensified level of inspection, knowledge production, and thus control.[34]

While Foucault does not deny a place for the kind of hermeneutics practiced by ethnographers like Geertz, he warns that the history of the subject *is* the history of interpretations. Because he argues that there is no deeper level of meaning to be revealed, interpretations are Foucault's data, not his mode of inquiry. Therefore, the delusions with which Foucault is dealing (political and otherwise) are not misunderstandings. Rather he is highlighting what amounts to a metalevel delusion within which particular delusions are wrought. This is the delusion of understanding itself, the idea that there is a truth or unmediated level of meaning to be discovered, a resting place for the mind in a field of concepts that opens reality to us. Accordingly, Foucault distances himself from the traditional conception of ideology inasmuch as he is not criticizing something masking the truth but showing how the very production of knowledge and truth is linked to systems of power.[35]

One way of underscoring the contrast would be to note that the Geertzian unmasking is one that aims at gaps in our conversations about society in general and the political dimension of social process in particular. These gaps are overcome when we achieve the appropriate figuration ("the capable word"). Our conversations about what is exotic thus begin to coalesce with our conversations about ourselves, and, as a result, we are enabled in the sense of being able to have better, less deluded conversations about ourselves. Foucault's delusion is the delusion that provokes conversations in the first place. Any discourse constitutes a delusion inasmuch as it administers dimensions of silence as soon as it begins; it establishes practices which force out other possible practices.

It is more appropriate, moreover, to use the metaphorics of scripting rather than conversation to characterize Foucault's notion of discourse. The prevailing discourses are not parts of persons' conscious awareness. Persons' perspectives are pre-scripted in the sense that meanings, subjects, and objects are sedimented in the dominant and thus most readily available discursive practices. When we reference an object in an available discourse, we reproduce it unreflectively. And, because we (our available identities) are scripted into these same discourses, we end up telling various "truths" about ourselves, be they medical, psychiatric, or political truths. Ultimately for Foucault the only way for an individual to avoid subjugation is by disavowing power, by refusing to be the self that power has scripted for that individual. What this involves is not improving conversations but constructing counter discourses, modes of writing which oppose the terms of power and authority circulated and recirculated in prevailing modes of discourse.

However, despite all of the antihermeneutic gestures in the Foucaultian approach, there are what I call "hermeneutic anchors" in Foucault's analyses. Foucault is an incessant politicizer; he thus wants to insinuate his analyses into conversations about politics and power. This much is clear from the very fact that Foucault is intelligible; while his analyses depart in many ways from ordinary discursive modes and thus create discomfort with the prevailing fields of analysis, they still communicate; they engage at least part of the ways of thinking/speaking already in circulation. He has shown that we in the modern age fail to incorporate the workings of power into our predominant political discourse because we neglect the normalizing power of disciplinary agencies and systems of "knowledge."[36] We fail to encode in our political talk the way that modernity has witnessed a structure of domination elaborated through the various mechanisms of power. These mechanisms are not to be understood as things operating from a distance in the control of the willed forces of individuals. Power is incorporated into our identities such that power functions through what is "known" about us.

This, then, is Foucault's main hermeneutic anchor. He commits his analyses to our ongoing discussion of politics and power. In arguing that the terms of the discussion have been disabling, he lines himself up with others, like Geertz, who are also trying to improve our political conversation. Foucault's hermeneutic anchor is tossed out explicitly in several places, but one general characterization he has offered should suffice for purposes of this discussion.

> The question I asked myself was this: how is it that the human subject took itself as an object of possible knowledge? Through what forms of rationality and historical conditions? And finally at what price? This is my question: at what price can subjects speak the truth about themselves?[37]

This statement is primarily a description of the genealogical mode of analysis, and Foucault's treatment of knowledge as a power-related practice draws us out of our customary discursive distinctions. But when we get to the "at what price" portion of his question, we are into the hermeneutic dimension of Foucault's project. We have been encouraged to recalculate the economies of the exercise of power within this altered way of representing the locus of power. Thus, genealogy reveals the process by which humans invest in the world with value; but as soon as we assume that we are already in a kind of world, we begin to ask value questions about it, and this kind of question about value is a hermeneutically inspired kind of question. Within the hermeneutics of value questions, Foucault is asking about the political costs of a disciplinary society in which that discipline, which is a form of power, is disguised within depoliticizing forms of discourse. He is inviting us to weigh the costs of this modern, delusional form of power which represents itself as something else. The bulk of his analysis is taken up with a figuration—the politics of the body — which focuses our attention on our former delusion, but then the conversation about the price we have been paying is offered. What does it cost to be dominated and subjugated in the names of healing, curing, nurturing, and educating?

The Ideological

It was important to sort out the different delusions to which interpretive theory and poststructuralist theory are addressed, because it is the latter construal which makes intelligible the assertion that the ideological dimension of discourse can be viewed as a form of writing that encourages a misreading. In keeping with an emphasis on the given distribution of discursive boundaries as constituting a set of practices, ideological scripting can be viewed primarily as a discursive mode that naturalizes and universalizes those practices, so that it appears that the world is being described rather than contrived. Once human enactments are banished from the value- and meaning-creation process, the effect is depoliticizing, for the assumption that a discursive mode delivers truth, rather than being one practice among other possibilities, discourages contention. In order to elaborate this notion of ideology as a form of scripting, it is necessary to ask, in addition, what it is that is scripted. In general, the misreading involved in one's succumbing to ideological thought is a failure to discern the power and authority effects which are part of the scripting of seemingly politically innocent objects, forms of subjectivity, actions, and events.

There are several perspectives that contribute to this general reading/writing metaphorization of the ideology problem. Because the style or representational practice of writing is so crucial to the ideology problem, it is useful to begin with Benita Parry's view, which states effectively the way ideology functions in contemporary capitalist systems. For her, ideology is "the system of representation through which individuals living their roles within the class structure of late capitalism learn to assimilate their existing positions and relationships as natural, permanent and conforming to a transcendental ethical plan."[38] Within this general approach it is possible to identify several thinkers who have elaborated relevant aspects of this kind of ideological scripting. For example, Roland Barthes's analysis of myth supports Parry's view insofar as he conceives mythical speech as a discursive mode that, among other things, "transforms history into nature."[39] Looking at a photograph of a "Negro soldier" saluting the French flag on the cover of *Paris match*, Barthes describes the kind of reading the simple, photographic mode of representation encourages. Read inno-

The Problem of Ideology

cently, the picture says "that France is a great empire, and that all her sons, without any color discrimination, faithfully serve under her flag, and that there is no better answer to the detractors of an alleged colonialism than the zeal shown by this Negro in serving his so-called oppressors."[40] In contrast with this innocent reading, Barthes's reading recovers the Negro soldier's history and shows how such a form of representation flattens him out and makes timeless and universal what has come about as a result of the functioning of a dominating form of power.

One way of interpreting Barthes's point is to note that ideological modes of representation encourage a form of misrecognition. When we relate ideology to misrecognition, we can find a similar and more fully developed view of ideology-as-naturalization in the work of Louis Althusser. To begin with, Althusser uses the notion of the "problematic," the set of theoretical assumptions that lends coherence to a particular terrain of understanding and, like Thomas Kuhn's paradigms, determines the sets of questions that will be relevant, permissible, and possible.[41] More important, the problematic determines what will be visible and invisible within the field of objects constituted by that problematic. The Althusserian problematic thus provides a prototype for one of Foucault's kinds of questions, his query about why one discursive formation rather than another comes into being, and his project of rendering articulate and visible those objects and subjects that have been pushed off stage and relegated to domains of unreason or marginality by existing problematics or, in his terms, prevailing discursive practices.

It is on the heels of the problematic that Althusser's notion of ideology appears. In his earlier discussion of the problem, Althusser distinguished sharply between science and ideology, regarding the latter as a form of discourse that "is not conscious of itself."[42] Whatever the value of this science/ideology split — indeed Althusser later apologized for overdrawing it — the analytic move which followed it is most relevant to this discussion. What Althusser proposes is a "symptomatic reading" as a way to detect the problematic of a discourse. This detection process, obviously modeled on Freud's psychoanalytic readings, is aimed at the gaps or absences in an ideological discourse as much as it is at what is manifest. For example, Althusser's reading of *Capital* credits Marx with such a reading in noticing that the English political economists had answered a question that was never posed. Marx noticed that the political economists produced an answer that valued labor in terms of the cost of reproducing labor power, but they had never posed the question in this way. This answer captured Marx's imagination, and he elaborated on it, but the development of that imagination required a kind of reading, a symptomatic one detecting ideological production.[43]

Coupled with his notion of symptomatic readings, Althusser construes ideology not as a system of ideas but as a set of practices. Ideology is, above all, the subject's lived relation to the real;[44] it thus makes it possible to be a social being. Althusser therefore rejects the traditional model of ideology as false consciousness, for consciousness is not the locus of ideology. In place of false consciousness, Althusser speaks of misrecognition, arguing that in the very process in which subjects are able to recognize themselves in social relations there exists also a misrecognition, a failure to see that their subjectivity is produced historically and materially by forces beyond their control. When Althusser says, in his well-known formulation, that "ideology interpellates individuals as subjects," he is referring to the process whereby misrecognition is generated.[45] Persons learn to objectify themselves, regarding their identities as natural and ethically appropriate rather than as impositions representing social practices. Thus, despite his disavowal that he has been concerned with ideology, Foucault's project of recovering histories of the formation of the subject can be construed as a form of ideological criticism within Althusser's conception of ideology. In Althusser's terms, Foucault is bringing to recognition what is misrecognized.

When we add Althusser's insights to the emphasis on ideology as naturalization, we emerge with an understanding that, on the one hand it is not surprising that human practices create boundaries around discourse, for without boundaries there could be no intelligibility and the lived interpersonal relations that intelligibility allows. However, on the other hand, when those boundaries are naturalized or treated as simply the parameters of what is thought to be real, we have what amounts to an ideological form of censorship. Here Pierre Bourdieu's approach is pertinent, for he has spoken of the way that orthodox forms of discourse impose a form of censorship wherein people are cognizant of an "overt opposition between 'right' opinion and 'left' opinion or 'wrong' opinion, which delimits *the universe of discourse.*" They fail, however, to access the "doxa," which Bourdieu refers to as the "universe of the undiscussed."[46] Critique of ideology within Bourdieu's model would amount to providing a discourse to allow discussion of what cannot be said within orthodox and heterodox discursive forms — a vehicle, in short, to render the pre- or nondiscursive articulate. This is an important part of Bourdieu's discussion for here he formulates what language can do it if is to be a politicized, nonideological vehicle. He notes that in situations "in which the everyday order . . . is challenged, and with it the language of order" there is a need for "extraordinary discourse."[47]

How, then, can we situate these views of ideology with respect to the more familiar approaches influential in the social sciences? The variety

The Problem of Ideology

of familiar positions on ideology tend to bifurcate. There are those that construe ideology as simply the set of beliefs and values persons use to orient themselves toward public affairs. Martin Seliger, for example, treats ideologies as simply sets of action-oriented beliefs which are organized into wholes at various levels of abstraction.[48] The other positions treat ideology as a form of false consciousness, the absorption into a point of view which alienates persons from "reality," from objects as they really are (in some versions), or from their real interests (in others). If we heed the Althusserian position elaborated above, we avoid the bind that would make it necessary to choose between these two options. Ideology is both a necessary discursive form inasmuch as it is a person's lived relationship with a social reality, and it is a type of misrecognition or misreading. Most important is Althusser's phrase that there is a misrecognition in the recognition. This formulation allows us to avoid the oversimplified notion of the real built into the view that ideology is false consciousness, and it recovers the critique of domination that we are liable to lose when we conceive ideology as simply some kind of belief system. Although we should resist Althusser's tendency to tie ideology too closely to one aspect of a society's functioning — its economic production system — and we should also resist Althusser's notorious, radical distinction between science and ideology, there are insights worth endorsing. To summarize, Althusser teaches that while ideology is represented as a set of ideas, it is a relationship which extends beyond them. A subject operating within Althusser's notion of ideology is innocent of its effects inasmuch as he or she is caught up in ideology's practical function of helping the subject to cope with everyday life as it is produced within prevailing socioeconomic structures. Althusser's subject can thus be understood ontologically rather than epistemologically, for the subject's modes of representation allow for a coherent form of practice within the reigning system of intelligibility. Ideology functions, as Althusser puts it, as an "indispensable practice essential to the historical life of societies."[49]

The misrecognition involved in ideology is thus a necessary misrecognition. It provides the kind of naturalized construction of the social reality that obscures a historically acute recognition of the constructed nature of the "real" while making everyday life appear coherent and unproblematic. It is thus the creation of a self, a socially meaningful identity that is both ideological and a necessary adaptation function for the individual.

But the development of the self is, at the same time, a dubious achievement inasmuch as it produces a docility toward the system of power and authority and an inability to read that system in an effectively politicized way. That misreading stems from the tendency of the individual to take the linguistic path of least resistance, to function within the set of categories, grammar, narrative, and rhetorical structures that provide relatively spendable social currency. Part of this tendency was recognized by Adorno when he noted that the mind tends to "mold itself for the sake of its marketability, and thus reproduce the socially prevalent categories."[50] Other dimensions were captured by Thomas Mann in his Joseph novels, where he emphasized the difficulty of reconciling diverse cultural traditions with outlooks represented in the grammars and narrative structures with which they understand themselves. Mann was particularly masterful at demonstrating with his writing style the linguistically based ideological structures within which persons function. For example, the third novel in the set begins with a misunderstanding between Joseph and the wandering merchants who have pulled him from the pit where his brothers had left him:

> "Where are you taking me?" Joseph asked Kedeema, one of the old man's sons as they were setting up the sleeping-huts, in the rolling moonlit lowland at the foot of the mountains called Fruit-lands. Kedeema looked him up and down.
> "Thou'rt a good one!" said he, and shook his head in token that he did not mean good at all but various other things such as pert or queer or simple. "Where are we taking thee? But are we taking thee any whither? No, not at all. Thou art by chance with us, because our father hath purchased thee from harsh masters, and thou goest with us whither-ever we go. But taking thee that cannot be called." "No? then not," responded Joseph. "I only meant: whither doth God lead me, in that I go with you?"
> "Thou art and remainest a funny fellow," countered the Ma'onite, "and thou hast a way of putting thyself in the center of things till one knoweth not whether to wonder or be put out. Thinkest thou thou 'Come-hither,' that we are a-journeying in order that thou mayest arrive somewhither where thy God will have thee to come?"[51]

One does not need an extensive analysis of the passage to grasp that what is at issue is the relationships among narrative, grammar, and ideology. Joseph is operating within a narrative which locates his personal destiny at the center and relegates the Ma'onites to peripheral, helping roles. The grammatical play of the passage reflects a struggle in which Kedeema disavows the privileging of Joseph's narrative. What distinguishes Mann's treatment here is its linguistic self-consciousness, its explicit attempt to render ideology as a series of linguistic mechanisms. In this instance, Joseph is involved in an ideological production insofar as he renders in discourse an account of his situation unreflectively; he treats as natural, universal, and uncontestable the narrative context in which the Ma'onites are involved in carrying out his destiny and the grammar of his statements, which deploy the relevant responsibilities for agency within that narrative.[52]

This kind of linguistic self-consciousness tends to be more evident in literary texts than in those produced by social and political analysts. Among the few examples is Joseph Gusfield's treatment of "the drinking-driving problem," in which he locates the dominant discursive practices in the debate over the issue as a "grammar of agency," which emphasizes the behavior of individual motorists instead of social, structural dimensions. Alert to how a set of literary devices can show the ideological investments in the debate, he goes on to implicate rhetoric and narrative as well. The "ownership" of the drinking-driving problem stems from the use of certain "root metaphors," such as the "criminal" or the "sick," and the narrative of the "killer drunk," one of many different stories that could be told, is shown to be part of a public staging that passes off a particular drama as if it were the only reality available.[53]

In effect, Gusfield reveals the valuational commitments harbored in the way public policy problems achieve their reality in language. The ordinary language of public policy is ideological to the extent that it poses as non-valuational. By shifting the genre of analysis from the descriptive/analytic to the literary, he turns our attention away from the referents of public policy language and toward how they are achieved through the style of their public inscription. His focus shows that representations of reality are ideological, and that to challenge ideological inscription requires a special kind of reading.

This attention to the style of a public-policy debate brings us still closer to a perspective on ideology constructed within a literary metaphor. But before summarizing that perspective, there remains a need to connect the discussion thus far with some of the familiar dimensions of ideology that have been identified by a wide variety of approaches. If we assume, at the minimum, that ideological gestures are gestures which represent an acceptance of some authority, we can identify three basic ideological strategies.[54]

The first is the general idea of legitimation, which has been emphasized in a tradition of analysis stretching from Weber to Habermas. If we are speaking of legitimation processes, such as the justification of the power exercised by a centralized state, we can separate them into two phases, both of which are involved in establishing a referent against which state control is vindicated. One is the authority of the referent itself. Some states draw their pattern of control and domination by claiming that their foundation experience is transcendental. For example, Geertz showed how the nineteenth-century Balinese state claimed to be representing a divine pattern. Modern states refer to traditions, to consensus, or, in cases where extraordinary or temporary patterns are installed, to crises. In each case, the referent is treated as something not to be problematized or treated as controversial. This treatment of the legitimation referent as an extra-discursive non-practice-related entity gives this phase of legitimation its ideological character.

The second phase or moment of legitimation has to do with the commentary or set of commentaries on the referent. Even if the referent is taken to be authoritative in principle, its features emerge in a commentary on those features. Just as the authority of a Jehova and a Jesus depends on the authority of their scriptors (Moses and the writers of the Gospels), the law — the referent establishing the authority of the state in tenth-century Iceland — was without force until it was referred to in a commentary delivered by a law speaker. Without this commentary, there was no referent and no legitimation one could turn to in one of ancient Iceland's few public processes, dispute resolution.[55] Even today, state authority depends on the legitimacy of the author or authorless script which inscribes the referents of that authority, whether it be nature, the general will, a combination of these, or some other recognized domain of justification.

The second conception of ideological mechanisms with a significant tradition is that of reification, emphasized in the writings of Lukács and Adorno, and, more recently, Jameson. The emphasis of thinkers concerned with this ideological mechanism has been on the loss of forms of social relations, which have a unity and coherence based on cultural tradition. When an object loses its original significance and becomes appropriated into a means/ends system of efficency, it is reified in the sense that it becomes a thing to behold in the contemporary, imposed system of values, and only a form of critical analysis can recover the meaning it derives from the developing social formation in which it came to have its more fundamental significance.

It should be clear why approaches to ideology that emphasize reification have benefited from both the Marxian and Freudian forms of reading. The structure of both Freud's approach to the object as a fetish that has lost its original psychic-value investment and the Marxian analysis of the commodity that has lost touch with its work-value investment provide much of the inspiration for contemporary reification approaches to ideology. Notable in this respect is Jean Baudrillard's discussion of the "vacation sun," which draws effectively on all the intellectual traditions contributing to our understanding of the reification mechanism.

> The vacation sun no longer retains anything of the collective symbolic function it had among the Aztecs, the Egyptions, etc. It no longer has that ambivalence of a natural force — life and

death, beneficent and murderous — which it had in primitive cults or still has in peasant labor. The vacation sun is a completely positive sign, the absolute source of happiness and euphoria and as such, it is significantly opposed to non-sun (rain, cold, bad weather).[56]

Baudrillard's approach to the fetish recalls the discussion above contrasting Geertz and Foucault's different notions of delusion. Like Geertz, Baudrillard regards the Marxian approach to social processes and meanings as insensitive to culture. Accordingly, Baudrillard moves away from the traditional Marxist emphasis on production and need fulfillment as sources of value and, like Geertz, emphasizes the symbolic exchange system. For Baudrillard, as for Marx, the fetishization of a commodity involves emptying it of its concrete labor, but that labor is a labor of signification, a collective process wherein objects take on their meanings within a social code.

For Baudrillard, as for Geertz, ideological thinking involves a loss of meaning, the substitution of a functional for a rhetorical, social logic in Geertz's case and the substitution of an empty system of signs for a symbolic, semiological process in Baudrillard's. Foucault's position differs insofar as he regards any system of meaning as a kind of perspective with delusions of its own. To privilege any code or discursive practice, cultural or otherwise, is to uncritically submit to a form of power. Foucault, with Geertz and Baudrillard, recognizes there are ideological mechanisms, such as the ones they describe at work within social formations and their meaning systems. But his archeological and genealogical analyses are designed to recover the silences administered in the production of those social formations. Unlike the traditional interpretive orientations which seek to recover meanings or the unities and coherences of a society that are hidden by ideological thinking, Foucault seeks to show that any unity or coherence is an imposed, arbitrary practice rather than an absolute foundation for a system of meaning against which one can judge deviations.

This brings us to the next traditional approach to ideological mechanisms, one with which Foucault's form of analysis articulates well: ideology as dissimulation. This mechanism has already been introduced above in the discussion of Barthes's and Bourdieu's treatments of ideological thinking as that which turns human practices and contrivances into something natural and timeless. The major ideological aspect that fits under dissimulation is a situation in which power or relations of domination pose as something else. Ironically, according to Foucault, one place they have posed as something else is within political discourse itself. Having reviewed this particular instance of dissimulation above — the discussion of the dominance of the sovereignty discourse and the resulting neglect of the normalizing power in so-called nonpolitical institutions – the mechanism can be illustrated with a fresh example. Among the objects created by disciplinary, normalizing forms of power is probably the most highly funded kind of object in the modern social sciences – what we call the "attitude."

How does power sequester itself in the attitude? The question to pose is why the modern person has been given attitudes. A genealogical approach would reveal, no doubt, that the emergence of the attitude coincided with the growth of mass media, particularly as it is used to sell products ranging from consumer goods to public policies. When legitimation processes for existing forms of power and forms of commerce were more direct, in that they were mediated through face-to-face occupational, tribal, or ritualistic membership groups, the social formation was such that it was not necessary to influence anything as socially unmediated as an individual cognitive orientation because power was always experienced through one's subsocietal affiliations. The modernizing and fragmenting of society, with its attendant development of a technological capacity for power and influence to act at a distance rather than having to be mediated through face-to-face relations, created the conditions of possibility for the emergence of the attitude. The increasing intensity in social-science surveillance of the attitude, therefore, reflects the complicity of social science and authoritative public agencies in the preoccupation with the problem of centralizing control. An analysis of ideology from the point of view of the dissimulation mechanism thus requires a reflection on language and genre. Because power often hides itself in other, nonpoliticized discursive practices, the critique of ideology requires a nonrespect for genre.

Finally, there is another ideological mechanism that is peculiarly modern because it is media dependent. This is what Jameson has called the "strategy of containment," which he illustrates in his analysis of the film, *Dog Day Afternoon*, a semicomic but in many ways profound treatment of various marginalized persons who are the rarely observed victims of modern industrialized society.[57] This containment operates in the first instance through simple naming. "To name something is to domesticate it, to refer to it repeatedly is to persuade a fearful and beleaguered middle-class public that all of that is part of a known and catalogued world and thus somehow in order. Such a process would thus be equivalent, in the realm of everyday social life, of that cooptation by the media, that exhaustion of the novel raw material, which is one of our principal techniques for deferring threatening and subversive ideas."[58]

There is another dimension to a strategy of containment as Jameson explicates it. In addition to the simple presentation and repetition of material that might be disturbing if it were a discovery not sanctioned by authority, is the structure of that presentation. It was Adorno who, more than any other, identified the kind of ideological production that fragments aspects of a social totality and thereby robs people of the ability to re-create the whole of which the fragments are a part. Adorno illustrated this fragmenting mechanism in his analysis of what he called the "regression of listening" effected when musical potpourris with fragments from various classical works are assembled and marketed. The result is a commodification of music wherein each fragment is sold or appreciated for its familiarity rather than its part in a composition as a whole. This fragmenting and commodification transforms the listener "into the acquiescent purchaser."[59]

Adorno subsumed the repetition of fragments and resulting loss of the totality under the rubric of reification, but the mechanism also belongs to the mechanism of containment. For example, Jameson absorbs this notion into his conception of containment in his analysis of the way that popular culture represents victimized classes. The showing of a marginalized person, such as the inept bank robber Sonny or the various exploited groups such as the low-status bank employees in *Dog Day Afternoon*, is not done in such a way as to politicize the film's viewers, for it "is not enough to constitute a class system, let alone to precipitate a beginning consciousness of class in its viewing public."[60]

Reading the Sports News

To pull all these dimensions of ideological production together, we can apply them to a seemingly innocent sports news item carried by most of the major networks recently. After a high school basketball star was murdered near his school, among those interviewed was a basketball coach from a university that had been recruiting him for their basketball program. He said that the young man was a "terrific package," because he not only played great basketball but also gave interesting, articulate interviews. He would, said the coach, be able to "sell our program" as well as help our team.

One of the most remarkable things about the statement is that we find it perfectly intelligible; we know what the coach means, and ordinarily, we would be prone to filing the statement among the "what-a-tragedy" sentiments which usually attend the untimely death of someone who seemed destined for success. However, viewed not as communication, that aspect of language invoked when we merely speak of things, but as part of a productive practice inviting inspection of its various linguistic dimensions, the statement can be found to exercise most of the ideological mechanisms and effects described above.

First of all, the lack of ironic or other self-conscious literary effects in the coach's statement — his confident and straightforward reference to "our program" and his unproblematic identification of the young man as a "package" — suggests that there is nothing reflective or playful in the remark. Going back to the aspect of ideology emphasized by Adorno, Althusser, and Parry, we can note that the statement constitutes the young man in "operational terms" (Adorno's expression for terms reflecting a self-interested partisanship). And these terms, because their application involves an objectification of both the young man and the coach, can be said to interpellate the people involved from individuals into kinds of subjects; they could both recognize themselves in the statement, but there is no apparent grasp of the history of the production of these kinds of subjectivity. Hence, as Althusser would say, there is a misrecognition in the recognition. It is as if, as Parry put it, the "system of representation" through which the participants see their roles is treated as "natural, permanent and conforming to a transcendental ethical plan."

The statement also invites the kind of analysis of ideology as naturalizing the historical that Barthes outlined in his analysis of myth. The black athlete (which the young man happened to be), when treated as a package, is robbed of his history. A historicized view of the black athlete would have us connect the use of black athletes to sell athletic programs with the exploitation and commodification of blacks (and other groups) from the landing of the slave ships onward, especially in light of what is known about the small percentage of college athletes who ultimately achieve educational or economic success.

It is also clear that the grammar and rhetoric of the statement as well as its implicit narrative structure, speak to a system of produced identities, which surrounds a politics of sports discernible only when the statement is assessed in terms of the specific ideological mechanisms outlined above. The specific ideological mechanisms of the statement hinge on the reading of it they promote. We accept its authority to the extent that we accept it as sports talk. Speaking first of all of the mechanisms of legitimation, this would mean that we regard the substance of the coach's commentary as legitimate — that the things he is referring to such as a "sports program," can be so regarded, and that he is a legitimate commentator, one who is appropriately placed to engage in sports talk.

But even a relatively short-term view of the history of sports and their connection with educational institutions reveals startling shifts in both what constitutes sport, who is involved in it, and the nature of the roles played by people who control and manage it. The original movement to promote athletic activity in schools began in England and connected the idea of athletic play and competition with the idea of educating the whole person. The guiding approach to value was connected to the good of the person as a developing individual. To the extent that there existed an ideological overlay, it consisted, among other things, in failing to be self-conscious about the class and other social commitments that remained silently in the background of what was meant by the whole person.[61]

Once we have even this very brief historical sketch, the statement becomes strange. The fact that a coach is making a public statement at all becomes startling rather than unremarkable, for the shift from the coach-as-teacher involved in encouraging healthy competition to the coach as director of marketing for a school's athletic program is a dramatic change in the identity of the coach as well as in the nature of the context for the games that athletes play. The major objectification calling out for analysis is closely tied to the coach-as-marketing-director. This is the athlete as a package. What metaphor could more tellingly exemplify our epoch in which almost everything, including the amateur athlete, has been commodified. All of this brings us dramatically in confrontation with the ideological mechanism of reification, the severing of the connection between an object and its original meaning system.

There are two senses in which this severing can be described. The more traditional interpretative sense is one that functions within the idea that there is some model of authenticity. Accordingly, those positing such an idea would seek a privileged way to describe the value of athletic endeavor and then regard commercialization and commodification as a kind of corruption or devaluing. However, within the Nietzschean/Foucaultian approach ideology of this kind is not treated as a kind of loss. Rather, the athlete as a commodity is simply the contemporary kind of objectification. It is not so much that the athlete has lost something of value as it is that the athlete represents another kind of valuing. The forces imposing meanings have changed, and if one can say that some kind of severing of the person from an identity has taken place, it is a severing of value in general from human practices. Practices make the athlete something that has meaning within particular discourses. The reification involved is the unproblematic or unreflective construction of the athlete/subject which resides in speech as though it were a perennial, non–practice-related phenomenon.

In opting for the second kind of understanding of reification my concern is to emphasize a different way of reading what is involved in constituting the young, black athlete as a package. What is ideological within this second conception is the understanding of the contemporary language practices surrounding athletics as simply referential. The individual in question was not naturally a package any more than he was anything else. What constituted him as a kind of thing was related more generally to the ownership of such things. What are regarded as sports, athletics, and the system of relations which might legitimately pertain to them operate within a discursive practice emphasizing selling programs, packages, and educational institutions living off their ability to publicize what they do.

In an earlier period the forces at work constituted sports and athletics in other terms. For example, the invention of sports as a Sunday pastime goes back to a struggle between the English monarchy and the Puritans. The birth of the Sunday sports day was, among other things, an attempt by King James to diminish the influence of Puritanism.[62] Once the sports Sunday was established by King James's decree, persons were given sports-related identities on the basis of their willingness or unwillingness and ability or inability to participate in the newly constituted pastimes. These identities, e.g., the religious fanatic or clumsy fool, were no less objectifications than are our current ones surrounding the contemporary sports system. The constitution of modern sports with an emphasis on virtuoso performance in front of mass audiences produces not only stars but also various marginalized identities, which extend downward in the status system to the "nonathlete" (a prevalent self-description). Ideology, as it emerges from the mechanism of reification thus resides in the making of a produced phenomenon into something considered a natural referent of speech. What is to be recovered is a nonreferential understanding of how a sports discourse does its work, the process wherein one kind of form — e.g., commercial language as imposed on sports — is opposed to another — e.g., a health-related, educational, artistic, or some other form of language/practice.

If we wish to speak of the ideological mechanism of reification as involving some kind of loss, the genealogical perspective I have just elaborated does not prevent it. We must recognize, however, that reification-as-loss operates at another level of analysis. Preserving the same ontology — namely that every form of discourse is an imposition of an order on an otherwise disordered world — we can still look within those forms of order for losses, contradictions, and incoherences. When we do this, we focus, not on the values that are given a birth in the imposition of a discursive formation, but on the values which are prized and at issue within that formation. For example, one can find aspects of modern sports commitments that range from the merely discourteous (a minor value system in our present social formation) to the inhumane, exploitative, and collectively disabling (value systems at the center of how we live); forms of understanding that hinder our ability to think the connection between sports as they "are" and these value systems are ideological in the more traditional sense of the term.

We also find the dissimulation mechanism closely tied to the mechanism of reification when we do an ideological analysis of the sports example. Dissimulation, like reification, involves suppressing the historical genesis of something. But the major aspect of dissimulation is the presentation of sports talk as if it were wholly cut off from other forms of discursive practices. For example, contemporary sports announcers cooperate in this dissimulation when in announcing college athletic contests they refer to "student-athletes." In a situation in which college athletes are recruited by coaches solely on the basis of their athletic ability and, it seems, their ability to help sell a school's program, the "student-athlete" utterance is a form of dissimulation. Evidence is overwhelming that when student-athletes get injured and can no longer play sports, they find their scholarship to the school withdrawn. This suggests that the student side of the hyphenated identity is merely ideological. To the extent that an identity applied to performers in college athletics emphasizes anything but a role in a commercial and prestige-enhancing venture — the primary kinds of values promoted in big-time college athletics carried by the media — there is dissimulation involved.

The dimension of what we think of as play that is part of sports and games at the time they are invented gets diminished in favor of their specularizing (spectator-enthralling) dimension, and fewer and fewer of those performing in such a game are playing. For example, football players (here the use of play is increasingly ideological) who, when the game was more like rugby, were all players in the sense of performing many different, talent-demanding moves — kicking, throwing, dodging, etc. — now take part in a so-called game that has a majority of roles which are monotonous, single-function tasks. The evolution of this sport bears a striking resemblance to the evolution of the modern technologically sophisticated factory. For how many who enjoyed the old games of football they played as children would the prospect of trying to maul the person across from you — the task of the blocker on an offensive line — be something that seems like play?

Finally, Jameson's notion of ideology as containment becomes relevant in the increasing mediaization of sport. In recent years, for example, the television networks hype college basketball games by placing them within a story. If the NCAA finals are to be played in city X, all games having a bearing on the championship are introduced as part of "The Road to X." What is thus narrativized is simultaneously the sequence of contests and the sequence of viewing. Of course, there are always other narratives not publicized, not only of those who failed at a sport and lost their athletic scholarships but also more subtle effects of the totality of the modern sports system. For example, the stories not told include those of persons marginalized as nonathletes and thus deprived of both status and the opportunity to play because play as a phenomenon is monopolized, even in elementary schools when the emphasis is on major sports, by spectator-oriented games whose performance demands increasingly select only a few virtuosos. Even critiques of sports which emphasize things such as boxing's brutality and commercialization in general tend to name problems but contain them insofar as they fail to represent the way a system of living as a whole is implicated in the sports phenomenon.

Having run through an example which exercises most of the ideological mechanisms, it is appropriate to reassert the overarching metalanguage within which the problem of ideology has been constructed here. Ideological production is to be regarded as a mode of writing that promotes a misreading of the value investment inherent in the meanings attributed to persons and things, a misreading involving the various mechanisms reviewed and applied above. But in keeping with the metalanguage of ideology employed here, the linguistic features of ideological writing need to be further elaborated. As I have already noted, it is most frequently literary theorists who have supplied the more interesting ideological analyses. Parry's analysis of Joseph Conrad is a case in point.

Parry emphasizes the ambivalence of Conrad's texts. On the one hand, Conrad makes use of irony and other distancing literary devices to disestablish "enshrined notions about the unassailable nature of existing social institutions and standards of conduct," but on the other hand, Conrad vindicates the idealistic intent behind colonialism as he denounces some of its forms of implementation.[63] As a result, a novel like *Heart of Darkness* undermines itself because while it provides a critique of excesses and insensitivities of colonialism, particularly its either/or forms of thinking, the force of the critique is "ultimately undermined by a discourse invoking a solidarity with the progenitors of a system based on and sustained by lies."[64]

An appreciation of how these ambivalent effects operate, however, requires a very specific treatment of Conrad's stylistic devices. According to Parry, Conrad maps the colonial mentality as a dichotomous interplay of black and white: "a Belgian woman clothed in black, wearing a white head-dress, a black moustache on a white face, dark eyes in a pale face, white eyeballs in a black face."[65] Conrad's treatment is directed to showing that this white/black figuration of the colonial mind leads to an unreflective, self-justifying absorption into a good/evil, truth/ignorance, chaste/defiled set of dichotomies used to contrast the colonizer with the colonized.

Conrad goes on to display the white/black dichotomy in a more ambiguous light, subjecting it to "a radical rearrangement subverting Europe's
customary imagery."[66] For example, white Brussels is represented on the
surface as a "clean white city," a "white sepulcher." Conrad then shows
it to be "the place from where a rapacious colonialism is organized."[67] This
rhetorical device, along with several others that Parry presents, creates
a level of functioning in *Heart of Darkness* that supersedes the surface
colonial adventure story. In general, Marlow's narrative, the major voice
in the novel, undermines itself because one can see how what Marlow
observes is created and imposed by colonialist ways of thinking. The novel
thus calls into question prevailing concepts of intelligibility: "it shows that
what is 'true' and 'real' is the human presence as modifier."[68]

While Conrad's novel is a strong attack on colonialist ideology, carried
out with a variety of literary mechanisms — rhetorical and ironic devices
most notably — much of its political force is blunted by a level of thinking
immanent in Conrad's textual practices. What he disavows with his writing
at one level (the colonial system of domination), he reinscribes at another;
while he creates a distance from colonial practices at their level of implementation, he valorizes an idealist doctrine of cultural allegiance.
Imperialism's "vile agents" are juxtaposed with beliefs in an ideal. "Although
[Marlow's] narrative abundantly validates his view of colonialism as
robbery and violence" and thus challenges colonialism's practices, the basic
ideology justifying colonialism remains in place for "his story concludes
with an affirmation of loyalty to Europe's illusory pure form."[69]

Power and Authority Reinscribed
in Social and Political Analysis

MEDIATION THEORY

These novelistic reinscriptions of existing forms of power and authority
are matched by the discursive productions we find in various social science
genres. One example emerges in the recent tendency to theorize alternative dispute-resolution procedures. It is an increasingly popular move in
recent years to take disputes outside of the normal, legal system of lawyers,
courts, prosecutors, judges, etc. If one takes as given the terrain within
which the dispute emerges, as well as all the identities attached to the
parties of the dispute, the economy of this move tends to militate in its
favor. Two aspects of this economy are immediately apparent. First of
all, with respect to some disputes the legal norms, which must be employed
once the parties legalize their disagreement, produce costs that threaten

various aspects of the disputants' well-being even more than the threatened loss of the dispute. Second, whatever the direct costs of the legal norms, the legal process leading up to the invoking and implementation of those norms imposes high costs. It should suffice to mention attorneys' fees, crowded court calendars delaying resolution of the dispute, and the proliferation of ideologically mystifying issues, which are all part of any adversary proceeding and tend to raise communication and information costs.

If we remain within this economic metaphor of conflict resolution, it is difficult to view alternative dispute resolution or "mediation" as anything but a wholly rational institutional development that ought to be encouraged at a practical level and theorized at an intellectual one. But however rational an institution may appear within one perspective, such as the one bounded by the idea of cutting the costs of disputes, there are alternative perspectives one can evoke which show the limited range of that rationality. All rationalities derive their cogency from some authority which, itself, must remain unquestioned if that rationality is to stand undisturbed and undisputed. For the purposes at hand, the rationality of mediation procedures requires a nonpolitical view of the distribution of society's legalities and illegalities, even though the turn toward mediation reflects a disavowal of the domain of the legal. (It is doubtful, one might imagine, that the existence of a well-developed system of alternative dispute resolution in the old Austro-Hungarian Empire would have sufficed to dissuade Franz Kafka from introducing us to Joseph K.)

What kind of disavowal is involved in the repudiation of the normal, legal route for dispute settlement, and what is the result? While mediation disavows the existing system of legality at the level of its intentions, at the level of its representational practice, it reinscribes the most significant aspect of that system, the part that legalities play in creating the meanings attached to persons, collective groupings, and actions and relationships.

To recover this aspect of the language of the law, we need a politicized view of how legal codes speak and what silences they represent. Insofar as existing legal codes represent historic political victories, the language of the law reflects the institutionalization of some values and interests and not others. Assuming that prior to institutionalization there exists, under most circumstances, a plurality of different value and interest positions, each of which would have given us a different legal discourse, the existing laws lack depth insofar as the diversity of demands and struggles prior to their emergence cannot be read in the univocal code. The narrowly politicized view of the law, which simply suggests that the laws favor a particular class or the interests of the few rather than the many, fails to record the potential diversity now hidden by the code, because what are usually regarded as the suppressed interests are based on what is already named and accounted for.

Thus, the political functioning of the law goes well beyond its role in enabling recognizable social groupings and limiting or impeding others. In the case of the criminal code — to the extent that we view the law as a set of strategies designed to prevent transgressions, however unequally those preventions may be administered — and in the case of the civil code — to the extent that we view it as simply designed to channel and resolve or control conflicts, however it may favor one kind of party over another — we lose our ability to read the law as part of an overall system of power.

This system of power functions as a productive, normalizing force. In the case of the creation of penalties for various kinds of offenders, this productive aspect of the law is reflected in how various offenses are differentiated. What a society is, among other things, is a set of people who are differentiated into various kinds of individuals and groupings. This differentiation frees certain persons to act in some ways and limits others, and this general regulation is managed, not only by responding to transgressions, but also by creating types of persons and collective groupings which are constitutive of the situations we can encounter. Foucault was speaking of this aspect of legalities when he referred thus to the functioning of penalties: "penalty does not simply 'check' illegalities; it differentiates them, it provides them with a general 'economy.'"[70]

Foucault's point is that the legal discourse represents power through its participation in reproducing the social categories by which a society is structured, as well as by restricting some people and reacting to their transgressions. Therefore, attempts to oppose or criticize the exercise of power by various social-control agencies — the legal apparatus, state apparatus, police, social work profession, etc. — reinforce that power to the extent that the critique or opposition reproduces the same discourse through which the institutionalized form of power operates. D. A. Miller has captured the irony of this couplet of disavowal and reinscription in his analysis of nineteenth-century police novels. Speaking of Zola's *Nana*, which portrays the brutality of the police toward prostitutes, he points out that:

> the police procedures that are censured in the story reappear less corruptly in Zola's method of telling it. . . . Zola wants to register the Parisian *fille* no less than the police. Nana is the title of a file, referring both to the prostitute who resists the record and to the novel whose representational practice has already overcome this resistance.[71]

A similar irony manifests itself in moves to resist or avoid the authority of the legal structure through mediation. There are numerous instances, but one stands out at the moment because it can be witnessed at present in municipalities in both Europe and America. There has been an increasing turn toward mediation techniques, rather than the police and courts, to get "squatters" off pieces of land. Where is power functioning in such a situation? Clearly the major dimension resides in the designation squatter. The existence of the squatter in legal discourse reinforces its position in political, economic, and social discourses.

There is nothing legible in the interaction between persons and ground that makes us say "squatter." The historical process whereby the "squatter" came into language is a process of struggle over what were to be legitimate claims to land use. In one kind of case, a classic one, the formation of a society in which a sedentary, agricultural, and commercial culture combines with a nomadic, hunting, and fishing culture, the land demands and political power of the former end up criminalizing much of the traditional land-use patterns of the latter. In such cases, what used to be the acts of fishing, hunting, and pitching the tent become various deviant acts such as poaching and squatting. The controlling discourses, which give value and meaning to the ground, result in a dispersion of legitimate and illegitimate identities and actions. The squatter, then, is a historically produced phenomenon with political significance. A thoroughgoing political approach to land-use conflict would call into question such identities as the squatter, rather than incorporate them into the conflict-resolution procedures.

Within this scenario, it can be seen how politically vacuous is the gesture toward negotiation and mediation. As long as the understanding within which there are squatters remains in place, there can be very little range in the outcomes of disputes in which squatters are involved. Operating within the squatter identity, squatters must inevitably relinquish their claims to land. Not surprisingly, therefore, what was considered the resolution of a recent conflict between squatters and the city of Honolulu was the forcing of the squatters off beaches where they were living and onto what amounts to a reservation on inferior public land. Unless the past is recovered in such a way that one begins to excavate the silences that were generated by the emergence of the prevailing authoritative discourses, what are sanctioned as conflicts in a society can only produce a marginal effect on the political process.

It is here that the political insensitivity of the new mediation theory becomes apparent, for it positively celebrates its ahistoricity, seeing itself as "more concerned with the present and the future than with the past."[72] The purpose of turning away from the past is the familiar "let's-forget-the-past-and-let-bygones-be-bygones" argument. Reiterated here, it amounts to an insensitivity to the standing that parties to a conflict bring with them as a residue from the past.

Mediation theory's neglect of the past is implicated in another of its

The Problem of Ideology

tenets, the avoidance of adversarial conflict-resolution procedures. Part of the adversarial dimension of what is called a "dispute" is sequestered in the identities of the participants. To return to our example, when squatters and landowners join in a nonadversarial conflict-resolution process, the adversarial part resides in the silent past. This adversarial dimension, no longer recordable in the discourse which disperses the landowner and squatter identities, remains as a silent possibility within either court battles or nonadversarial mediation processes.

In keeping with mediation's nonadversarial self-understanding, much is made of the so-called neutrality of the mediator. Mediation, as two mediation theorists have put it, is the "process by which the participants, together with the assistance of a neutral person or persons, systematically isolate disputes and reach a consensual settlement that will accommodate their needs."[73] But as noted above, the partisanship involved in a mediated dispute precedes the dispute-settlement structure; it exists in the identities of parties whose conflict is being mediated and in the silenced controversies immanent in the way official and authoritative social discourses lend meanings to actions (recall Brecht's remark, "What kind of crime is it to rob a bank compared with owning one?") and objects (e.g., real estate). It is therefore relatively insignificant that the mediator happens to be neutral, for most of the partisanship is involved in the dynamic that creates kinds of persons and the controversies in which they find themselves.

Related to the neutrality claim is yet another ideological aspect of mediation theory's celebration of its conflict-resolution advantages. Mediation theory trades on what Baudrillard has called a "naive anthropology" of need fulfillment.[74] As the above passage implies, mediation theorists assume that a society's conflict-resolution process is directed toward accommodating, through structures of decision making, the needs of its individual members. The mystification in this idea of needs becomes apparent when one takes any object involved in a dispute — e.g., the residence of a couple that is separating — and inquires into its meaning and value. The modern residence, as Baudrillard shows, has changed its meaning. It is now more of an object of consumption than a place symbolizing a hereditary space which locates persons in an organic relation to others.[75]

The concept of a need hides the meanings that surround the individuals in any given dispute. What are silenced by an anthropology of need fulfillment are the processes that value objects and determine their meanings for the persons involved. Mediation is no more politicized than legal structures here, for it does not invite reflection on the dynamic, structural effects that give objects their significance. Rather, it empiricizes the object, taking its meaning as unproblematic.

There is, however, a slight shift involved in moving into mediation discourse from the legal discourse. This is a shift away from rights and toward wants. More generally, it is a shift away from the individual rights-oriented discourse which implicates and empowers legal codes and personages and toward a psychological discourse which implicates the psychological codings that can empower either experts or lay persons. Within this psychologically oriented discourse, the subject is asked to probe beneath the surface discourse of captious demands made in the heat of controversy to the latent conflict involving wants and needs. But where does the self derive interpretations of its wants? A mediator's injunction to find the hidden text of controversy may be effective inasmuch as it may find an agenda of controversy that could not have been managed had it not been brought into communicative discourse. But, once again, the scripting of the contemporary self-understanding is a political scripting. The injunction to the mediated subject to tell the truth about himself or herself, to produce a list of "real" wants and demands, is no less political than that involved, as Foucault has shown, in the confessional.[76] The subject's finding of that "truth" is always the acceptance of some aspect of power and authority. In finally submitting to each other, the mediated participants submit to a power immanent in a discourse in which their selves are imposed, whether that discursive constitution of selves evokes the practices of health, economics, psychotherapy, etc.

Modern mediation theory tends to encourage a psychological form of reflection and understanding of the self and thus to encourage a preemptory consensus or rapid closure, rather than a political form oriented toward disclosing values and interests that may function outside of the participant's discursive competencies. A politicized form of reflection would disclose the forces that bring the particular persons to certain kinds of disputes and other parties to similar disputes; it would seek to recover the genealogy of such disputes and thus the formation of warring classes of many relatively advantaged and relatively disadvantaged parties. But because of the individual dispute orientation of mediation as a structure for conflict management and its absorption into a psychological code, it can only perform a social control rather than a political function.

Finally, the absence of this politicizing function is evident in mediation theory's notion of discourse. Language is metaphorized as clarity. What is encouraged is good communication. But, as has been implied in our previous analysis, discourse is a resource, not a transparent means of communication. The statements in a discourse can be viewed on the basis of the assets they distribute, even as they appear to operate innocently in communication. Because mediation's psychologized notion of reflection operates within the transparency model of discourse, it fails to encourage a linguistic form of reflection, one that would help the participants to his-

The Problem of Ideology

toricize their conflicts and seek conflict resolution at a level that addresses the functioning of power and authority as they operate to legitimate a limited range of disputes. Mediation's model of discourse helps it to perform the same function as other social-control agencies, even the ones (e.g., the legal) which it disavows. It re-creates power and authority, allowing them to do their work in silence, free from controversy.

THE POLITICS OF MANAGING "CRIME"

Two studies in the area of public policy related to criminality provide further instances of the reinscription of existing structures of power and authority. These were conducted by James Q. Wilson, one on criminal investigation and the other on the efficacy of punishment. Written in a conventional public policy/public administration style, both studies can be shown to yield a different kind of interpretation when read within a politicized literary perspective that emphasizes the representational practices immanent in the writing.[77] The first one, *The Investigators*, loses its ideological innocence when we pay attention, not to the statement of motives (in which Wilson declares himself to be innocent of partisan or polemical purpose), but to the grammar and rhetoric of the text. When we do this, we find that at the level of textual practice Wilson has created, in general, a legitimating pamphlet for the existing power structure, and, specifically, an apology for the FBI and DEA (Drug Enforcement Administration).[78]

This legitimation/apology consists primarily in Wilson's uncritical use of the prevailing discourse of "criminal investigation." He describes and analyzes the two investigative agencies using the language that they use to describe themselves and their adversaries. He invites us to visit a world of subjects/objects called "investigators," "informants," "extremists," and "drug traffickers," and he describes their conduct in language that we ordinarily associate with the genre of business or administrative job-performance evaluation. There is thus a complicity between the genre in which Wilson writes and the practice of investigative agencies, and the effect of such a complicity is a failure on Wilson's part to politicize the field in which he works. For example, a "drug trafficker," for Wilson, is one so identified by investigative agencies. Large pharmaceutical companies, whom some would want to recruit into this category (for they traffic in more dangerous drugs than any other "drug dealers"), receive no mention. In short, Wilson does not approach the language of investigative conduct from the point of view of the historical processes which have resulted in the proliferation of various criminal identities. He treats criminal roles as if they were self-selected, rather than as nominations which emerge from complex power-related processes.

But Wilson's depoliticizing rhetorical gestures can only be appreciated when contrasted with a politicizing mode of inscription which resists a complicity with power- and authority-reproducing representational practices. In an extension of the remark quoted above, Foucault has spoken of penalties in a way that provides a politicized contrast to Wilson's rhetorical complicities:

> Penalty would . . . appear to be a way of handling illegalities, of laying down the limits of tolerance, of giving free reign to some, of putting pressure on others, of excluding a particular section, of making another useful, of neutralizing certain individuals and of profiting from others. In short, penalty does not simply "check" illegalities; it differentiates them, it provides them with a general "economy" and, if one can speak of justice, it is not only because the law itself in the way of applying it serves the interest of a class, it is also because the differential administration of illegalities through the mediation of penalty forms part of those mechanisms of domination.[79]

Wilson participates in this "general economy" inasmuch as he employs the predominant codes of law enforcement and crime prevention rather than stepping outside the discourse of the administration of criminal investigation and opposing it with a politicized understanding. Moreover, his genre of writing provides a grammar of absolution, for he nominates the "task" as the appropriate initiator of action, arguing that a properly administered investigative agency would allow the task to determine the behavior of the investigator. Apart from this ֿgrammar, which absolves investigative practices by making the task an agent, is an important rhetorical commitment, revealed when we interrogate task at the level of its metaphoricity. When we do, we find a rhetorical commitment in Wilson's text that undermines his explicit political motive, a recommendation that the task replace the prevailing, "top-down" (rigidly hierarchical) model for running investigative agencies that Wilson criticizes.

If we regard a task, not simply as a thing to be done (a job or performance), but as something that has meaning within an institutional context which prescribes roles within criminal-investigation hierarchies, we see it in a more revealing interpretive context. It turns out that its meaning within an organizational context is close to its linguistic origins, for "task" is a metaphor deriving from *taxa, taxara*—Latin for "a fixed payment to a king or feudal superior."[80] Although the connotation has changed to accord with modern modes of authority and sovereignty, it is still the case that a task determines conduct only because it implies an organizational hierarchy and the duties associated with it. In performing a task, one is deferring either to an individual or to an institutionalized collectivity in authority. Wilson's political program is thus vacuous inasmuch as top-down administration, for which he would substitute the task, is simply reintroduced, more subtly, in a management-by-task model.

It should be noted that there is nothing unusual in the personal motivation behind Wilson's analysis of the investigators, and there is evidence of an extraordinary level of skill in the structuring and consummation of his inquiries into the administration of public policy. Most contemporary public-policy analyses could be selected for this kind of inspection of representational practices with a similar result. What evinces a motivation in Wilson's analysis, like other public-policy studies, is the discourse of public policy itself, which has a built-in clientele. The clientele for Wilson's study is the police, FBI, DEA, and similar agencies. If we render controversial the clientele for public-policy analysis and do not assume we are simply serving the implicit political programs implemented by bureaucratic personnel, we are forced to reflect on how to speak. It becomes problematic as to what grammatical and rhetorical moves are appropriate, and, at a minimum, we find ourselves privileging a political rather than a bureaucratic/efficiency code.

However, it is not easy to be convinced that Wilson's polemical postures are merely inadvertent or textual when we inspect his more recent analysis "Thinking about Crime." Here he not only purveys a conservative, system-celebrating ideological posture as if it were simply scientific inquiry but also denounces what he calls the "radical critics of America," claiming that these critics might be right about the need for changes in our criminal justice system, but that "to the extent that they propose anything but *angry rhetoric*, they would have us yearning for the good old days when our crime rate may have been higher but our freedom was intact" (my emphasis added).[81]

Wilson's insinuation that the only possible radical criticism of American institutions would substitute some form of rigid political control for our supposedly benign market system is belied by the existence of nations with a high rate of employment, a low crime rate, a low level of inequality, and the "freedom" of which he speaks. But this part of his claim is less interesting for present purposes than his remark about rhetoric. Wilson does not sound angry, but there is a rhetorical dimension to his language, and if there is a characterization appropriate to the rhetorical content and force to the writing in "Thinking about Crime," we are again led to the genre of the apology. Wilson's apology belongs to a typical, fairly sophisticated genre of apology for inequality in America, and it emerges, as before, in the "rhetorical motions of the text," displaying itself in a variety of ways.

One of the most immediately apparent features of the text is the omnipresence of the scientific code. The language comprising this code contains the terms familiar to scientific experimentation. For example, "findings" are reported in the language of probability, and in the quantitatively oriented terms of weighing, measuring, etc. There is a discussion of the "probability of imprisonment for drug dealers," and he speaks of "hard to measure factors" and "hard to observe" persons. And once the evidence is "weighed," the public-policy options that Wilson adduces are all entertained within the same weighing and balancing metaphors, making his conclusions appear logical rather than polemical:

> All this means that it is difficult but not impossible to achieve desired deterrent effects through changes in the law. To obtain these effects, society must walk a narrow line—the penalties must be sufficiently great to offset, at the margin, the benefits of the illegal act, but not so great as to generate in the criminal justice system resistance to their prompt imposition.[82]

The political insensitivity of this kind of analysis has already been discussed above in connection with *The Investigators.* Unlike Foucault, who sees penalties as responsible for the creation of subordinated subjects, Wilson treats these subjects as the natural referents of statements and neglects the processes wherein persons and activities are assigned criminal identities. The weighing and balancing figures of speech, which appear both in the scientific code and in the code of policy calculation, presume that there are unproblematic things to be weighed and measured. But there is a political process involved in creating the objects of the kind of penal science immanent in Wilson's thinking. To recover this political process, one needs to think of the social codes aiding and abetting an analysis in which the explicit linguistic vehicle is the scientific code. As Heidegger put it, "Science always encounters only what its kind of representation has admitted beforehand as an object possible for science."[83] What Wilson's neglect of this "beforehand" amounts to is a depoliticizing gesture, a failure to examine the power and authority assets and liabilities his various ways of speaking deliver. In addition to the scientific code, which is Wilson's primary analytic device, are the rhetorical commitments which arrive along with the code of individualism running through his discussion. Marxists, structuralists, and, in fact, theorists of almost every interpretive stripe have long recognized that a focus on the actions or attributes of persons blinds us to the structures or wholes within which attributes of individual persons, their actions, and the things they contemplate have meaning. For example, as I have pointed out elsewhere, to describe an individual as "disabled" is to exonerate disabling social structures, the performance demands of which create the meaning context within which disabled identities are produced.[84] Lurking in any attribute of an individual is a disguised social formation or structure, but the language within which Wilson analyzes crime and punishment is almost totally nonstructural. He presents an individual decision-making model in which a criminal is construed as one who has chosen between making an honest living and a life of crime. Crime statistics then become simply the sum of individual choices on the life-of-crime side of the selection process.

The ideational force in this kind of thinking is very much like the one we encounter in individualistic approaches to explaining inequality. Unless we realize that, for example, an individual said to "own capital" indicates a disguised relationship among individuals (a realization that requires structural-level figures of speech), such that X's poor position is understood to be related to Y's favorable position in the economic system, we are left with only individual-level explanations (e.g., poor motivation or bad luck) for the differences in income levels.[85] Similarly, the absence of structural imagery in Wilson's discussion of crime leaves him with no explanatory or interpretive resources when his individual-level model yields puzzling conclusions. Resisting a structural language which would provide a meaning-context or interpretive frame for understanding both the way persons end up in criminal role assignments and, more important, how such assignments develop, Wilson is forced back into the naive empiricist use of the scientific code. In one of the few places where he refers to the notion of structure, or, as he puts it, "economic conditions," he dismisses the issues such a frame evokes, noting that such conditions are "hard to measure." Within the strictures of such a methodological and political imagination, which cannot articulate views of structure and process, it is not surprising to find this amusingly self-evident statement presented as a serious, scientific conclusion: "Perhaps if ex-offenders had more money, especially during the crucial few months after their release, they would not need to steal in order to support themselves."[86]

But having money relates to what I pointed out about owning capital; it is a disguised relationship. Mr. X can have money only to the extent that something else happens in the totality of relations within which he functions. Wilson's failure to think about crime is thus represented in the grammatical and rhetorical commitments in his text. Grammatically speaking, he lacks verbs and overuses nouns, e.g., he wonders about how to treat criminals but fails to wonder about how things become criminalized. Rhetorically speaking, there is an overreliance on the scientific code, which harbors the metaphors of measurement (weighing, balancing, observing, etc.) and the individualism code with its metonymic commitment to representing persons in terms of their criminal attributes.

Recovering for a moment the dialogic impetus in Wilson's essay on crime and punishment, it will suffice to note that, unlike the "radical critics of America" to which he refers, Wilson does not give us angry rhetoric, but he does give us rhetoric. His insensitivity to the polemical dimensions of rhetoric in general, through his almost exclusive reliance on the code of science and his reification of the identities of persons (the "drug dealers," etc.) and their acts ("drug dealing"), renders him politically unperceptive. Whatever he thinks he is up to, his discourse fails to think about crime inasmuch as it fails to produce a pedagogy, a way of thinking/speaking that would reveal how and why modern society has created the reality implicit in the everyday language (and the public-policy analysis language) of crime and punishment.

With this analysis as background, how can we arrive at a more linguistically self-conscious model of writing for the social sciences in general and political analysis in particular? The common wisdom has it that social scientists should avoid ethically charged language in the descriptive or explanatory part of their presentation. This is sometimes construed, as it is by James Q. Wilson, as a matter of presenting the "evidence" (evidence that has emerged from social scientific investigations) in relatively nontechnical language, and then evaluating the alternative policy options in light of that evidence. But descriptions of evidence contain evaluations. Figures of speech and rhetorical and grammatical structures of discourse are not simply extra means of expression used to represent thoughts. What is thought is produced by the figuration of the text. For example, the employment of an individualistic discourse allocates responsibility for crime to persons whose conduct has been criminalized. Such a discourse is part of what Foucault calls the "mechanisms of domination," for it speaks in the language of the administration of penalties. Policy analysts who speak in the ordinary way, which is familiar to policy makers and the public at large, are letting the prevailing power structure play ventriloquist. When they let the existing structure of domination speak through their mouths, the alternative policy responses proffered for meeting "the situation" are predetermined by the interests that constitute "the situation" to begin with.

Policy analysis, then, is necessarily a polemical practice. Once we recognize that its value, the resources it lends, and the kinds of persons it presumes and creates come about through its grammatical, narrative, and rhetorical strategies, we are in a position to rethink the relationship it has with its clientele. In one respect, vocation of critical analysis is the same within this productive approach to discourse as it is in the representational approach: it is supposed to provide analysis. But the kind of analysis is different. Rather than accepting and reifying the subjects, objects, and surface relationships deployed by the languages of public policy and of everyday life, it makes available the practices that have produced the referents of that language.

Conclusion: Toward a Critical Posture

If ideological production, particularly the recycling of the prevailing system of power and authority, lurks in the ready-to-hand language, the responsibility of the social/political analyst must be located in the problem of writing. In this conclusion, therefore, I will explore the tactics of linguistic evasion necessary for what I will call a "politicized" form of writing. This is a form of writing that is conscious, not only of the need of being intelligible and of therefore connecting itself to political problems as they are understood by many, but also is conscious of how power and authority are sequestered in the language of those understandings. By using the prevailing social categories and observing the prevailing boundaries among kinds of discourses — economic, political, aesthetic, etc. — we are reinscribing power and thereby undermining any purportedly political analysis we might undertake.

Before rehearsing the various mechanisms for linguistic evasion in political analysis, it is worthwhile to explore the efforts of someone who was faced with a similar problem. For example, Charles Darwin recognized that his *Origin of Species* was a radical departure from the prevailing ways of thinking. But he recognized, at the same time, that prevailing linguistic practices were antithetical to his project. More specifically, as Gillian Beer has shown, "Darwin faced four major problems in precipitating his theory as language."[87] The first two problems were intrinsic to discourse as it exists as a medium of exchange between persons. The first is that language is anthropocentric in that it places man at the center of signification (something with which Thomas Mann was wrestling in his Joseph novels, discussed above); and the second that language, at least of the European variety, does not separate out intentions of a person or author. Indeed, had Darwin been able to use the language of the Hopi Indians, he would have had a linguistic medium much better suited to think and express his position.[88] The third problem was that Darwinian theory had no place for an initiating creator, but the notions of selection and preservation both tend to raise the "by whom" kind of question. Fourth, the natural history discourse, which Darwin had inherited, was saturated with natural theology. This placed him in the dilemma of having to represent the struggles with the old, teleological doctrine of natural theology in a language that favored his opponent. Thus, he had to "write against the grain of his discourse."[89]

In tracing through Darwin's correspondence and early drafts of his *Origin,* Beer is able to show how he employed various grammatical, rhetorical, and narrative devices to carry out his linguistic struggle. For example, Darwin shifted the structure of his narrative by shifting from a preservation imagery to a survival imagery, changing such expressions as, "the preservation of favored species in the struggle for life" to "the survival of favored species in the struggle for life." His changes tended to emphasize variability rather than development and distance him still further from the teleological mode of thought built into the language of natural history.[90]

Darwin's language problem is our problem, and one of the primary modes of resistance and evasion that has a politicizing effect is one already introduced above in the discussion of the arbitrary boundaries imposed between the variety of forms of discourse. Beer's analysis of Darwin is a case in point in that it treats a scientific discourse as if it were a literary text. The point is that a major form of politicization, or resistance to an ingrained form of power and authority, is failure to observe the boundaries of genre. Indeed, one of the major political-control mechanisms in a society is the boundary between what is thought to be part of a political discourse and what belongs within other discursive practices. What we need then is an expression for the kind of politicizing disrespect that questions the boundaries we use to delimit discursive practices, that shows us the power and authority immanent in the production of separate genres. Jameson's idea of "transcoding" is serviceable here. It is a mechanism by which those whose vocation is the critique of existing glosses on reality manage to "break out of the specialized compartments of the (bourgeois) disciplines and to make connections among the seemingly disparate phenomena of life generally." It is, more specifically, "the invention of a set of terms, the strategic choice of a particular code or language, such that the same terminology can be used to analyze and articulate two quite distinct types of objects or 'texts,' or two very different structural levels of reality." Through this invention, he goes on to say, "the compartmentalization and specialization of the various regions of social life (the separation of the ideological from the political, the religious from the economic, the gap between daily life and the practice of academic disciplines) is at least locally overcome, on the occasion of a particular analysis."[91]

There are abundant examples of such "transcoding," a relatively nonpolitical example of which is Lévi-Strauss's discussion of games and rituals.

> Games . . . appear to have a *disjunctive* effect: they end in the
> establishment of a difference between individual players or teams
> where originally there was no indication of inequality. And at

the end of the game they are distinguished into winners and losers. Ritual, on the other hand is the exact inverse; it conjoins, for it brings about a union . . . or in any case an organic relation between two initially separate groups.[92]

Lévi-Strauss's transcoding here helps us to relate the two seemingly disparate phenomena to a powerful social process dependent on a cultural one, the creation of meaning by the alternation of identity and difference. While Lévi-Strauss gives us a relatively politically innocent form of transcoding, two of Foucault's terms in his studies of the birth of the prison exemplify a highly politicized form. He refers to education, social work, psychiatry, etc., as part of a process of "normalization" wherein a variety of disciplinary agencies help to create a docile labor force by giving persons identities that render them susceptible to surveillance and regulation. Insofar as various knowledge disciplines and administrative agencies contribute to this form of regulation, Foucault includes them in what he calls a society's "carceral" network.[93] Foucault thus uses a terminology that takes the prison outside of the boundaries it has acquired in the prevailing way of speaking. In so doing, he has given us a code with which we can conceive the control dimensions of processes which appear benign and apolitical within the old, fragmented speech practices of education, nurturing, curing, etc. This transcoding gesture enlarges the arena for political talk. Rather than reinscribing political power by maintaining the divisions that allow it to operate unnoticed — in what Foucault calls its "disciplinary mechanisms" — he highlights political functions, extending them conceptually outside of the narrow arena of problems of rights and legitimate authority to the domains of knowledge and regulating administration.

Closely related to transcoding is a rhetorical aspect of writing of which Paul Veyne has taken note in analyzing histories of science. "When a historian stresses the dependence of the history of science in relation to social history, he is writing a general history of an entire period and is obeying a rule of rhetoric that prescribes the building of bridges between his chapters on science and those on society."[94] The rhetorical dimension of historical accounts, which Veyne describes here, is not so much the figuration in the prose as it is the juxtaposition that is countenanced in the genre of historical writing in a given period. When he states that "history is the realm of juxtaposition," he is making the point that what is the case, as historians construct it, turns out to be a function of the connections which are part of the legitimized practices for writing within a particular discipline — the history of science in this example. The ideology of the historical text within such an understanding emerges as the pattern of juxtapositions constitutive of what an event and nonevent are.

Transferring Veyne's point about the science/society relationship to another domain, we can imagine a challenge to prevailing ideologies consisting in writing with a new set of juxtapositions. For example, in his history of mind-control sects, Donald Meyer juxtaposes the content of theological commitments with sociological, psychological, and political forms of writing. In so doing, he sunders the commitment to theology as an individual spiritual commitment and shows its relationship to the alternative modes of social control emerging in the American political culture. Meyer's text, by dint of its juxtapositions, mounts a challenge to the American ideology of individualism, one of the ideational supports of which is the separation of religious belief from the sciences of psychology, sociology, and politics.[95]

Less subtle than the general pattern of juxtaposed discourses in a text are the juxtapositions of individual terms. The challenges to prevailing ideological investments which such a textual strategy perform was elaborated by Kenneth Burke under the rubric of "perspective by incongruity." Burke contrasted this concept with that of "piety," which he defined, after Santayana, as "loyalty to the source of our being." Piety, moreover, functions as a "system-builder," a desire to round things out and fit experiences together into a unified whole." Piety, in short, "is the sense of what properly goes with what."[96]

"Perspective by incongruity," which Burke saw as the essence of Nietzsche's style, consists in "taking a word usually applied to one setting and transferring its use to another setting."[97] An example of such a transfer, according to Burke, is Thorstein Veblen's expression, applied to bureaucracies, of "trained incapacity," used to alert us to the irrationalities built into bureaucratic processes, proffered as the height of the rationalization of public administration. What Burke emphasizes then is a mode of writing that challenges ideological modes of thinking (writing and reading). Urging that pieties ought to be broken or dissolved, he states that "planned incongruity should be deliberately cultivated for the purpose of experimentally wrenching apart all the molecular combinations of adjective and noun, substance and verb, which still remain with us. It should subject language to the same 'cracking process' that chemists now use in their refining of oil."[98]

Burke's strategy of planned incongruity, like the transcoding and juxtaposition shifting, is designed to disturb, denaturalize, and dislocate our imaginations so that we are able to problematize and question what passes as the natural and ordinary. All of these strategies have more specific linguistic features, but before turning to this level of refinement, one more, very powerful problematizing and ideology challenging mechanism must be ventured: it is the mechanism of historicizing. Certainly we owe to Marx

The Problem of Ideology

as much as to anyone the insight that the valuation attached to things which seem wholly appropriate, natural, and universal can be recovered when we discover the historical process by which they came to be. And much of contemporary, Marxist-oriented criticism and analysis emphasizes this historicizing mechanism. For example, Jameson's above-mentioned review of the film *Dog Day Afternoon* turns especially on his historicizing of what appears marginal in the film when one employs the usual narrative reading habits and follows the star, concentrating on his fate.[99] Describing the police operation outside the bank where Sonny (Al Pacino), the major character, is holding hostages after having bungled the holdup, Jameson says:

> It is no accident indeed that the principal circuit of communication of the film passes between the mom-and-pop store in which the police have set up their headquarters, and the branch-bank—the real-life original was appropriately enough a branch of Chase Manhattan—in which Sonny is holding his hostages. Thus it is possible for the truth of recent urban history to be expressed within the framework of the bank scenes themselves: it is enough to note, first, that everyone in the branch is nothing but a salaried employee of an invisible multi-national empire, and then, as the film goes on, that the work in this already peripheral and decentered, fundamentally colonized space is done by those doubly second-class and underpayable beings who are women, and whose structurally marginal situation is thus not without analogy to Sonny's own, or at least reflects it in much the same way that a Third World proletariat might reflect minority violence and crime in the First.[100]

Jameson's historicizing interrupts for us a scene that is so familiar it lacks a history. To think about existing institutions and discursive practices in terms of a political problematic it is necessary, at a minimum, to recognize that what "is" was not always the case. This recognition allows us to see, for example, that what was once owned by religious institutions is now owned by medicine, social work, and prisons, inasmuch as many of our ways of identifying who and what we are eschew theological language and incorporate the discursive practices of these modern institutions. We only see these identities as a matter of ownership when we are able to view the historical dynamic of change in this ownership.

This latter mechanism of historicizing is propitious for bringing us to a consideration of the specific linguistic features of politicizing, ideology-challenging forms of writing. Historicizing is reflected, for example, very specifically by a characteristic type of grammar, particularly the displacement of simple nouns by verbs and nominalizations. Instead of referring to criminals and sick persons, for example, politicized language invokes historical, political processes by noting that an object, person, or problem has been "criminalized" or "medicalized," or it employs nominalizations such as criminalization, medicalization, urbanization to indicate that what is has been brought about.

The next aspect of politicized writing invokes figures of speech. Among other things, rhetorical structures are always immanent in even the purist descriptions, a point that was elaborated above. What politicizing language does, as Ricoeur has put it, is to employ impertinent figures of speech that have the effect of challenging prevailing notions of what is pertinent. Among the more dramatic politicizing impertinences is Foucault's metaphor of the body, which he uses to convey the way that the operation of power can be read. In order to show that what we are — our individual and collective identities — are impositions of power rather than natural developments, Foucault speaks of "the penetration of bodies" to represent education, training, and "socialization."[101] The replacement of dead tropes that are thought of as literal with such disturbing and defamiliarizing figuration gets our attention and alerts us, as do Foucault's verbs and nominalizations, to the "is" as an imposition of an order, something resulting from practices.

Taken together, the grammatical and rhetorical play of politicized writing calls existing narratives into question. For example, by showing how various modern forms of subjectivity have been created — the psychologized person or the collectivity that has become a population — Foucault's writing style challenges modern forms of teleological thinking which imply that man is simply fulfilling a destiny rather than being molded or shaped (or participating in a self-construction). Prevailing identities of persons, things, and relationships embody implicit naturalizations, narratives that are unquestioned when they are sequestered in what appear to be descriptive or explanatory accounts. Even as seemingly nonideational a discipline as paleoanthropology has been shown to be driven more by its implicit narrative than any other mode of thought. For example, the employment of such conceptions as the "turning point," used to refer to the time when man descended to the ground, presupposes a story with a beginning, middle, and end.[102]

This implicit narrative in paleoanthropology is evident throughout the writings in the human sciences. If one assumes that, as Foucault has put it, "there is no prediscursive providence which predisposes the world in our favor," we must look upon every discursive production, even those by the human sciences, as impositions. Narrative imposition has been involved even in the traditional critiques of ideology. For example, critiques of modern capitalism often presuppose a prior existence in which a form of rationality existed in the relationship of persons to each other and to their object world. Then modern capitalism comes along and creates a fall into unreason or a forgetting of reason. Often the story ends with an imagined world of perfect or ideal rational consciousness. Such stories or narratives of the rise and fall of ideology are just as ideological as those popular in the late 1950s and 60s, which told stories about the end of theology.

A challenge to ideology is relentless politicization in the form of questioning the implicit narratives, grammars, and rhetorics that reproduce and reinforce forms of power and authority. I have mentioned just a few of the discursive mechanisms available for this challenge, most of which are fairly obtrusive. It should be noted, however, that even a seemingly realist genre of writing can be ideology challenging. In addition to the familiar literary effects of the neologism, oxymoron, or otherwise disturbing figure of speech, there can be a similar impact from simply simulating a typical literal genre of writing in such a way that the simulation comes across as parody. Much of the writing of Kafka, Beckett, and Handke functions this way.

What a politicized form of writing must do, in general, is somehow disturb us, force us out of our narrative habits by giving us an experience of discord in both our relation to things and to each other, by making unfamiliar, through transcoding or refiguring or otherwise recontextualizing, what has been familiar. This writing can reorient our valuations by dislodging privileged subjects, objects, and relationships in our conventional discursive practices. Our failure to be politicizing animals in our roles as social and political analysts has stemmed largely from what Samuel Beckett has called a failure to "feel the words in our mouths." Strategies that are politicizing then — to continue Beckett's metaphor — are strategies which make our words chewy. Writing styles that manage to tease our jaded palates are likely to force us to examine what we have been eating, and, as a group of social and political analysts, it should make us self-conscious about our roles in conspiring with those who have offered a bland depoliticizing diet.

2 READING BIOGRAPHY

Introduction: Scripting an American Hero

My decision to attempt a political reading of biography began with a reflection on the biographies of famous Americans, which constituted much of my leisure reading during my elementary-school years. The pleasure I derived from accounts of the early exploits and later accomplishments of Benjamin Franklin, George Washington, Clara Barton, Andrew Jackson, Anthony Wayne, and George Armstrong Custer, among others, was doubtless related to the ethical force of the writing. These people were cast as exemplary heroes, enacting exciting deeds with which the reader was meant to identify. Personal inspiration and approbation of the persons and deeds associated with America's emergence as an independent nation were the almost-inescapable productions of these life histories for children.

It does not take a sophisticated reading to classify these as pious biographies, and here I am using piety broadly in Kenneth Burke's sense, which extends the concept beyond its theological implications to refer to any representation of something in a way that celebrates its appropriateness.[1] More specifically, these biographies are pious inasmuch as they produce early American heroes as sacral emblems of the rightness or appropriateness of America's founding and early institution building. Biographies such as these, in creating these sacral emblems, smooth out and make untroubled the lives they treat, which has the effect of hiding the structural economies of personal success versus failure and the individual and collective costs borne for the paths some lives are able to take.

The emotional loading of these pleasurable reading experiences coupled with the reinforcement received from the usual curriculum running from school social studies through American government, tended to defer a reconsideration of these early biographies. Nevertheless, there were two experiences that helped distance me from them, and because a discussion of these provides a context for the readings which are to follow, they are worth elaborating.

The first is an encounter with a biography of a wholly different kind

This chapter was previously published in a slightly different version as "Reading Biography," *Philosophy of Social Sciences* 16 (1986): 331–65.

of person, *The Autobiography of Malcolm X*.[2] The reading of this biography was revelatory from several perspectives. Most notable perhaps was the enormous gulf between the positive, relatively detached, and calm self-appraisal in the autobiography and the treatment of Malcolm X in the media. Here was a man whom the press had fanaticized. This is not surprising, for it was one thing to be a black civil-rights advocate in the 1950s and 60s but quite another to be a champion of black separatism. Civil-rights advocacy produced a generally negative identity in the South and a relatively controversial one in the North, but at least the issues surrounding that identity fell within the official, rights-oriented political discourse, the boundaries of which were relatively uncontested in the North and South. But here was someone impugning the prevailing political discourse, arguing that it could never adequately encode the interests of black Americans. Moreover, in seeming to advocate a form of separatism and in questioning the circumstances surrounding America's founding (as a slave-holding society), Malcolm X was questioning a piety which had deepened since the Civil War, the idea of the importance of one nation at all costs. In any case, for the American press and broadcasting media, Malcolm X was exemplary; he was the exemplar of the fanatic, and identifying him as such was instrumental in maintaining our political peace of mind.

In this context, the autobiography was profoundly unsettling because it did not read like the ravings of a lunatic. Malcolm X's ideas and the policy implications he drew from them came across as reasonable and coherent within the narrative of his and, by implication, many blacks' experience of American institutions. At a minimum, this different kind of biography helped introduce me to a different America and a different kind of reflection on a life, one designed to question established pieties rather than reproduce them.

The second kind of provocation for a reconsideration of the biographies of early American heroes was my reading of accounts which presented these same personages far less sympathetically. At one extreme, for example, it is not difficult, as several writers have demonstrated, to cast an Andrew Jackson and a George Armstrong Custer as perpetrators of genocide, and increasingly, at a lesser extreme, it has been possible to discover a Benjamin Franklin who is less than an unalloyed hero and genius, standing for almost every positively appraised aspect of the American character. When I couple these two kinds of reflection-provoking experiences with my current interest in questioning genres of meaning production that perform legitimating functions for existing systems of power and authority, a political reading of biography becomes irresistible.

This declaration, of course, calls for some clarification as to what the genre of biography is, but because we have Benjamin Franklin on the line at the moment, it seems sensible to reflect a bit further on the concept of piety introduced above. This is especially appropriate because for me, the childhood Franklin biography made the strongest impression and because Franklin has been an object of both extraordinarily pious treatment and some fierce demythologizing.

Like the childhood biography I read, *Ben Franklin: Printer's Boy*, many of the more pious treatments of Franklin were encouraged by Franklin's autobiography, which not only provides these treatments with their basic narrative sequence and the events upon which they focus, but also seems to have been undertaken with the encouragement of a secular form of piety in mind. One aspect of the Franklin legend is relatively well documented. Correspondence surrounding Franklin's decision to write his autobiography reveals that he was encouraged to cast himself as an ideal model for the appropriate American character. But the task became more than simply exemplifying the ideal character; it extended as well to valorizing the context within which such a character ought to function. Franklin was encouraged to do no less than construct his autobiography as an advertisement for America. One friend from whom Franklin had solicited advice on the autobiography project said quite unequivocally that he could think of no "more efficacious advertisement" of America than Franklin's history. "All that has happened to you," he reminded Franklin, "is also connected with detail of the manners and situations of a rising people."[3]

That Franklin took the advice and began shifting the emphasis in the autobiography, which he had already begun some time before, was clear from what he said. "What had gone before he had written for his family; 'what followed,' he said in his 'memo,' was written . . . in compliance with the advice contained in these letters, and accordingly intended for the public."[4] This conclusion of a Franklin analyst is hard to escape: "when Franklin resumed his story, he did so in full self-consciousness that he was offering himself to the world as a representative type, the American.[5]

There is also abundant textual evidence that Franklin conceived the rest of his autobiography as a pious mission. It comes across as a narrative about success and the importance of hard work and perseverance in achieving it. In emphasizing his humble origins and his combination of ingenuity and industriousness, Franklin is also telling a tale about America as a place congenial to such success aspirations. There is no sophisticated sociology to be found, no hints that there is such a thing as an opportunity structure which sorts persons of different types onto different social rungs (or casts them outside the society altogether, as was the case with the "Indians"). Indeed, one cannot find much evidence that there are different types of persons in terms of how fortune, assisted by the aggression and acquisitiveness of the well placed, might help distribute outcomes which are conferred irrespective of persons' virtue, energy, ambition, and ingenuity.

Along with Franklin's explicit personal-success narrative, which celebrates the American context in which his successes are achieved, is an implicit narrative, which has been picked up by the above-mentioned children's biography and biographies of other early Americans seen as heroes. This might best be termed a "destiny narrative." Reminiscent of hagiographies and pious treatises on the life of Christ, this narrative, penned by Franklin's biographer and other pious biographers, treats every episode in a life as a sign of future achievement. In the theologically aimed biographies, the function of such destiny narratives is clear, they are aimed at showing that a divine hand is guiding each episode. The life described is described in the service of a moral imperative: the necessity of accepting the divinity of that guiding hand.

In the case of the secular pieties delivered by the Franklin autobiography and various other similar biographical treatments of Franklin and others, the moral imperative is more subtle, for it encourages an ideological reading of American heroes. The suggestion is that famous people deserve their fame. Everything in their lives is a sign of their future greatness. By implication, no aspect of the American social formation can be faulted, for the social-status distribution system is wholly appropriate. For example, early in the narrative Franklin says, "I was generally the leader among boys and sometimes led them into scrapes of which I will mention one instance as it shows an early projecting public spirit."[6] In speaking of his early reading, he mentions Dr. Mather's *Essays to Do Good*, "which perhaps gave me a turn of thinking that had an influence on some of the future events of my life."[7] To put the matter briefly, the style in Franklin's autobiography is a still-typical representational practice, that which constitutes a textual apology for American institutions and, by implication, a silencing of class contention, individual failure, social dislocation, and other aspects of peoples' lives which would be disturbing to the peace of mind of one who wishes to think that no one pays a disproportionate price for the success of others.

To highlight the piety/impiety distinction and its ideological implications, it is useful to consider, briefly, a wholly different treatment of the Franklin legend contained in Herman Melville's novelistic biography, *Israel Potter*.[8] Even apart from the debunking treatment Franklin receives at Melville's hands, the novel as a whole serves as a counterpoise to the pious political pedagogy in Franklin's treatment of himself in his autobiography and in biographical derivatives of the autobiography. Indeed, it would appear that Melville's project was very close to mine. His sources for the drafting of the novel were biographies, and that he was consciously crafting a novelistic parody of pious biographies is confirmed in his remark, "the many episodes and sketches that constitute the materials of Israel Potter are made to cohere ostensibly by the device of biography."[9]

The major contrast between *Israel Potter* and the biographies Melville was parodying is created by his focus on an ordinary person instead of a hero, an interest which had captured Melville's imagination and politicized much of his work during the period in which he was writing *Israel Potter*. Moreover, in elaborating his common-man theme, Melville shows us an America that spawns failure, frustration, and dashed hopes. The inversion of the Franklin image is effected by casting him as yet another vehicle for frustrating the hopes of the common man. When Israel Potter meets the famous Dr. Franklin, his expectations are constantly violated. Expecting, for example, to be served wine and pastry and to receive other amenities, he is disappointed, and Franklin accompanies every deprivation he dishes out with a brief sermon that makes a virtue of it. At one point the exasperated Potter exclaims, in reference to Franklin's visits from adjacent quarters, "Every time he comes in he robs me . . . with an air all the time, too, as if he were making me presents."[10]

Ultimately, Melville's Franklin is, in one analyst's apt characterization, "a paternalistic moralist whose ethics reflect an irremediable inability to understand the problems and desires of the common man."[11] Melville's ironic style captures a Franklin who rhapsodizes about simple virtues which are insensitive to the differences between those who can afford such virtues and those who cannot. The so-called virtues (Poor Richard-style homilies) amount to alibis for inequality. What comes through most powerfully in Melville's Franklin parody is the historical continuity of the effects of the ideology of sacrifice. In Franklin's hands, it serves as a mystifying success narrative, which, like the current economic myth of the small business becoming a large venture through hard work, hides the inequalities in a social formation. Today, the ideology of sacrifice, insofar as it is embraced by those who have to make the largest ones, serves as an impediment to an effective class consciousness among the oppressed. It blocks a politicized self-understanding that would serve to uncover forms of domination and subjugation, which are hidden in a rhetoric which absolves human practices of their worst consequences.[12] Melville's consummate ironic style is one of piety's worst enemies. But in addition to the biographical parody there are other ways to politicize biography, to read lives in ways that make more palpable the functioning of power and authority. As a first step toward inquiring into those ways, it is appropriate to speculate on the boundaries of the genre.

Biography

What is a biography, and should it be distinguished from an autobiography? In what follows, I plead for a rather relaxed approach to boundary drawing, primarily because the boundaries shift radically when one moves from one theoretical orientation to another. For example, at one extreme is the orthodox Freudian position in which all writing is autobiographical, at least at a latent level. Given, on the one hand, the narcissistic impulse to advertise oneself in one's writing and, on the other, the social proscription against blatantly demanding attention for personal feelings and episodes, the writer disguises such wish-fulfillment fantasies by displacing them on other objects and events or on another life (in the case of the biography or intellectual portrait). As Freud put it, the author "bribes us by the purely formal — that is, aesthetic — yield of pleasure which he offers in the presentation of his phantasies."[13] Supporting the Freudian model, Samuel Schoenbaum collapses the genre of biography into auto-biography stating that "biography tends toward oblique self-portraiture."[14]

Freud generally encoded the problem within a dialectic between individual desire and fantasy on the one hand and the collective nature of language on the other, which demands a transpersonal level or socially mediated form of expression and thereby frustrates wish fulfillment. Elaborating on this model, we can note that given that language is invested with institutional meanings, which have a history that precedes the desires anyone might want to express, and given the complexity of social roles — intellectual among others — various language practices have the effect of disallowing excessive self-preoccupation. The writer is faced with entering a meaning system that has, among other things, built-in knowledge and evidence demands, epistemological codes which severely restrict a narcissistic development of the text.

Freud's model, which pitted a narcissistic attempt to appropriate one's writing against the forces of institutionalized social codes, rendered him acutely sensitive to a need in his own writings to blunt the potential charge that psychoanalysis itself could be subject to displacements and thus to the same suspicions to which he subjected the discourses of his patients. This is treated below in an analysis of one of Freud's biographies. What is significant at this juncture is that Freud's dialectical model sets up the other end of the theoretical continuum on the meaning of biographies. This is the poststructuralist or textualist position which deauthorizes texts, claiming that the grammatical, narrative, and rhetorical structures in texts exceed, in their meaning-delivering effects, any intentional structure the writer may wish or try to impose. Accordingly, textualist theory uses the concept of displacement in a different way from its functioning in Freudian theory. It is used not to suggest that the work in question is hiding wish-fulfillment fantasies but to refer to the displacement of the author by the text. It is to suggest that the inherited styles with which texts are written produce the meanings a text delivers.[15]

This textualist position is ably demonstrated in an analysis of one of Freud's texts. While Freud tried to suggest that he relied on an unmediated form of observation in order to vindicate his interpretations, it has been shown that observation for Freud was just as mediated as it was for his patients. More specifically, Neil Herz makes the case that while Freud ascribed his interpretation of E. T. A. Hoffman's story "The Sandman" to a psychoanalysis with a structure that is observational and scientific, his inconsistent interpretation of the story can be laid to the irreducible figuration embedded in the psychoanalytic discourse.[16]

This brings us to a more comprehensive statement of the textualist position within which, in contrast with the Freudian position that reduces all texts to autobiography, no text is profoundly either biographical or autobiographical insofar as any writer inevitably is controlled to a large extent by representational practices which make statements by dint of their own institutionalized rhetorical motions. No author, according to the textualist position, wholly controls the text, and at times, the writing practices within which the "author" functions actually undermine the intentional argument he or she is attempting to produce. At a minimum, the textualist position, which shows how any speaker or writer operates within inherited discursive practices, resists attempts, Freudian or otherwise, to reduce the meaning of a text to an intentional structure. This leaves us with an encouragement, first of all, to forego a rigid distinction between biography and autobiography and, second, to avoid definitely classifying works as a whole into biographical and nonbiographical genres. That which purports to be wholly biographical may influence librarians, but as soon as we are involved in a practice more complicated than book shelving, the search for unambiguous classifying gestures becomes futile.

It is less misleading to say that texts contain a biographical code to the extent that there is a reference to a life, either that of the author or someone else, and that in some texts this code predominates, thereby inviting official and unofficial classifiers to say "biography" or "autobiography" and, where relevant, implement the consequences of the utterance (e.g., shelving it among other volumes that have invited the same utterance). Of course, the existence of the biographical code will always be a theory-mediated identification and will thus always be subject to dispute. My interest is therefore not in the classification problem but in the politicizing or depoliticizing implications of biographical codes, in assessing what is being effected by the way that lives are inscribed, not in placing a genre as a whole on some continuum of epistemological/political credibility.

The biographical impetus varies widely in its design, even when a bio-

Reading Biography

graphical code occupies a small part of a text. For example, there was a small, pious biographical code insinuated in a series of televised basketball games during the National Collegiate Athletic Association championships. The competition as a whole was cast in the form of a story called "The Road to Lexington," in reference to the place where the final four teams in the competition were to meet. The network's use of explicit story imagery was doubtless part of a strategy for attracting viewers: get them involved in the story and they are bound to stay with it to its conclusion. But while the major plot of the story focused on the competition, there were many other small stories within the general plot, several of which were biographical vignettes, intermittent stories about the lives of various people associated with the competition — players, coaches, etc.

In terms of the network's obvious interest in finding biographies that could be sustained throughout the big story, some of the writers' instincts did not pan out. The early elimination of some teams had the effect of leaving around a lot of unfinished biographies. But one fairly short biographical vignette did pan out, and it is worth highlighting because its implicit pedagogy reinforces my point about the pervasiveness of pious biographies. This biography, written as much by the camera work as it was by the pre-scripted and impromptu remarks of the commentators, focused on a small part of the life of an old man watching the competition from the stands. He was a retired trainer, employed in that capacity for many years at Villanova, the "school" whose team eventually won the NCAA championship. As the tournament progressed and Villanova's chances continued to improve, we were introduced to a man who had worked hard and selflessly for his school without having been rewarded by seeing its basketball team win the national championship. This hard-work-and-loyalty theme was pushed hard, partly because the network was constructing a small legend on a limited budget and partly because the potential story being written was that hard work and loyalty pays off. This story paid off because when Villanova won the final game, the network was able to finish the biography. The camera's eye, aided by more and more frequent verbal references, intensified its gaze on the old trainer, and although he suffered from an illness which rendered him impassive throughout the proceedings, whatever emotions he failed to display were lent to him by the commentary. Most significant for present purposes is the theme of the story, a theme very close to the one contained in the autobiography of Ben Franklin: the theme of hard work and loyalty paying off. In addition, the biography of the old trainer said, by implication, that America is a great place and college basketball is part of that greatness. Nothing but fulfillment and well-earned rewards were dispersed along "The Road to Lexington."

This is not the place to rehearse all the disappointments and structurally engendered deprivations connected with America in general and amateur athletics in particular or to elaborate on the implications of the increasing specularization and commercialization of what was once a form of play. Suffice it to say that one of the biographical codes embedded in "The Road to Lexington" was performing a pious political function.

Biographical codes pervade the knowledge enterprise as well, and here, as elsewhere, their functions are diverse. Biography tends to find its way into philosophical texts, for example, to the extent that the content of the philosophical position and its associated presentation requirements (form and content are especially inseparable in this genre) suggest the relevance of the life experiences of the philosopher. Exemplary here is what many regard as Nietzsche's autobiography, *Ecce Homo*, which in many ways is to the life of Christ what *Israel Potter* is to the life of Benjamin Franklin and other American heroes. Nietzsche's figurative construal of himself as the Anti-Christ is inextricably linked with his philosophy, which undermines all positions, Christianity among others, that locate meaning and value in a supersensuous realm, transcending human experience and practice. At great pains to distinguish his thinking from what had gone before, Nietzsche expresses this difference in a biographical code. "Listen! for I am such and such a person. For Heaven's sake do not confound me with any one else!"[17]

In addition to his playful modeling of his life and thought as a counterpoise to the life and teachings of Jesus Christ (to which the "heaven's sake," meant ironically, is a contribution), Nietzsche's resort to the biographical code is connected with his notion of the need for a self-understanding to make effective thoughts happen. Heidegger noticed that, although more biographically oriented than some of Nietzsche's other writings, *Ecce Homo* was not, stylistically speaking, a departure, because of Nietzsche's general "habit . . . of having an explicit and dogged self-reflection accompany his labors in thought."[18]

This doggedness to which Heidegger refers represents Nietzsche's conviction that the story of his life has led up to his thought. Nietzsche casts that story as one of his becoming increasingly healthy to the point where he is able to achieve the "thought of thoughts," which for him was the thought of the "eternal return of the same." This health metaphor was Nietzsche's way of figuring a freeing of oneself from the burdens (or sicknesses) he associated with forms of ethical thinking which deflect value creation onto some extrahuman agency. Urging others to achieve this degree of health, Nietzsche, remaining within a biographical code and quoting his own creation, Zarathustra, who exhibited perfect health, states, "Now I bid you lose me and find yourslves; and only when ye have denied me will I come back to you."[19] Again, the pedagogy takes an ironic turn, reversing Christ's teaching both in the structure of the statement and, by implication, in the theory of value it represents.

Biographical codes have found their way into sociological texts for similar, knowledge-related reasons. For example, it becomes an appropriate epistemological subject in Harold Garfinkel's ethnomethodological perspective in which reality is treated as an accomplishment of the human subject involved in an ongoing task rather than a static field of objects to be apprehended in passive, disinterested cognitions. Within such a perspective it is sensible to imagine that among the accomplishments toward which persons direct their activities in everyday life is the accomplishment of a coherent, socially marketable identity. Because most people acquire such an identity in the normal course of events, the energy they spend in working to mold a social self is done relatively economically and unobtrusively because they can resort to the usual scripts for which the eligibility requirements for their use is not in question.

It was therefore a propitious decision on Garfinkel's part to undertake an analytic biography of Agnes, a person in the process of preparing for a sex-change operation when Garfinkel began his investigation.[20] What made Agnes especially interesting from an ethnomethodological point of view was his/her extraordinary difficulty in the task of accomplishing a reality that most people have from birth, an unambiguous gender identity. Whatever sexual ambiguity we could discover in the average person were we to wax theoretical and resist the ordinary facticity of everyday life, such theorizing occasions rarely intrude on people's self-concepts. Most persons are able, without contention or energetic scripting, to think of themselves as a natural (100 percent, as Garfinkel puts it) male or female. Agnes's ambiguity thus played into Garfinkel's theoretical hands, because his/her possession of both male and female sexual insignia before the operation — a penis and breasts — led Agnes to strive to pass as unobtrusively as possible. Agnes tried to script that passing in such a way that it could be construed as an overcoming of an initial error of identification and an achievement of what could be considered the true sexual self rather than a choice among two different possibilities.

The case is thus also propitious for my purposes because if we take the situation as a whole — Agnes attempting to pass and Garfinkel constructing a narrative of the passage — we are confronted by at least two biographical codes, one primarily analytic (Garfinkel's) and one ideological (Agnes's). From an analytic point of view, the biographical code in Garfinkel's text functions in the service of sociological and scientific codes, for Agnes's story is offered as evidence of the superiority of ethnomethodological truth. The extraordinary lengths to which Agnes went to accomplish a consistent gender identity provided an exemplary case to show how "reality" is an accomplishment. And it provided an opportunity to work off Agnes's situation and argue that it is only in the process of managing everyday life that persons in general create social realities.

The other brief biographical vignettes, those of Agnes's family and her boyfriend, Bill, represent Garfinkel's extension of Agnes's problem to people in general as he scrutinizes their reality-management activities related to their association with Agnes's ambiguous social presentation. There is also a biographical code (autobiographical in orientation) embedded in Garfinkel's account inasmuch as he was involved in counseling Agnes and represents this role in a first-person narrative. This biographical code, like Agnes's, functions in the service of ethnomethodological truth. Like Freud, Garfinkel employs the scientific code to distance the autobiographical part of his investigation from his observations. The autobiographical dimensions he highlights are all designed to show that he took pains to situate himself in such a way as to know what was going on and, further, that he did nothing to intrude in a way that would compromise the data (Agnes's developing reality-management strategies).

The confrontation of biographical codes we can discern as Garfinkel scripts Agnes and Agnes scripts her/his gender tells us, among other things, about the pervasiveness of the biographical code. It asserts itself in intellectual endeavors as scholars try to manage knowledge production and in everyday life as persons try to manage the self and the other (both "real" and internalized).

Biography, Truth, and Value

It is in the light of this realization of the significant social-control dimensions of the biographical code that I approach the question of what kinds of biographical scripting tend to reinforce existing control structures in a society (as Agnes's certainly did) and what kinds tend to challenge them (as Garfinkel's did, albeit in a very limited way, given the lack of a reflective dimension to his own writing). Another way of putting this is to imagine a continuum with management at one end and politicization at the other. Biographies or biographical codes can then be placed on a continuum on the basis of the extent to which they support management and thus help to sell various control- and allegiance-producing institutions or, on the contrary, provoke thought about the existing system of truth or the political power and authority systems these truths support.

All biography has an ethical or valuational component, for there is no neutral way to script a life. Because there is no unmediated form of truth against which to judge biographical truth, the interesting question becomes one of how biographies function. And within this how question, as I have suggested, the interesting political questions surround the effects in biography which either invite belief in and allegiance to some authority or raise questions about it. When we turn to this kind of question, we find it difficult to separate out the various textual mechanisms. At a minimum, the rhetorical force of any fragment in a biography or biographical part of a text must be judged in terms of the rhetorical force of the text as a whole. Erich Auerbach's observations on part of Abraham's biography in the Old Testament provide an instructive example. He calls our attention to a seemingly trivial part of the text, the place where it is written that when Abraham began his journey with his son Isaac they began "early in the morning."[21]

Auerbach finds that there is no clear coherence in references to time if one surveys the rest of the episode. For example, it is not mentioned, he notes, "at what time of day did Abraham lift up his eyes and see his goal." Auerbach concludes that "early in the morning" is given not as an indication of time but for the sake of its ethical significance; it is intended to express the "resolution, the promptness, the punctual obedience of the sorely tried Abraham."[22]

Interestingly, the piety of the biographical vignettes and codes in the Old Testament work in a different direction than do the pious biographies of early Americans. Rather than emphasizing a person's ability to work out a destiny through individual effort and ingenuity, the rhetorical force of the Old Testament places destiny in God's hands. As Auerbach summarizes it:

> The stern hand of God is ever upon the old testament figures; he has not only made them once and for all and chosen them, but he continues to work upon them, bends them and kneads them, and without destroying them in essence, produces from them forms which their youths gave no grounds for anticipating.[23]

Whereas early American heroes displayed the American character who was capable, as was Benjamin Franklin, of raising up himself or herself, the representational style of the Old Testament is such as to portray God as determinative in any raising up (or casting down as is often the case). Indeed, as Auerbach states, "The concept of God held by the Jews is less a cause than a symptom of their manner of comprehending and representing things."[24] Divine control and the necessity for obedience is the agenda. For the purposes at hand, however, what becomes interesting as Auerbach treats the Old Testament text, is how it represents this necessity for obedience. In comparing the Old Testament with Homeric texts, Auerbach argues that Homer's writing does not invite interpretation, for "the Homeric poems conceal nothing, they contain no teaching and no secret meaning."[25]

The Old Testament, however, as a pedagogical/religious text presents episodes which extend into the shadows. In contrast with Homer's rich and seemingly complete descriptions, a narrated reality, the story of Abraham and Isaac "is dark and incomplete, and since the reader knows that God is a hidden God, his effort to interpret it constantly finds something new to feed upon."[26] Clearly, much of the ethical force of the Old Testament is connected with its textual strategy of inviting interpretation.

Auerbach's analysis demonstrates unambiguously that the ideational aspect of a text inheres in the representational practices it reflects. In reading biography in a political way, then, the interesting dimensions of that reading must raise the question of how the biographical code or biographical text (those texts in which the biographical code is predominant) works. Within this context, one reads biographical codes not to find out about who wrote them or how faithful they are to the "facts" but how it is that they contain meanings, how certain representational practices do their work, a work that can be arranged along a continuum of political challenge versus pious inscription of some aspect of entrenched power and authority.

Knowledge, Style, and Biography

When we are dealing with biographical codes as practices rather than as disinterested representations to be judged as true or false in the traditional, empiricist sense, it raises the issue of how to construe the relationship between biography and knowledge. Here, my emphasis is on the theory of knowledge immanent in the text itself, because there is an intimate connection between the way knowledge is represented and ideologies legitimate aspects of power and authority. The knowledge-related aspect of textual practice connects with ideology particularly in relation to the text's implicit claim to authority. For example, ethnographers are more likely to write in the first person than are social scientists who study cultures from a distance with aggregate data. For the former, the knowledge claims they wish to advance inhere in the implied claim that first-hand contact is a requirement for understanding an exotic culture, for ethnography as method is conducted within an epistemology that privileges direct contact between the analyst and the subject of observation. The authority of the text is established, as James Clifford has shown, with a series of grammatical gestures which establish the ethnographer's presence in the field of data and link the ethnographer to the reader as the reader's observation surrogate. For example, the first-person narrative is employed to represent the fact of first-hand contact and the related privileged place of the ethnographer for making knowledge claims; the second-person (e.g., "if you were a Nuer," one of Evans-Prichard's statements) is used to implicate the reader in the text, and the third-person is used in order to imply an objective level that will connect the study to a scientific, knowledge-validating code.[27]

Similarly, the grammatical gestures in a biographically oriented text represent the text's implicit theory of knowledge in general or its position on the relationship between the biographer and knowledge in particular. A striking contrast can be drawn here between Henry Adams's *The Education of Henry Adams* and J. J. Rousseau's *Confessions*. The former is an example of an approach to knowledge that requires self-effacement, for Adams strove to keep the focus off himself as the writer and subject of the account and on the historical forces to which he ascribed far more shaping power than the will or actions of the individual. In his meditation on the nature of the psyche and its role in orienting the individual, Adams metaphorizes the mind with mechanical, balance-related imagery suggesting that what helps to keep a person in balance is artificial and acquired through habit. "Sanity" he refers to as "unstable artifice."[28] Indeed, Adams saw the writing of his autobiography as a way of maintaining his precarious balance.

The Adams force metaphor then comes into play as he construes "man" as a force but one whose power is relatively feeble compared with the historical forces of technology and social change. It is a "fiction" he asserts, that a society learns through the force of its consciousness. "The fiction that society educated itself, or aimed at a conscious purpose, was upset by the compass and gunpowder which dragged Europe at will through fruitful bogs of Learning."[29] Within this epistemological perspective, which argues for the relative superiority of historical forces over individual or social consciousness in the meaning-creation process, Adams's use of a third-person narrative to distance himself becomes a coherent gesture.

Rousseau's various autobiographically oriented texts are also directed toward a representation of the knowledge problem, but offer a useful contrast with Adams's style/view because of their first-person narrative structure. However, Rousseau's first-person voice does not distinguish his project from Adams's as radically as the contrast in styles might make it appear. Even though Rousseau's grammar gives us a world seen through an individual's eyes, he saw his quest for self-knowledge as a vehicle for understanding the other. Rousseau's autobiographical texts are ambivalent, for in some places he seems to be saying that he has offered himself as a model and that anyone would do for such purposes, but in others he seems to be claiming uniqueness for his autobiography.

For purposes of comparison with the Adams autobiography Rousseau's ambivalence is less important than the imagery he uses to figure the knowledge problem. In contrast with Adams's model of the play of forces between the consciousness and impersonal historical developments, in which the latter forces overwhelm the former, is Rousseau's more mind-centric formulation in which, as one analyst put it, there is "an epistemological dialectic between knowledge of the self and knowledge of the other."[30] And, unlike Adams's position, which privileges the forces of historical change, Rousseau advances a thesis that situates the individual in a process of self-invention. Accordingly, Rousseau's episodes, like his use of the first-person narrative, become intelligible when viewed as demonstrations of his view that the meanings emerging from social change must be read in terms of how they are registered in an individual's self-consciousness. For example, Rousseau's description of the intolerant and angry reactions with which his writings were met tell us more about how he learns to take courage in his views than they do about the structure of authority in his historical age. Rousseau tells us how he handled "libelous" assaults on his reputation and not about what, during his time, was "libelous" and what forces are reflected in general in what is regarded as going beyond the bounds of reasonable criticism.[31]

It should be noted that, although Rousseau's first-person narrative coheres with other stylistic dimensions of his autobiographical writing in promoting an intentionalist rendering of knowledge and meaning issues, a first-person narrative can cohere with other, radically different epistemological orientations. While Rousseau's preoccupation with self-reference supports his subjectivist rendering of knowledge and meaning, Nietzsche's first-person narrative constitutes a critique of ordinary (including Rousseau's) self-reflection. Mingling his self-reflections with a carefully developed series of ironic tropes and metaphors, Nietzsche scripts himself with rhetorical gestures designed to show how reality in general is not available to the mind, whether it deploys itself in a self-reflective mode or otherwise. Nietzsche says, through the style of his autobiography, that reality is a product of perspectives which are rhetorically mediated. The self for Nietzsche is caught up in an uncontrollable play of figuration. "The involuntary nature of figures and similes is the most remarkable thing; one loses all perception of what is imagery and metaphor."[32]

While Nietzsche's autobiography in effect disavows most understandings of knowledge in general and the knowledge relevance of biographical writings in particular, Freud's biographically oriented study of Leonardo da Vinci is exemplary of the epistemologically self-conscious text which functions within conventional positions on knowledge.[33] In his Leonardo study, Freud is eager to show how psychoanalysis will explain not only Leonardo's extraordinary achievements but also his general work style (his tendency to leave works unfinished) and some of the specific details in his work (the Mona Lisa's smile in *La Gioconda* and why Mary's mother, St. Anne, appears as youthful as she does in *The Holy Family*). Freud is emphatic both explicitly and textually: his Leonardo study is to help vindicate psychoanalysis as a scientific, truth-delivering discipline. "Let us lend an unprejudiced ear for a while to the psychoanalytic work, which after all has not yet spoken the last words," he says in a typical grammatical gesture which removes his voice from an entanglement with the writings of his study.[34]

It is psychoanalysis inscribing the text as Freud innocently holds the pen. This gesture is not surprising given, on the one hand, Freud's psychoanalytic account of how a biography is usually written and, on the other, his desire to claim a disinterested, scientific posture in the production of his biography of Leonardo. On biography in general, he states, "Biographers are fixated on their heroes in a very peculiar manner. . . . They devote themselves to a work of idealization, which strives to enroll the great man among their infantile models, and to revive through him, as it were, their infantile conception of the father." This desire, he goes on to say, leads to a valorizing style in the biography, which in idealizing the hero, covers over "the traces of his life's struggle with inner and outer resistance. . . ."[35]

Freud distances himself from this psychoanalytic model of writing a biography, not only with the grammatical gestures with which he ascribes the text more to psychoanalysis itself than to himself as a writer, but also with an indirect, textual strategy which, ironically, reinstates one's suspicion that Freud may be subject to the psychoanalytic mechanisms from which he seeks to claim immunity. In his explicit discussion of his motives for writing *Leonardo*, Freud seeks to reassure the reader that he is not doing the opposite of what he claims biographers usually do; he is not trying to destroy the image of Leonardo as a legendary hero. He urges the reader not to "flare up with indignation and refuse to follow psychoanalysis because in its very first applications it leads to an unpardonable slander of the memory of a great and pure man."[36]

Here again it is psychoanalysis and not Freud we are following, but this distancing gesture, achieved by making psychoanalysis the author of the study, is less interesting in this instance than the indirect distancing Freud achieves by distancing himself from other biographers. At a manifest level, the reassurance that he is not destroying a legend is offered to try to avoid outraging readers who, upon seeing a legendary hero demeaned, might then not be open to seeing how psychoanalysis provides a scientifically sound interpretive procedure. But at a latent level, Freud's reassurance, when considered in the context of what he has already said about the fixations of biographers on their heroes, serves to extricate him from a (Freudian) psychoanalytic reading of his own text, a reading which, however, becomes irrepressible when one notices that this distancing gesture is a form of displacement.

Both of Freud's textual gestures, then, serve to implicate psychoanalysis as a disinterested science and remove him as a person with a psyche and its attendant motivations from the text. Nevertheless, Freud was, among other things, a writer, and any knowledge that might emerge from his Leonardo biography must be considered in the context of his writing problem. At an explicit level, Freud's Leonardo study fits somewhere between the emphases of Adams and Rousseau because the emphasis is on an interaction of inner and outer forces, which produce "the behavior of the personality."[37] However, when we pay attention to Freud's struggle with his knowledge problem as it manifests itself in his writing, this knowledge must be reflected back into the text's ambivalences and ambiguities. "Knowing," as it emerges from Freud's text, like any form of knowing, has to be read in the context of how it emerges. Freud's attempt, whether disingenuous or delusional, to ascribe his study to disinterested science would, if successful, make us misread his *Leonardo*. We would fail to see the disguised polemic — the selling of psychoanalysis and the depsychoanalyzing of his own account — which the biography serves. And, ironically, we would fail to achieve fully the pedagogy that Freud's version of psychoanalysis offers because we would be deterred from a symptomatic reading of Freud's text.

Political Biography

There is another type of biography which encourages a similar type of misreading. This type, what is called the contemporary "psychobiography," is also a knowledge-oriented form of biography, situated within the methodological practices of social scientists. As in the case in the Leonardo biography, which is written in a way that encourages us to read with an emphasis on the scientific code, the prevalent social-science genre of psychobiography and life history offers its lives within a scientific, knowledge-accumulation code. In contrast with Freud's studies, however, the new psychobiography manifests relatively little ambivalence and ambiguity with respect to knowledge claims. Freud, steeped in a complex hermeneutic of suspicion, knew too much and thus had to suspect himself. This self-suspicion, as I have shown above, left its textual traces.

In contrast, the new psychobiographers know too little. Having little suspicion of discourse in general, they fail to make their own discourse an object of scrutiny. As a result, the emphasis in psychobiographical texts has been on a very standard, empiricist kind of knowledge vindication.

Rather than reviewing several examples, it can suffice for present purposes to examine a recent overview of life histories and psychobiographies, because the self-understanding within which it is written constitutes more of an advertisement for the genre than a critical analysis. The major knowledge emphasis of William McKinley Runyan's *Life Histories and Psychobiography* comes across as a kind of ecumenical empiricism; he expresses the hope that we can piece together several different biographies of the same person so that each one, written from a different perspective, will form a component of an "optimal biography." "The optimal biography," he states, "will often be an integrative or synthetic one, which recognizes and takes into account a variety of more particular perspectives, weaving them into a more comprehensive and multifaceted representation of the life."[38]

Here is the epistemological rub: the idea that lives are "represented" by an unobtrusive, scientifically oriented form of discourse. With this idea, central to a bankrupt version of empiricism, comes a failure to appreciate that biographers are writers who participate in representational practices, and that their texts impose meanings on lives. When one recognizes the existence of these practices, the knowledge problematic shifts from the accumulation of so-called facts about a life to the writing itself. Why, one might ask, are some lives described and others not, and why are the descriptions cast in psychological-versus-political or other rhetorical modes of writing? What do the representational or discursive practices of various historical periods tell us about what is regarded as important, authoritative, and legitimate? Moreover, to the extent that we seek a politicized form of knowledge, we pose such questions in political terms, asking, for example, "at what price" are various individual and collective identities formed and recycled in biographically oriented texts, i.e., how are forms of power and authority implicated in the economies of the discursive formations within which the biographical code functions?[39]

The naive accumulation impulse, which treats the biographical text as a case study and seeks to explain behavior, fits into the more unreflective wing of the scientifically oriented branch of social-science practice. This emphasis is depoliticizing, even as it produces what are called "political biographies," inasmuch as it is unreflective about both how various practices produce scientific questions about behavior and how official forms of power and authority establish residence in the categories and kinds of utterances that are available to the psychobiographer. Runyan is aware that alternative explanations of figures such as Daniel Ellsberg serve different political motives, but he treats motives as extratextual causes.[40] As a result, he is unaware of his own language as he speaks of treating "behavior" and trying to improve and aggregate "case studies," and, more generally, he fails to appreciate that he and the "biographers" about whom he writes are writers operating within representational practices that contain political motives of their own.[41]

Runyan's text (and the biographically oriented texts about which it is a commentary) is thus a relatively pious political text. What politicizing gains it achieves in questioning the interests served by different approaches to a life, it relinquishes with its style, the way that it represents, unreflectively, persons and their relations. Such a militantly representational orientation to discourse, one which construes language in general as a transparent mode of communication and scientific discourse in particular as a wholly technical, representation-oriented tool, can only serve a business-as-usual kind of politics; it can only support and help reproduce the forms of power and authority manifested in prevailing discursive practices.

How, one might ask at this point, does one write a biographically oriented text in a language that is aware of itself or, as Nietzsche and Heidegger might put it, in a language that "thinks"? It is not surprising that one tends to find answers to this question by turning to the literary or poetic genre of writing, because it is becoming increasingly apparent that literature can be a hyperpoliticizing genre. Those examples in which a text's own linguistic practices are foregrounded show how language practices impose forms of authority.[42] It is therefore reasonable to expect a different style in a biography written by someone who is both aware that writing is a form of practice and that the writer's ability to control meanings is severely compromised by the control dimensions inherent in the preexisting discourses. Such a writer tends to produce a text in which the biographical code is intermingled with a critical code, a text that uses rhetorical gestures that open up the authority of the text in which they appear, and also open up the problem of how textuality or linguistic production in general has the effect of either summoning and installing authority or calling it into question.

Although there are abundant examples, I will introduce here Peter Handke's biographical eulogy to his mother, a text that is best read along with some lines from his poem, "Changes during the Course of a Day."[43]

> As soon as I step out on the street — a pedestrian steps
>   out on the street.
> As soon as I enter the subway — a subway rider enters the subway . . .
> As soon as I see the incredible — I become a witness.

> As soon as I enter the church—I become a layman.
> As soon as I don't ignore an accident—I become a busy-body . . .
> Then someone crawls out from under a thicket in the park and
>   becomes a suspicious subject.
> And when the car makes a sudden stop in front of me—I become
>   an obstacle . . .
> Then I am seen by a figure in the dark—and become a figure
>   in the dark . . .
> Then someone stumbles over me—and I become a body.
> And when I am then stepped upon—I become something soft.
> Then I am wrapped up in something—and become a content. . . .[44]

Without going into an extended discussion of the philosophy of language, it should be evident that Handke understood the constitutive effects of practices on human identities. What we are, the meanings we have as persons, are epiphenomenal to our discursive practices. Inasmuch as our meaningful existence is connected to the existing linguistic enactments that produce the meanings in everyday life, only linguistically evasive strategies will allow us a distance from the subjugation we experience merely by having to affirm our identities by engaging in ordinary speech. What Handke's poem provides, among other things, is a poetic version of one of Althusser's insights into ideology. Handke's poetic demonstration that meaningful subjects are epiphenomenal to language practices is equivalent to Althusser's remark that "ideology interpellates individuals as subjects."[45] We learn to recognize ourselves, according to Althusser, insofar as we are familiar with our society's system of meaningful identities. But there is, says Althusser, a misrecognition in that recognition; unless we wax critical, we are not aware of the historical forces involved in producing these identities and the practices which maintain them. Our ideological orientation to everyday life motivates us to adjust to the given identities and deflects us from a questioning of the conditions which lend us a kind of subjectivity.[46]

Handke's biography of his mother focuses on this ideological problem. He portrays his mother's adjustment strategies and, at the same time, overcomes the misrecognition they represent with his textual strategies. We witness Handke's construal of his mother's subjugated form of self-recognition as he describes a woman who was especially hard-pressed in achieving a satisfactory adaptation to the socially invested system of meaning.

> And so an emotional life that never had a chance of achieving
> bourgeois composure acquired a superficial stability by clumsily
> imitating the bourgeois system of emotional relations, prevalent
> especially among women, the system in which "So-and-so is my
> type but I'm not his," or "I'm his but he's not mine," or in which

"We're made for each other" — in which cliches are taken as bind-
ing rules and any *individual* reaction, which takes some account
of an actual person, becomes a deviation. For instance, my
mother would say of my father: "Actually, he wasn't my type."
And so this typology became a guide to life; it gave you a
pleasantly objective feeling about yourself; you stopped worrying
about your origins, your possibly dandruff-ridden, sweaty-footed
individuality, or the daily renewed problem of how to go on
living; being a type relieved the human molecule of his humiliat-
ing loneliness and isolation; he lost himself, yet now and then he
was somebody, if only briefly.[47]

While Handke's mother appears to have been a linguistic thrall, Handke's
manner of scripting that thralldom is authority challenging rather than
adaptive. Although the prose manifests a simple descriptive or realist style,
there is a parodic dimension in the descriptions. Whenever Handke comes
to a description he finds worth contesting, he either places it in quotations, which shifts the discourse from the third to the first person or he
mocks the statement by putting parts of it in large, billboard-size
characters. Referring to his mother's suicide, for example, he says, "I would
like to represent this VOLUNTARY DEATH as an exemplary case."[48] And,
speaking of a news item from the financial section of the paper, he describes
what he calls an "apologia for the economic principles of the Western
World." "Property, it said, was MATERIALIZED FREEDOM."[49] His mother, he
states, "TOOK EVERYTHING LITERALLY."[50] Handke, with his parodic style, dis-
solves the literal, showing its construction in a way that distances us from
what is taken as the "real." By deviating from stylistic norms in his writing, he reveals the norm ladenness of what passes as innocent description.[51]

We are now in a position to contrast the usual genre of what we call
"political biography" — what is taken unproblematically as political biography — with biography that is political (as is Handke's) by dint of its style
or method of deviating from the norms for representing the dominant
reality. As an example of the former, it is useful to choose a well-executed
political biography that has something valuable to offer as long as we
remain within a relatively conventional and uncontested model of what
constitutes the domain of the political. Among the best of this type is Doris
Kearns's treatment of the former American president, Lyndon Johnson.[52]
The text, as its title, *Lyndon Johnson and the American Dream*, implies,
offers us a dialectical model that places the development of the individual
in the context of the forces in the political culture that play a role in shaping
him. In this sense, the focus is a familiar one, which, like Freud's treatment
of Leonardo, sees the shaping of a person's personality and life choices
as a result of an interaction between inner and outer forces.

Kearns's Johnson biography is not a pious one at the level of its explicit content. It appears to seek neither to create nor destroy a legend. However, as is the case with all biographies, even the supposedly nonfictional, there is a plot; it is organized, in this case, around the theme that Lyndon Johnson was the quintessential political animal. Given the kind of story that Kearns was writing, the portrayal of the younger, pre-presidential Johnson is necessarily taken up with a search for signs of his political motivations and abilities. For example, picking up the story during Johnson's college years, we learn that he put together a winning political coalition to take control of campus politics. To do this he had to break the power of an entrenched power coalition whose control could be understood, not simply on the basis of the number of its supporters, but also on its ability to control the discursive agenda, the conceptions about what was at issue in student politics.

In describing this episode, in which Johnson's political tactics included an attack on the prevailing political agenda, not simply a strategy of collecting votes, Kearns shows a keen appreciation of what constitutes politicization: "The key to Johnson's strategy for increasing the power of the White Stars turned on his ability to render political things that previously had not been—that is, to make new matters negotiable."[53]

This statement on what constitutes politicization is wholly compatible with the way I have been using the concept in my readings of biography. But Kearns's conception of what it means to be political is not manifested in her textual practice as she writes the Johnson biography. She does give us a well-articulated version of an individual's political tactics and also a grasp of the institutional contexts that are congenial to those tactics. For example, there is an excellent section pointing out how Johnson's personal qualities made him fit the political process in the Senate better than the White House. This part of her investigation is summarized in her claim that Johnson's failure to be as effective a president as he was a senator "demonstrates that talent for public life is not a unity, but that there are distinct, often contradictory talents, which are relevant to success in one area of public life and not in another."[54]

But Kearns's treatment of the workings of political institutions and her ability to discern through Johnson's political life the nature of politicizing strategies provides a basis for political understanding only if we remain within the official discourse on American political life. At the level of style, Kearns's writing is depoliticizing. Her figuration locates the domain of the political within political institutions as conventionally understood—the congress, the presidency, etc., and she relies on the old checks-and-balances metaphor of the pluralist understanding of American politics. She notes, for example, that "non-governmental" institutions such as the media have the effect of countering executive or presidential control over political understanding.[55]

Without going into an extended criticism of this kind of political pluralism, it should suffice to mention that we can construe the media as a counterforce to presidential power only if we equate power with the will and success of a person instead of viewing it in terms of the prevailing modes of thought which control the agenda of politics, the enshrined realities that are manifested not only within the prevailing political discourse but also by what are taken to be nonpolitical discourses. Foucault's insight that a major aspect of the functioning of power in the contemporary world is our tendency to absorb the notion of power into the problem of controlling and limiting executives is apposite here. In reinforcing the conventional notions of power and authority in her writing, Kearns fails to carry out the kind of politicizing she ascribes to Lyndon Johnson, "to render political things that previously had not been."[56]

In effect, Kearns helps to administer political silences by narrowing the political discourse to the official kinds of political talk. What she designates as a counterforce to presidential discourse — what appears in the media — is parasitic on presidential discourse; it remains within the acknowledged orthodox and heterodox views, expressed mostly from the executive office, on what presidents ought or ought not do. Indeed, historically speaking, politics for the media is increasingly rendered as presidential talk.[57] When politics is thus mediaized, the very form of a medium, the economies of which make presidential speech its major object, carries an ideology (an effect which Jameson calls the "ideology of form").[58] In a society that is increasingly fragmented, counterpolitical discourses, those which might convey politics with something other than the trope of politics-as-presidential-speech, are increasingly silenced. It is in this sense that the ideology of Kearns's text lines up with a mediaized political ideology and works against the explicit notion of politicization that animates the story she tells about Lyndon Johnson.

The dimensions of the political life of a society that are missed or silenced in Kearns's treatment are precisely those emphasized in Norman Mailer's *The Executioner's Song*.[59] Although in some ways the narrative is focused on one biographical code — the life of Gary Gilmore from his youth to the time of his incarceration and execution in a Utah jail — the Gilmore biography moves in and out of focus as Mailer treats several lives at once. Indeed, one of the brief advertising blurbs on the back of the paperback edition conveys an effective summary of the ideologically challenging force of what Mailer has called a "true-life novel." James R. Frakes of the *Cleveland Plain Dealer* states, "There's no such thing as a minor figure. . . . All turn out to be complex, quivering human beings."

In avoiding the kind of structure of the so-called nonfiction biographies, such as Kearns's, that focus on a single life and place others in supporting roles, Mailer achieves a different representation of political life. Rather than getting a recycling of the typical academic view of politics as presidential, congressional, and media approaches to the issues which find their way into official discourse, Mailer provides glimpses of family politics, small-town politics, the politics of law enforcement, of adjudication, of the media, film making, and publishing. What Mailer ultimately provides is a comprehensive mapping of the American political culture. In so doing, he never explicitly attacks the ideological narrowness immanent in other kinds of treatments. It is the form of the Mailer text that opens up so many different kinds of questions about power and authority.

Mailer's "true-life novel" provides a very different kind of "true" than that which one gets from other genres, and, ironically, that "true" subordinates much less to its story line than many nonfiction approaches which function within analytic perspectives. Mailer's true is a true in the Heideggerian (and early Greek) sense of truth as uncovering. The workings of American institutions are not strained through one kind of perspective on the political, which allows us only one model of their consequences (e.g., the checks-and-balances-among-executives-legislatures-and-the-media model). Rather, they are read in terms of how they achieve their meanings through the pressures they place on a variety of different kinds of lives. The many voices in Mailer's story, which is a virtual jumble of biographical codes, convey, among other things, a different understanding of crime and punishment than that which one gets from the traditional public-policy discourse.

When we discover in Mailer's text the kinds of identities with which people struggle as they become subjected to official discourses, we observe the pressures that the creation and dissemination of kinds of criminality and penalties create at different levels in the society. We are reminded of what Foucault has described in his treatment of penalties (discussed in chapter 1), not in terms of what they prevent but in terms of how they help maintain a structure of social differentiation and control.

> Penalty would . . . appear to be a way of handling illegalities, of laying down the limits of tolerance, of giving free reign to some, of putting pressure on others, of excluding a particular section, of making another useful, of neutralizing certain individuals and of profiting from others. In short, penalty does not simply "check" illegalities; it differentiates them, it provides them with a generalized "economy" and if one can speak of justice, it is not only because the law itself in the way of applying it serves the

interests of a class, it is also because the differential administration of illegalities through the mediation of penalty forms part of those mechanisms of domination.[60]

That Mailer should achieve so rich and politicizing an approach to biography in a novelistic genre, when the explicitly political biography tends to be politically impoverished at the level of its style, is not surprising if we pay attention to the "ideology of form" as it relates to the novel as a representational practice. Whereas Handke's challenge to linguistically entrenched authority takes the form of parody, carried out with various pseudodescriptive statements, Mailer's challenge emerges from the very form of the novelistic genre.

M. M. Bakhtin has supplied us with a powerful conceptual mapping of how a novel provides such a form. In speaking about the way language functions in various genres of writing, Bakhtin sets up a tension between "centripetal forces," those "forces that serve to unify and centralize the verbal-ideological world," and the "centrifugal" forces which operate against this unifying tendency.[61] All societies contain what Bakhtin calls "heteroglossia," many (contending) voices.

> At any given moment of its evolution, language is stratified not only into linguistic dialects in the strict sense of the word . . . but also . . . into languages that are socio-ideological: languages of social groups, "professional" and "generic" languages, languages of generations and so forth.[62]

Bakhtin goes on to describe the novel as that form of writing which exemplifies heteroglossia or the internal stratification of language maintained in the midst of the unifying, centripetal tendencies of a society. He points out that while various poetic genres of writing "developed under the influence of unifying, centralizing, centripetal forces of verbal-ideological life, the novel — and those artistic-prose genres that gravitate toward it — was being shaped by the current of decentralizing, centrifugal forces."[63]

What a novel in general is — and Mailer's novel is exemplary here — is a form with "a diversity of social speech types and a diversity of individual voices, artistically organized," according to Bakhtin.[64] In optimally exploiting the novelistic genre, Mailer has made it serve as a challenge to a unifying political language that would encourage us to read our political culture within the unifying language of the official political discourse. Throughout *The Executioner's Song* the prose style shifts as it is adapted to the kind of person whose life is in focus at one moment or another. Toward the end, for example, Mailer accentuates Gilmore's voice by approximating the form of the epistolary novel as Gilmore speaks through his letters to his girlfriend, Nicole. As a result of his orchestrating of the many different voices, Mailer's novel is far more politicizing than "political texts" in general and the political biography in particular, which join themselves with, in Bakhtin's terms, the "forces that serve to unify and centralize the verbal-ideological world" by failing to either diversify or reflect upon the language practices within which they operate.

Conclusion: Political Biography

Given my emphasis on the power and authority resident in prevailing discursive practices, it is appropriate to conclude with an examination of some biographical writing which explores, in one way or another, the ideational investments of a society's discourses. For this purpose I treat Sartre's biography of Flaubert and two of Foucault's edited volumes, *I Pierre Riviere . . .* and *Herculine Barbin,* which contain various official and analytic documents juxtaposed to the autobiographical statements of Riviere and Barbin.[65]

Sartre introduces his study of Flaubert as a primarily epistemological biography. Describing the subject of his study, he says, "It's subject: what at this point in time can we know about a man."[66] But this problem of "knowing" for Sartre emerges from what he recognizes as a densely political problematic, one to which he had addressed himself in his *Search for a Method,* where he tried to synthesize his early existential commitments with an intellectually adequate version of Marxism.[67] This is not the place to review the twists and turns of Sartre's struggle to bring his synthesis into a coherent discourse. At a minimum it is evident that he was seeking an adequate philosophy within which contemporary affairs, as he saw them, could be effectively politically encoded.

The synthesis Sartre effected and ultimately applied to his Flaubert study is in many ways more of a synthesis of Marxist and Freudian modes of textual analysis than it is an existentialist/Marxist synthesis. Relatively little of the discursive traces of existentialist philosophy remain, except in those places where Sartre tries to draw some implications for child rearing (which I discuss below). Sartre emerged from his "search" with the view that psychoanalysis is complementary to Marxism in attempting to understand someone like Flaubert. One can read the "relations of production" through the way the individual develops within the affective and ideological matrix of the family. "Psychoanalytic monographs — if it were always possible to have them — would by themselves throw light upon the evolution of the French family between the eighteenth and the twentieth century, which in turn would express in its own way the general evolution of the relations of production."[68] Sartre felt that the mediation of Marxism through psychoanalysis prevented one from adopting a vulgar Marxist position which tends to dissolve "real men" into caricatures. "Marxism ought to study real men in depth, not dissolve them in a bath of sulphuric acid."[69]

In addition to the existentialist, Marxist, and psychoanalytic influences, there is another theoretical commitment we must appreciate to see why it made sense for Sartre to exercise his political imagination through a biography of Flaubert. This is his commitment to writing as a politicizing act, a way to reverse the pacifying and dislocating effects of dominant discourses. Sartre argued that there is an alienation from oneself that results from the inability to give expression to one's own experience within the confines of the ideational rhythms of public language. Sartre celebrates the power of new ways of making words as a counterforce to the theft of personal experience that the public discourse represents. *"Les mots font des ravages quand ils viennent a nommer ce qui n'est etait vecu sans nomination."*[70] In light of this, we see the attraction of Flaubert not only because he was a writer but also because of the personal struggle he had to undergo to manage language. Flaubert was a "little boy badly anchored in the universe of discourse," as Sartre puts it in referring to Flaubert's relative slowness in learning to speak and read.[71] This coupled with Sartre's more or less Freudian interpretation of Flaubert's writing — that Flaubert was objectifying himself in his work — leads Sartre to the claim, "It is necessary to resort to biography" to look at "the facts collected by Flaubert's contemporaries and verified by historians."[72]

There is an abundance of themes in Sartre's Flaubert biography, but one stands out for analytic purposes here. This is the theme suggested by the quote on the young Flaubert being "badly anchored in the universe of discourse." This peculiarity of the young Flaubert sets up the kind of story Sartre wanted to tell, one which constructs a tension between a person's ability to think and act in a self-directed, authentic way — here is the irrepressible existentialist code asserting itself — and the tendency for a society's unifying ideological modes to impose themselves and, to use Bakhtin's term, "ventriloquate" themselves through the individual.[73]

Sartre begins to introduce an explicit imagery of the young Flaubert being forced into language when he has nothing of his own to communicate. Even though the "notion and need for communication" are present in him, according to Sartre, his words are "strangers" because, belonging to others, they "cannot designate his own experiences."[74] However, Sartre does not render this linguistic struggle as an individual battle. The biographical code often gives way to the social, analytic, and political codes as he represents the content of the imposed language/ideology which comes out of the society's public discourses and is mediated through the key persons in Flaubert's family, his parents. While he casts Flaubert as one who, in an unhappy condition, little loved and linguistically inept, attempted to "clarify that condition through discourse," Sartre's level of discourse moves from the individual to the ideological/critical as he states that Flaubert was a victim of false consciousness, believing he was clarifying his condition but actually "obscuring and mythifying" it with resort to "the ideologies of his time," one "faith" from his mother and the other "scientism" from his father. At this point, Sartre's questioning of Flaubert's life is: "How was he penetrated by bourgeois ideology."[75]

This ideological penetration was especially intense in the Flaubert family, according to Sartre, because it was an ambitious, upwardly mobile family, operating within an ideological narrative that justified their high status. "The Flauberts are *awaited* at the summit of the social scale – any delay is an injustice. When they finally get to the top, they will have *become*, in spite of malicious persons and their intrigues, what they were all along."[76]

Like Freud's emphasis in his Leonardo study, much of Sartre's analysis shows how Flaubert's early development affected the content of his work. But the interpretations of the work, which are very Freudian in orientation (and not completed), are less significant for purposes of this analysis than the other major emphasis, Sartre's treatment of how a self emerges in a linguistically alien world.

Sartre's politically oriented critique of ideology is most in evidence in this aspect of the study, and, as I have noted, he offers a treatment of the ideational force of the prevailing public discourses, showing how they penetrate the imagination and self-understanding of the individual. He also provides an insightful analysis of the specific ideological mechanisms of those discourses. For example, he shows how the mechanistic and rationalistic structure of bourgeois thinking allows it to both dissolve the myth that sustained aristocratic privilege and, at the same time, justify a self-interested position vis-à-vis the working class.[77]

However, in his approach to the developing self, a generalized analysis for which Flaubert provides a convenient exemplar, Sartre overemphasizes the family narrative at the expense of less politically impoverished social codes, and, as the narrative progresses, he slides from a political code to the existential/ethical code familiar from his earlier writings. Where the biography could have taken a political turn in which Sartre might have developed the link between how a self is constructed in a historical age and what the relationship is between that self or kind of identity and the workings of power and authority, it gropes instead for a language of authenticity and romanticizes the presocial self.

Sartre works out his ethical injunctions from a radical distinction between nature and culture. Speaking of the "human animal" in general, he characterizes the passage from nature to culture as an abdication of the individual's "native poetry."[78] And, extending this imagery through his construction of Flaubert's socially purloined sensibilities, he says, "Culture, for him, is theft: it reduces the vague and natural consciousness to its being other, to what it is for others."[79]

These musings, which hark back to Sartre's earlier writings, reexpress his conviction that there is no telos or abstract reason in the world and that socially constituted imperatives are not productive of a true self. For the still-existentialist Sartre, the individual person makes a meaningful existence by shaping it through action. Wanting people to feel a mandate to make a meaningful existence, Sartre combines this point, which sits somewhere between an ontology and an ethical position, with a meditation on the disabling effects of being, like Flaubert, an unloved child. Ascribing Flaubert's passivity to his impoverished emotional life in his early years, Sartre promulgates an ethic of child rearing. He argues that all children need a "mandate to live," a sense that they are valuable and thus have a license to be active in creating meaning. This ethic clearly connects with Sartre's general philosophical commitment that the world cannot issue a meaningful or true summons. Whatever truth a person can live is self-created.

However one might evaluate that ethic and the scrutiny of Flaubert's life which Sartre offers as support for the causal links he supplies, the ethical mode that asserts itself in Sartre's text plays an ultimately depoliticizing role. The power and authority relations that Sartre emphasizes in his discussion of the way social ideologies are mediated and imposed through the family slip into the background as they are displaced by Sartre's individual-oriented, existentialist, ethical language.

Sartre's focus on the social self as an imposition of both an emotional prehistory and a verbal/ideological public discourse sets up a comparison with Foucault's use of biographies, which are also written in service of a pedagogy about the way a self is shaped. But while there is a surface similarity in their emphases on the social self as imposed, Foucault's writing, while similarly ethically motivated, asserts the political over the ethical. This privileging of the political in Foucault's investigations has roots in his ontological position. Departing from empiricist models of truth, which seek a domain of unchallenged facticity as a warrant for the value of a discourse and also departing from interpretive theory's injunction to recover the dimensions of the self which are unthought within society's manifest discourses, Foucault treats all discourse as a false arrest of experience.

We must not imagine that the world turns toward us a legible face which we would only have to decipher; the world is not the

accomplice of our knowledge; there is no prediscursive providence which disposes the world in our favor. We must conceive
of discourse as a violence which we do to things, or in any case
as a practice which we impose on them; and it is in this practice
that the events of discourse find the principle of their regularity.[80]

Here, in Foucault's Nietzschean ontology — the prediscursive as disorder
and all order as human imposition — is the root of his politicized problematic. Because all meaning is not, as Sartre would have it, to be judged
on the basis of an ethic of the authentic self but in terms of the economies
of that discursive practice, Foucault's analysis treats any self as an ascrip-
tion, as part of that discursive economy. Indeed, the only selves to be
found are those produced by the practices of a given historical age. The
problem, then, is not to truly know the self but to map out how it is that
what is taken to be knowledge is productive of kinds of selves. Foucault
thus treats self-knowledge as one of a variety of injunctions through which
power manifests itself. It is the constitution of persons' identities in various
periods that gives us insights into the working of power.

Foucault's publication of the autobiography or memoir of a nineteenth-
century hermaphrodite, Herculine Barbin, was an offshoot of his investigation into the history of sexuality, in which he sought to demonstrate
how sexual identities, e.g., the development of an increasingly intense preoccupation with "sexual perversions," were produced by an age more and
more concerned with surveillance and control.[81] Although, in a conventional sense, Herculine's memoir, a story of a young person with both
female and male sexual "insignia" (to use Garfinkel's term) is not Foucault's
text, his introduction, and the documents of the case which he packages
with the memoir serve to explicate how a society's exercise of power works
through the imposition of sexual "truths."

Herculine's sensitively told story reflects an intelligent human being seeking love in a situation which has a structure that must ultimately destroy
her/him. Classified first as a girl, this sexually ambiguous being gets
involved in a scandal after living in a convent and developing affectionate,
physical relationships with other girls. The discovery of the sexual ambiguity leads to ostracism and legal measures which force the young person,
now officially classified as a male, into a way of life at odds with his long-
developed emotional orientation.

How is such a story a politicization of the biographical code? Part of
the political dimension of Foucault's analysis comes through the choice
of the subject. Imagine the usual choice for biography being drawn from
a four-by-four table, constructed by the dichotomies of important-versus-
unimportant persons, cross classified with important-versus-unimportant
events, as shown below.

Persons

	Important	Unimportant
Important (Events)	a	b
Unimportant	c	d

The most familiar biographically oriented text comes from the "a" cell, where one finds important people involved in important events. Failing that, one finds biographies of the "b" and "c" types, produced because at least one dimension is "important." "D" types are hard to find (except those paid for by the "unimportant" person who has had a banal existence).

Foucault's choice of Herculine Barbin, like Garfinkel's choice of Agnes, is made partly for analytic purposes. Foucault's contention that our political discourse is king centric, focused on the limitations of sovereign power, has led him to attempt to show another increasingly apparent dimension of power. This is what he calls "normalizing" power.[82] The way a society inscribes itself on the body, the way it intensifies the creation of identities available to scrutiny and the production of forms of power/knowledge, can be read in the experiences of some individuals. Foucault not only selects from the "d" cell of the table but, in effect, also implicitly raises the question about how such a table is constituted, how it is that persons and events gain value in the economy of a society's discourses.

Herculine Barbin's story becomes "important," according to Foucault, when we pay attention to when it occurs.

> Brought up as a poor and deserving girl in a milieu that was almost exclusively feminine and strongly religious, Herculine Barbin, who was called Alexina by her familiars, was finally recognized as being "truly" a young man. Obliged to make a legal change of sex after judicial proceedings and a modification of his civil status, he was incapable of adapting himself to a new identity and ultimately committed suicide. I would be tempted to call the story banal were it not for two or three things that give it particular intensity.[83]

What gave it this intensity, Foucault asserts, is that it happened in a period in the nineteenth century in which a more and more intensive set of investigations into sexual identities was being carried out. It was a period in which types of persons were being classified in a society in which the developing ways of administering itself allowed less slack in characteristics and behaviors of persons. The story takes place, in short, in an age more concerned than any previously in enforcing sexual "truths" among others. Because, for Foucault, there is no true self, sexual or otherwise, he sees attempts at imposing rigid boundaries on persons' identities as a major dimension of the operation of power and authority. The documents of court proceedings, a scientific investigation, and media coverage all show how various disciplinary practices, beginning to assert themselves in Herculine Barbin's age and continuing into the present, have been complicit in inscribing this "truth" and thus complicit in extending a normalizing power.

The Pierre Riviere volume is also constructed as an autobiography or memoir, combined with other documents. The Riviere case, a case of a young man who "murdered" his mother, sister, and brother, would also fit in the "d" cell of the above four-celled table, if one takes as the measure of importance the values of his age. As Foucault puts it, "Riviere's case was not, then, a 'notable crime'." Again, however, the case serves Foucault's analytic of showing how power functions within discursive practices thought to be nonpolitical. His interest in publishing the documents of the case relates to how the case was situated at "the intersection of discourses."[84] Those that intersect include the discourses of the cantonal judge, the presiding judge of the assize court, the minister of justice, the parish priest, the major, villagers, and the "murder." In presenting the case, Foucault offers us a frame of reference for understanding the politics of discourse.

> I think the reason we decided to publish these documents, was to draw a map, so to speak, of those combats, to reconstruct those confrontations and battles, to rediscover the interaction of those discourses as weapons of attack and defense in the relations of power and knowledge.[85]

Here it is important to note the difference between Foucault's and Sartre's images of what is involved when a discourse predominates. For Sartre, the ideological effect of public discourses is to be figured as loss, as something that penetrates and robs the individual of a "native poetry" and possibility for self-authenticating action. Foucault also uses a penetration metaphor, but, in construing all selves as impositions produced by discursive practices, he turns to an imagery of struggle rather than one of the recovery of authenticity. And, in his explicitly political statements, he urges not the Sartrean ethic of child rearing but an injunction to "refuse" the self that modernity has authored.

> Maybe the target nowadays is not to discover what we are but to refuse what we are. We have to imagine and to build up what we could be to get rid of this kind of political "double bind," which is the simultaneous individualization and totalization of modern power structures.[86]

Foucault's publishing of the Pierre Riviere documents, particularly his inclusion of Riviere's memoir in his own words, is one of his many efforts at showing how our discursively engendered, familiar world of individual and collective identities, objects, and relations has an underside of silence. Alternative, resistant discourses, subjugated forms of knowledge, when disclosed and presented, show how our lived realities are actually forms of practice.

What is remarkable about Riviere's statement is its political sophistication. All the official discourses cast Riviere as a maniacal killer, who had matured from a strange, antisocial child. Those discourses all appear aimed at reinstating the community's peace of mind by recruiting Riviere into an irrational category. By contrast, Riviere's narrative reads, among other things, like a treatise on the political economy of marriage agreements, focusing on the injustices they perpetrate in general and on the afflictions suffered by his father as a result of his marriage agreement in particular. In describing his decision to kill his mother (and those siblings he felt had sided with her in the harassment of his father), he casts himself within a religious discourse of sacrifice.

In addition, Riviere offers us another level of analysis that is missing from the discourses in the other documents. He achieves a distance from his personal situation, and speaks of how different civilizations had different power structures reflected in the different authority relations within their families. He complains that a society that would allow such a marriage structure as existed in his age, should not refer to itself as existing in "the age of enlightenment."[87]

Foucault's text does not function, ultimately, to suggest that Riviere's "crime" should have been condoned then or, in retrospect, now. It suggests, rather, that we give the episode an alternative kind of reading, a reading which is suggested by the rhetorical force of the text, delivered through the arrangement and juxtapositions of the documents. The text has the effect of saying that instead of simply placing Riviere's story within a familiar and politically pacifying language of criminal justice, we should construe the functioning of Riviere's biographical code in a political way, for it is engaged in a struggle with criminalizing and other pacifying codes. Taken as a whole, the assembled documents provide something that I have suggested we must do if we are to read biography in a politicizing way. The documents, Foucault states, give us a key to the relations of power. When we examine what are taken to be disinterested, knowledge-oriented discourses within Foucault's kind of politicized analytic, they can be seen to be "both tactical and political, and therefore strategic."[88]

3

THE CONSTITUTION OF THE

CENTRAL AMERICAN OTHER

THE CASE OF "GUATEMALA"

Introduction: Finding Guatemala

Although a recognized territorial state appears in the title of this chapter, my intention is not to invoke and then work within the interpretive codes familiar to those involved in inquiry in the fields of "comparative politics," "international relations," or "foreign policy." Rather, the main intention is to extend an analysis begun in Tzvetan Todorov's demonstration that Central America in general and Guatemala in particular were not so much discovered as imaginatively preconstituted by the Spanish conquistadors. In effect, what is now called "Guatemala" was already there in the Spanish imagination, an imagination engendered primarily by two acquisitive practices — the search for inanimate sources of material wealth and animate raw material for spiritual domination. In his semiotic approach to the constitution of the "Other" in the early history of the European domination of the Americas, Todorov's argument amounts to an elaborate gesture of placing quotation marks around the word "discovery," for the burden of much of his analysis is to show that what the Spanish discovered was their own mentality.[1]

The main emphasis of my analysis is to bring Todorov's insight more up-to-date by showing that the kind of mentality which Todorov ascribed to the Spanish conquerers persists in the way Guatemala is constituted within the American foreign-policy discourse. However, this is not to imply that mentalities operate in isolation. Although the analysis here is not explicitly focused on the political economy of international domination, a guiding assumption is that the various agencies of the American state which are involved in external relations operate primarily to promote and

This chapter is a revision of a paper by Alfred Fortin and Michael J. Shapiro originally prepared for delivery at the twenty-seventh annual convention of the International Studies Association, Anaheim, Calif., 25–29 March 1986.

protect the flow of capital investment as it spills over the United States' domestic boundaries. Rather than rehearsing this familiar theme, which is controversial only for both naive and cynical apologists of American capital, I emphasize the modes of representation abetting this widely orchestrated form of domination by making it acceptable and coherent within the dominant ethos that constructs domestic selves and exotic Others. They are modes of representation that embrace the "operational terms" of the powerful, and their main effect is to encourage domestic allegiance to the state in general and its leadership in particular.

It is to be expected that government agencies and commissions are involved in reproducing and putting into circulation discursive orientations that both mystify the exploitive relationships of the United States to Latin America and seek to blunt criticism of its effects. In this analysis, I take a close look at a recent such discursive enactment by a special presidential commission, the Kissinger Commission, which purported to "discover" something about Central America; but part of my analysis is directed toward showing that academic social science, which thinks of itself as functioning within a frame that distances it from contemporary policy in order to provide critical perspectives, often operates within these same discursive practices that constitute an unreflective apology for American neoimperialistic practices.

The choice of Guatemala rather than another object of the Kissinger Commission report is relatively arbitrary. A recent speech by the new Guatemalan president, Marco Vinicio Cereza Arevalo, provides a useful point of departure, because it evokes the recent history of both U.S. and domestic military domination. As one might expect, Arevalo sees his role as one of holding off interference by both the United States and the Guatemalan military as he attempts, in his terms, to "implant democracy." That he stood on U.S. soil as he spoke represented his cognizance of the U.S. threat to his nation's autonomy. The other threat, a domestic one, is addressed discursively.

> We have to deal with the army of Guatemala to be able to establish a real civilian government. We have to deal with a society that is not accustomed to sharing its wealth and opportunities. And we have to deal with the confrontation inside the country, where people are fighting and dying.[2]

While there are many interesting aspects of Arevalo's statement (including where he was standing when he made it), his reference to Guatemalan "society" is what should most immediately engage an analysis such as this, which focuses on how Guatemala resides within the dominant American foreign-policy discourse. This discourse is oriented by a preoccupation with what inevitably directs the ideational commitments of modern nation states with significant capacities for violence outside their borders: these are their security needs as they see them and the preservation of economic/ strategic control over processes and events believed to be relevant to their ability to maintain those aspects of their domestic way of life connected to powerful commercial interests.

Within the predominant American foreign-policy discourse, circulated and reproduced by academicians, policy thinkers, and journalists, Guatemalan "society" is a mere fact. A discourse in which the major code is geopolitical is accordingly dominated by such things as "regime ideology" and the foreign-policy behaviors of leaders. This creates a depluralized and dehistoricized model of the society within which the leaders function. Whereas, within Guatemala, the contests for leadership resonate with meanings connected to a history of colonial and class relations, from the point of view of interested observers like the United States, the contest is revalued along more simple axes.[3] The kinds of questions allowed to emerge are such things as: is the leadership predictable or unpredictable in terms of its attitudes and permanency of its regulating institutions, or what direction will its policies take with respect to both foreign investments and regional cold-war games and contests?

The Language of Analysis

Much of the discursive style of the above introductory remarks is familiar to anyone who has paid attention to American foreign policy in Central America. Among other things, it locates the author in the critical camp of those who favor less interventionist policy. But there are stylistic gestures which go beyond the usual forms of partisanship operating within what are recognized as contentious aspects of U.S. foreign policy. One is the placing of quotation marks around the object of analysis ("Guatemala") in the title of this chapter. The implication in so doing is to indicate that there is no natural or unproblematic way to identify or represent Guatemala, that I, like U.S. foreign-policy makers am involved in a practice even as I employ one of the more simple linguistic functions, mentioning the name of something. Kenneth Burke expressed well the political nature of that which makes us self-conscious about our modes of representation. Turning our attention to the problem of authority immanent in any practice with which we convene what it is that constitutes a society, he noted that "in theories of politics prevailing at different periods in history, there have been quarrels as to the precise vessel of authority that is to be considered 'representative' of the society as a whole."[4]

Although there are relatively few quarrels about whether one should say "Guatemala" and thus let oneself be governed by the prevailing geo-political mode of representation, to do so is to engage in the continuation of a complex, historically developed practice. Guatemala is part of what we think of as the international system, a historically produced set of relations among nations. The predominant grammar of this international system has all of the individual nations performing as subjects and objects in the practice of international speech, a set of statements, regarded as intelligible, which issues from national units. But these units, which are consolidated both in the recognized system of territorial boundaries and in speech practices, embody histories of struggles over how those units are to be represented and understood. The ordinary grammar employed in contemporary discourses, whether of national leaders, journalists, or social scientists, constitutes a forgetting of those struggles which, if they had ended in other ways, might have engendered other grammars and categories. The use of the dominant, intelligible grammar and category-set of international speech thus helps to reinforce a consolidated understanding of these national units, an understanding which accepts both the importance of existing international boundaries and the dominance of whatever person or group (regime, class, ethnic group, etc.) manages to control domestic relations and attract recognition from the international community. As for groups who lost the struggles to maintain their practices (and have them be the ones that are intelligible), to the extent that we are reminded of those "Others" whose practices no longer control prevailing understandings on their old turf, the reminders are represented in other than a political code. For example, recently the Aztecs and Mayans appeared in one of the most sophisticated European newspapers not as victims of violence but as commodified perpetrators of it. In this recent advertisement in the travel section of the *London Times* we are encouraged to conjure up their exotic practices in our imaginations as we visit their old haunts.

The Constitution of the Central American Other

When we seek to make intelligible the politics of the Central American region we do not think of Aztecs and Mayans (nor of their descendants), for within modern speech practices, to invoke the name of a country as territory is to participate in a representational practice that belongs to what Foucault called the "tactics and strategies of power," which have no use for the historical continuities, discontinuities, and fates of early indigenous groups. This is not the kind of power one associates with the active manipulations of a conscious, individual actor but rather the power immanent in the historical process through which any entity acquires an identity. The geographic "knowledge" we invoke in our naming helps, in Foucault's terms, to put into circulation the tactics and strategies involved in the "demarcations" and "control of territories."[6] Thus, to the extent that one accepts and unreflectively reproduces the security-oriented, geopolitical discursive practice, one engages in implicit acts of recognition of the existing power and authority configurations.

The kinds of strategies and tactics implicit in the prevailing discursive practices are difficult to discern, however, inasmuch as one tends to receive them in the form of seemingly unproblematic descriptions. For example, it is matter of course that most books which claim to speak about a country begin with a map in the opening pages. This representational practice is so familiar it seems natural (i.e., not a practice), but this representation of bounded areas partakes of a venerable rhetorical gesture: the map is a spatial trope which, far from simply representing (natural) boundaries, is an aggressive practice, delivering up the discursive territory within which legitimate speech about bounded areas can occur.

It is important to recognize that the boundaries of legitimate speech are both arbitrary in some respects and nonarbitrary in others. Most significantly, they are arbitrary in the sense that they are one kind of practice among endless possibilities, and to realize this is to be able to ask why this practice as opposed to others. At the same time, they are nonarbitrary in the sense that one can inquire into the historical conditions within which one way of making a world was dominant so that we now have a world that power has convened. For example, the territory we now unreflectingly refer to as "Southeast Asia" has only recently acquired such a stable linguistic/geopolitical identity. A recent investigation disclosed that prior to 1942 there were no standard boundaries for the expression. During World War II, map makers responded to an interested public that was following the developing allied military movements. Accordingly, the maps enclosed territories on the basis of the unfolding military strategies. As the investigator put it,

> Making war meant making maps. The National Geographic
> Society made them in unprecedented numbers, making nearly

twenty million in 1941–42, including for the first time a Society map of "Southeast Asia" to enable Americans to "follow every move by our land, sea, and air forces to crush the Japanese."[7]

The map makers were responding to a regional name made popular by the Pacific Command, and the subsequent strategies and tactics of the cold war have reinforced the boundaries of the area, "Southeast Asia," which now slips so effortlessly from our lips.

Accordingly, to the extent that we are unreflective about the practices shaping international speech, we allow Guatemala to announce itself as a spatial domain unproblematically. In naturalizing the Guatemalan entity, boundaries are accepted and space consigned. "Rebels" or "terrorists" who violate this space by the kind of travel and behavior not authorized within the imposed security-oriented or trade- and commerce-oriented meanings acquire delegitimated identities. One way to illustrate the relationship between the prevailing geopolitically oriented discourse and the power configuration that it represents is to note that the ability to impose meanings on the space known as Guatemala has never been in the hands of Guatemala's most numerous group, the "Indians." They have existed, since the Spanish invasion, within a space given meaning and value by the conquistadors and then owned and operated partly by the conquistadors' descendants and partly by the vagaries of commercial and political processes produced outside their territory. The process of expropriation of the meaning of the area began with Columbus's first act, when he is said to have "discovered" bits and pieces of the New World, an act of naming.

> The first gesture Columbus makes upon contact with the newly discovered lands (hence the first contact between Europe and what will be America) is an act of extended nomination: this is the declaration according to which these lands are henceforth part of the kingdom of Spain. Columbus disembarks in a boat decorated with the royal banner, and accompanied by the royal notary armed with his inkwell. Before the eyes of the doubtless perplexed Indians, and without paying them the least attention, Columbus offers a deed of possession to be drawn up.[8]

Even today's map as space and as name has an inheritance of signifiers that hark back to this deed of possession. The original possession was an old form of imperialism which took on a meaning in connection with Spain's search for gold and souls. Possession today is also two-fold, connected to wealth and power as before, but a secular power. The current production of the meanings territories acquire relates to the security concerns of "major powers" and the commercial concerns of many residing within those powers. The primary "disposition of space" of which Foucault has spoken in remarks to geographers, is a disposition imposed within the security-oriented discourse.[9] Now Guatemala is, among other things, considered a pivotal country which inhabits vital space, "vitality" having a meaning imposed by the contemporary conquistadors.

The international system in general and Guatemala in particular represent, therefore, not innocent sets of objects attracting orderly speech practices; they are parts of a system that has been conjured up in policy-related speech practices over the centuries, practices that have predominated over other possible alternative practices. To say this is to say, among other things, that we could have it otherwise. In evoking the idea of the "United States," for example, we could refer not to an administrative unit controlled by the federal government but rather to the process by which white Europeans have been consolidating control over the continental domain (now recognized as the United States) in a war with several indigenous ("Indian") nations. This grammar, within which we could have the "United States" in a different way — as violent process rather than as a static, naturalized reality — would lead us to note that while the armed hostilities have all but ceased, there remains a system of economic exclusion, which has the effect of maintaining a steady attrition rate among native Americans. The war goes on by other means, and the one-sidedness of the battle is still in evidence. For example, in the state of Utah, the life expectancy of the native American is only half that of the European descendant.

There is little tendency to evoke this latter kind of grammar to treat what we call the "United States" because it is not an effective grammar with which to do business, as "business" is understood by those who contribute disproportionately to recognized discourses. It does not allow one to negotiate within the dominant discourse which produces "foreign-policy problems" for national leaders, journalists, multinational businesses, or social scientists. For example, a recent *Time* magazine feature article on the death of thousands of workers at a Union Carbide plant in Bhopal, India, represented the incident with a photo of suffering victims and a large title that said, "Environment" (figure 3.1).[10] If we bracket issues in the politics of meaning for the moment, the obvious implication to be communicated by the juxtaposition of the photo and headline was that we should understand the Bhopal incident as a pollution accident. A relatively trivial political explanation of the choice of the headline would have us speculate about interdepartmental competition at the magazine. Perhaps the personnel in charge of the environment department asserted their rights or demands for a cover story after not having had a turn for a while.

Clearly, however, the practices contributing to delivering up *Time's*

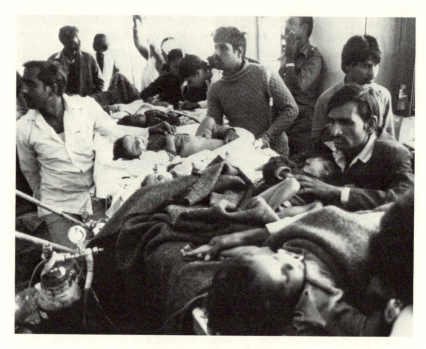

Environment

TIME/DECEMBER 17, 1984

Fig. 3.1. *Bhopal, India.* Copyright 1984 Time Inc. All rights reserved. Reprinted by permission from TIME. Photograph copyright 1984 by Raghu Rai and Magnum Photos, Inc.

Bhopal incident as a problem of the environment are deeper and more broadly distributed than the competitive structure within the editorial system of the magazine. One can speak usefully here of a kind of ideological scripting of the allocation of danger around the globe. Within this scripting, controlled by the dominant modes of representing problems of foreign policy and international politics, events involving the use of weapons against foreign nationals on their soil get recruited into the foreign-policy discursive space, while killing them with pesticide chemicals does not. Business interests in powerful nations with sophisticated health- and safety-conscious populations find themselves, with the complicity of their governments, exporting their more dangerous forms of working. Taken as a whole, this can be thought of as a general pattern of policy making. Those nations with strength and thus a disproportionate share of well-being and safety for their populations tend to increase this kind of international inequality by exporting dangers. And those groups (collaborating classes) in the host nation who, because of domestic inequalities, are protected from the dangers while benefiting from the activities, contribute by encouraging their importation.

In this context, the effect of *Time's* Bhopal coverage is to help maintain the kind of discursive space that exonerates the foreign-policy making of powerful nations and collaborating weaker ones from one of the more deadly effects of international politics, the allocation of danger. Within the discursive space of "environment," we are more prone to invoke the concept of the accident or, at least, to limit responsible agents to the occupational safety and health practices of the corporation involved instead of politicizing the event by locating it within the discursive space of policy making in the international system. Indeed, the international system, which excludes from its politics the importing and exporting of dangers is something that we help maintain. Insofar as *Time's* feature on Bhopal is intelligible and unsurprising, insofar as the *Time* editorial staff's glassy-eyed stare at the world can unreflectively and unproblematically produce the Bhopal story as an environmental incident, the resident practices that give us the "international system" are assured a stable purchase on our understandings.

Modes of representation are thus significant practices, and the insight that no representation is innocent of practice has been shown effectively in Rosalind Krauss's analysis of two different prints of a landscape photograph *Tufa Domes, Pyramid Lake* (figure 3.2).[11] O'Sullivan's original photo on the left evokes a mysterious, aesthetic mood. As Krauss notes, "three bulky masses of rock are seen as if deployed on a kind of abstract, transparent chessboard, marking by their separate positions a retreating trajectory into depth." By contrast, the photolithographic copy of the same

Timothy O'Sullivan. Tufa Domes, Pyramid Lake (Nevada). *1868.*

Photolithograph after O'Sullivan, Tufa Domes, Pyramid Lake. (*Published in King Survey report, 1875*).

Fig. 3.2. *Tufa Domes, Pyramid Lake.* Reprinted by permission from Rosalind E. Krauss, *The Originality of the Avant-Garde and Other Modernist Myths* (Cambridge: MIT Press, 1986), p. 132.

photograph on the right is "an object of insistent visual banality." What was rendered mysterious in the original photo, according to Krauss, "has been explained with supplemental, chatty detail."[12] We see a definitive shape of the lake's farther shore, and the water ripples and rock shadows are similarly rendered with sharper contrasts. The important point that Krauss is making in comparing the two different prints of the same photograph is that the difference in the representations reflects a difference in practices.

> They belong . . . to two separate domains of culture, they assume different expectations in the user of the image, they convey two distinct kinds of knowledge: in a more recent vocabulary, one would say that they operate as representations within two separate discursive spaces, as members of two different discourses.[13]

What explains the difference then is their discursive contexts. O'Sullivan's original photograph belongs to a practice of art photography oriented toward softening boundaries, while the photolithograph, which appeared on a publication called Systematic Geology, belongs to a practice oriented toward sharpening boundaries.

Similarly, the dominant representational practice within which we have a political grasp of the international system is one that sharpens boundaries, national boundaries in this case. There are relatively few challenges to the national boundary-sharpened discursive space engendered by the dominant discourse of national-level policy makers, journalists, and social scientists. Even much of the discursive orientation of peace researchers is parasitic on that of the most pious of cold warrior's insofar as it observes the traditional international system grammar. Perhaps the major contemporary challenge to this grammar is generated by the Greenpeace organization whose confrontations with various nations stem from their strategy of violating discursive spaces as they violate boundaries or what are known as "territorial waters." Within the challenging discourse of Greenpeace, national boundaries are softened and the living things within those boundaries — animals and humans alike — are rendered with greater clarity. Within the Greenpeace discourse, for example, Mururoa becomes a human population whose health is endangered by French nuclear tests rather than simply a territory under French jurisdiction. Indeed, unlike Time, whose journalistic discursive practice helps to maintain the prevailing, geopolitical orientation of the grammar of the international system (which had the effect of depoliticizing the Bhopal incident), Greenpeace has generated a discursive practice that would encourage an extranational, political response to the health problems within the administrative control of a single nation.

In sharp contrast with Greenpeace's discursive practice is much of the academically oriented study of foreign-policy decision making, which, by dint of the modes of representation it practices, tends to operate as a linguistic appendage of policy making itself. For purposes of illustration, one piece of analysis stands out because of its treatment of Guatemala. The focus of the study, Force without War, is on what the authors call "the use of discrete military moves to influence a particular situation."[14] This decisionist way of speaking is typical of much of the study of decision making in the social sciences and is linked to one of the primary legitimating moves of decision-making practice. When decision makers understand themselves to be responding to what they call a "situation," which they see as a set of events independent of the practice-related perceptions through which they are apprehended, they are effectively exonerating the practices with which they construct the world that requires what they think of as "decision making."

The authors of Force without War, the major effect of which is one of supplying a pseudoscientific vindication of aggressive U.S. foreign policy, aid and abet this form of legitimation with a variety of grammatical/rhetorical gestures. For example, using the passive voice, they note that if "memories of the Vietnam conflict recede from the American consciousness, the nation may once again more frequently employ its armed forces for political objectives, especially if an increasing number of 'opportunities' are presented by the international environment."[15] The slight inhibition represented by the quotation marks around "opportunities" has little moderating effect on the rhetorical force of the statement. The authors help to make the world safe for U.S. military adventurism by taking attention away from the interpretive actions which make the "international environment" and "opportunities." In their statement, the subject/actor becomes the "international environment" which presents opportunities. In addition, the concept of the "political" in the statement is conveniently depluralized (along with that of the "environment") so that, in keeping with the ambitions of a scientific analysis, many cases can be aggregated. The effect of this flattening and simplifying of the world — moves common to policy-making discourse as well as this form of pseudoscience — becomes especially evident when one examines one of the cases.

Force without War allows Guatemala a brief appearance under a section of the study called "Aggregate Analyses." Guatemala appears in a table of "Incidents in which Strategic Nuclear Forces Were Involved." The "incident" involving Guatemala turns out to be "Guatemala accepts Soviet Bloc Support."[16] This is precisely the kind of denarrativization that was central to the United States' legitimation of its participation in destroying Guatemala's democratic institutions. If the story were extended we would learn that Arbenz first sought American military aid and was refused and, more important perhaps, that the lack of security felt by the Arbenz regime, which was finally expressed in the acceptance of Soviet bloc support, is tied to a whole series of American moves that made it reasonable to feel a threat. It is not worth rehearsing all the ways in which Guatemala's treatment in *Force without War* constitutes an impoverished, dehistoricized image. To summarize, the mode of representation for "Guatemala" (among other things), which is implicitly vindicated with resort to the scientific code, is best understood as an implicit vindication of American foreign policy. And the ready acceptance that such "studies" achieve is less a measure of readers' explicit acceptance of American foreign policy as it is an indication of the tacit acceptance of the representational codes with which the study identifies subjects, objects, and events. What we may think of as the "reality" of the "international system" is inextricably bound up with these codes. Therefore, to seek a critical understanding of any of the objects in that discursively engendered system, one needs a level of analysis that is sensitive to how that object is produced and maintained.

Foreign Policy as the Constitution of Otherness

A sensitivity to the representational codes, which constitute the subjects, objects, and characteristic grammars as a whole within foreign-policy discourse, calls our attention to a process of foreign-policy making that tends to be neglected because it is presupposed and implicit in the recognized process ordinarily construed as "foreign-policy making." This implicit level of "policy" is the process of making foreign or exotic, and thus different from the self, someone or -thing. Given the usual esteem within which the self is constituted, the exoticising of the Other almost invariably amounts to the constitution of that Other as a less-than-equal subject.

This discursive function, which is immanent in the exchange of understandings we identify as "international relations," is evident at very basic levels of social organization. Remarking on how representational practices reflect the production of otherness, Jacques Lacan speaks of two young children — brother and sister — reading "Ladies" and "Gentlemen" on two different restroom doors at a railway station.

> For these children, Ladies and Gentlemen will be henceforth two
> countries toward which each of their souls will strive on
> divergent wings, and between which a truce will be the more
> impossible since they are actually the same country and neither

can compromise on its own superiority without detracting from the glory of the other.[17]

Gender policy, as it is practiced in everyday life is thus foreign policy; it is the predominance and acceptance of a discourse with which one makes strange something which one could instead identify or accord the status of another self with equal dignity and importance. How foreign policy of this kind operates within a more politicized domain and at a larger level of aggregation, that of the state, has been pointed out by Paul Veyne. Discussing ancient Rome's imperialistic practices, Veyne offers an ironic reversal. "Rome incarnates an archaic form, not of imperialism but of isolationism. She denies the pluralities of nations; she behaves as Momsen said, as if she were the sole state in the full meaning of the term."[18]

In effect, Rome adopted one of two possible ways that Veyne identifies as the options for achieving security: "to share semi-security with another from day to day, or to seize the definitive whole security for oneself by placing another in a total insecurity."[19] In opting for the "isolationist" strategy, Rome was engaged in a total denial of otherness. For a variety of reasons, modern strategies are less radical on the issue of otherness. Plurality is accepted between nations and varying degrees of otherness are recognized and permitted. Undoubtedly, this has a moderating effect on the level of direct, armed violence in the modern world. Pacification and containment of the Other is the dominant practice, and to the extent that it is practiced in a totalizing way, it is waged more with economic than military strategies.

Nevertheless, there exists a powerful impetus to violence in the form of armed interference by the modern state, and, as was the case with Rome, its ideational supports can be linked to foreign policy, to the ways in which the self and the Other are constituted and estrangements between the two are effected. For example, Foucault has located an important shift in the eighteenth century, which he associates with a growing concern with measuring the working vitality and resources expended by a people. The consequence was that when governments began thinking of themselves as involved with their "populations" instead of merely people, the mobilization for war became more intense. Because the idea of a "population" became a code for a variety of conceptions and measures of vitality, what was perceived to be a stake in relations among states was the "life" of the population. As a result, one now kills in international conflicts, according to Foucault, "in order to go on living."[20]

The making of the Other as something foreign is thus not an innocent exercise in differentiation. It is closely linked to how the self is understood. A self construed with a security-related identity leads to the construction

The Constitution of the Central American Other

of otherness on the axis of threats or lack of threats to that security, while a self identified as one engaged in "crisis management" — a current self-understanding of American foreign-policy thinking — will create modes of otherness on a ruly-versus-unruly axis. For example, American knowledge of other, nonsuperpower states in the contemporary discourse on the international system is often in terms of the idea that most of the Others are indirect threats. Their squabbles with other lesser states may spread and draw in larger states which are construed as direct security threats. In seeking to determine how such an object as Guatemala is produced as a kind of foreign object, then, we must turn our attention not only to the modes within which we have represented Guatemala but also those within which we have represented ourselves.

Given that an understanding of the way that an Other is situated requires us to know the value and meaning attached to the self, what are relevant dimensions of self-understanding? If we assume that the modern self has a value and meaning based on the idea that it is a moral/grammatical entity, it still contains many of the traditional attributes ascribed to selves: it speaks as well as is spoken of, and it is assumed that its natural existence constitutes a moral existence. Within this model we can expect that any Other that is accorded the same status as the self — it is seen as another equally worthy self which happens to reside in a different field of practices — will be accorded the same prohibitions and restrictions from harm or interference as well as the same entitlements. However, to the extent that the Other is regarded as something not occupying the same natural/moral space as the self, conduct toward the Other becomes more exploitive.

Consider, first, those Others that have operated on the farthest extreme of the self/Other dimension of the human regard. For Homo sapiens it is probably the case, as Bataille has argued, that animals were the first Others regarded as radical nonselves. Accordingly, Homo sapiens' self-recognition — their notion that they constitute a separate form of being — is inextricably tied to making Other the animal. Analyzing the Lascaux wall paintings, Bataille, departing from the simple materialist accounts in which the hunting scenes become expressions of the fantasies of hungry hunters, asserts that Lascaux is the place where man expresses his sense of moral superiority over the nonself, the animal.[21]

That this difference, considered natural, is also a moral difference is reflected in our current discursive practices. For example, we find no euphemisms or distancing grammars and rhetorics in references to our position vis-à-vis animals in the food chain. It is quite permissible (except within a few heterodox thought systems and public movements) to say we "slaughter" animals in places called "slaughter houses." By contrast, we tend to launder the violence that humans perpetrate on each other. Governments are always involved in the process of allocating life and death with lon-gevity-affecting acts within their health, education, and welfare policies as well as in their general fiscal policies. But the discourses within which such policies are represented rarely connect them with their deadly con-sequences. Even in the familiar discourses on war, which is a practice undertaken with injury, harm, and death as primary objectives, there is a tendency toward a grammar and rhetoric of administration along with other distancing linguistic practices which deflect attention from war's major constituting motives.[22]

None of this is surprising, for certainly most of our practices are centered. We know who we are, and, rather than seeking to extend the reach of the "we," we appropriate, often violently, the world of others—persons, animals, and landscapes—in a way that allows the familiar dis-courses containing that "we" to maintain their various economies. Our interest in these Others flows from what we understand and prize in our ongoing personal and collective wants and needs as we understand them. Only within certain more open knowledge games do we seek to make fragile and problematic the very grammar of self-understanding and thereby allow the Other not only to be something besides a thing *for us* (where the "us" is considered stable or fixed) but something that can pro-vide an instance for relocating that "us."

It is worth exploring the structure of the discursive practices dedicated to destabilizing ordinary understandings of the self, for it helps us to under-stand better how to situate the more appropriating discursive practices, viz. "foreign policy," which operate within a more self-assured and unreflec-tive self-understanding. One of the more remarkable examples is Barry Lopez's recent study of the arctic region. Noting at the beginning that he is concerned with "how a desire to put a landscape to use shapes our evalua-tion of it," he effects a writing practice that distances him from the ordinary uses characteristic of industrialized portions of North America.[23] In dem-onstrating what that distancing requires, both by what he says and how he says it, he emphasizes the difficulty one has in overcoming the more familiar practices that hamper finely tuned discernments in an unfamiliar territory.

Our first difficulty in seeking a less appropriating understanding of the Arctic is that our practices have developed in a temperate zone.

> Difficulty in evaluating, or even discerning, a particular land-scape is related to the distance a culture has traveled from its own ancestral landscape. As temperate-zone people, we have long been ill-disposed toward deserts and expanses of tundra and ice. They have been wastelands for us; historically we have not

> cared at all what happened in them or to them. . . . It is pre-
> cisely because the regimes of light and time in the arctic are so
> different that this landscape is able to expose in startling ways
> the complacency of our thoughts about land in general.[24]

What is it that attunes Lopez to his/our complacency as compared with
those who create a more appropriating and objectifying mode of confrontation with the unfamiliar? A few lines later he discloses his general knowl-
edge-gathering practice as he speaks of the need for a "more particularized
understanding of the land itself," and notes that this is to be gained by
treating the landscape "as if it were, itself, another sort of civilization we
had to reach some agreement with."[25]

Lopez extends this practice to the arctic inhabitants, pondering two kinds
of difficulties we have appreciating the way a narwhal's world is constructed:

> First, ours is largely a two-dimensional world. We are not crea-
> tures who look up often. We are used to exploring the "length
> and breadth" of issues, not their "height." For the narwhal there
> are very few two-dimensional experiences – the sense of the water
> it feels at the surface of its skin, and that plane it must break in
> order to breathe.
>
> The second constraint on our appreciation of the narwhal's
> world is that it "knows" according to a different hierarchy of
> senses than the one we are accustomed to. Its chemical senses of
> taste and smell are all but gone, as far as we know, though
> narwhals probably retain an ability to determine salinity. Its tac-
> tile sense remains acute. Its sensitivity to pressure is elevated – it
> has a highly discriminating feeling for depth and a hunter's sensi-
> tivity to the slight turbulence created by a school of cod cruising
> ahead of it in its dimly lit world.[26]

To deepen the contrast in the kind of understanding within which Lopez
is working here, one needs only to do an imaginative comparison between
his epistemological meditation on the narwhal and the perspective on the
tuna maintained by such users as the personnel of fishing fleets and the
average luncheon crowd.

Finally, Lopez addresses himself in the same spirit to some of the Arctic's
human inhabitants, those called "Eskimos." Keeping his attention on discontinuities in ways of making worlds, he notes that, among other things,
the Eskimos do not grasp the separation we have from our world, our
degree of objectification and depersonalization of the land and animal/
others. Lopez is not romanticizing the harmony of the Eskimos with their
surroundings here, but rather is once again setting up a pedagogic mode

for treating difference. It seems, for example, that the Eskimos use fear rather than belief as a central epistemological category:

> Eskimos do not maintain this intimacy with nature without paying a certain price. When I have thought about the ways in which they differ from people in my own culture, I have realized that they are more afraid than we are. On a day-to-day basis, they have more fear. Not of being dumped into cold water from an umiak, not a debilitating fear. They are afraid because they accept fully what is violent and tragic in nature. It is a fear tied to their knowledge that sudden, cataclysmic events are as much a part of life, of really living, as are the moments when one pauses to look at something beautiful. A Central Eskimo shaman named Aua, queried by Knud Rasmussen about Eskimo beliefs, answered, "We do not believe. We fear."[27]

Many would be tempted to use this anecdote as an excuse to exoticize Eskimos, to place them in a different cognitive and moral space. But if we follow Lopez's discursive strategy, allowing the Eskimos to help us learn who we are, and add to that a genealogical strategy, reflecting on how the world we understand has been historically invented, the Eskimo shaman's remark on fear can help disclose the discursive economies immanent in the way we use the idea of belief.

Within this general strategy, our first reaction might be that the Eskimo is saying, among other things, that beliefs are an extravagance. The pattern of need fulfillment and the survival demands placed almost daily on the Eskimo make it sensible to link knowing with fearing in contrast with an agricultural/industrialized society in which survival for most is bureaucratized. With our level of bureaucratization, the average person is so estranged, both in terms of knowledge and responsibility, from what there is that might be feared, it is almost impossible, however desirable it might be, to link knowledge and fear as effectively as does the Eskimo.

"Belief" becomes a relevant human identity of people who have, among other things, a complex division of labor with respect to survival and even with respect to lower-level value issues. Moreover, the sheer size of industrialized and centralized populations, along with the growth of a mediaized, technological structure of communication, make cognitive categories for receiving information more significant than the kind of alertness that fear implies. When face-to-face ways of coordinating collective action and maintaining authority are surpassed, and legitimation for such things as national-level policy requires media such as print, voice-at-distance, and remote visual signs, attributes of the receptivity structure, such as belief, related to a person's acceptance of remote authority, become relevant.

The Constitution of the Central American Other

Certainly, beliefs have a significance beyond their role in power relations, but the modern concern with influence and coordination of collective efforts in non–face-to-face situations is undoubtedly very much implicated in the central role the belief and similar cognitive categories play in academic disciplines, private concerns, and public agencies. And, most important for present purposes, is how this meditation on belief, inspired by the difference revealed by the remark of the Eskimo shaman, discloses who we are and contrasts with a perspective that would simply exoticize or objectify the Eskimos and place them within a lesser cognitive, social, and moral/developmental space.

We can further exploit the Eskimo shaman scenario for purposes of understanding the contemporary foreign-policy discourse. Lopez's view of why the Eskimo is afraid provides the point of departure; to repeat, "They are afraid because they accept fully what is violent and tragic in nature. It is a fear tied to their knowledge that sudden, cataclysmic events are as much a part of life, of really living, as are the moments when one pauses to look at something beautiful."

This Eskimo acceptance of the vicissitudes of chance or fortune provides a marked contrast with the history of the strategic discourse component of foreign-policy thinking. Bradley Klein has pointed out that in the history of people's perspectives on danger from foreign threats, what began in the sixteenth century as the acceptance of fate and chance (*fortuna* in Machiavelli's civic history) passed through a variety of alterations until what was once the "defense" of one nation has become a "security" policy.[28] Modern security represents the ultimate in leaving nothing to chance. The number and intensity of interests congregated in modern superpowers, for example, has resulted in a comprehensive level of surveillance and intervention all over the globe. Within this intensification of the security-oriented gaze, the meanings of landscapes and people everywhere are subjected to an intensified form of objectification. There are ever more categories and predictive scenarios, for the modern security-oriented discourse can tolerate no surprises or uncertainties, not only because of a relation to defense of a state but also to the perceived connections with ongoing domestic ways of life.

The constitution of the Other in Central America, then, is intimately bound up with this modern security discourse, and nowhere is this more evident than in the recent *Report of the President's National Bipartisan Commission on Central America*, which is, among other things, a polar opposite to Barry Lopez's way of treating the Other. To inquire into its general orientation as well as its details, it is useful to go back to the discursive production that preceded it.

We are back, then, to "Guatemala," whose indigenous population as an Other for the Spaniards and then their descendants, the Ladinos, has occupied an ambiguous place. At times the so-called Indians have been sufficiently estranged in the imaginative constructions of the Spaniards or Ladinos that slaughter has been easily justified (the primary strategy of the European North Americans in the first two centuries after their arrival), while at other times, the Indians have been construed as a kind of imperfect copy of the self. This kind of Other has justified a variety of policing strategies, ranging from oppression and exploitation to improvement, Christianization, etc. To understand the way that a technology of the Other has directed ideational foundations of foreign policy, it is instructive to hark back to the relations between Guatemala's indigenous population and the gold- and soul-hungry Spaniards who subjugated them.

In brief, the first Spanish–Indian contact provides an exemplary case of the production of otherness, for as Todorov has maintained, the contact was of an intensity previously unrealized both because of the radical difference between the two civilizations and because of the meaning that this difference took on for the Spanish. They accorded the Indian a kind of otherness so far outside their moral inhibitions with respect to human selves, they could comfortably perpetuate the "greatest genocide in human history."[29]

How the original Central American peoples are as Others for us is not wholly unambiguous, but, at a minimum, the discourse with which we produce our origins leaves them in a silence. In locating the Spanish rhetorically as discoverers of the "New World" (and as "conquerers," which implies a different role in a narrative than "slaughterers"), we reproduce the original Indians, not the Spanish, as the Others inasmuch as we trace our origins to that which we have called the European "discovery" of the "New World." As Todorov remarks, "We are all the direct descendants of Columbus, it is with him that our genealogy begins, insofar as the word *beginning* has a meaning."[30]

From the time of the Spanish "discoverers," the Indian voice has not contributed to the discursive practices in which the nations of the New World entered into the kind of talk that produced the "international system." The first scripting of Guatemala into international speech was with the pen of Cortés's infamous captain, Pedro de Alvarado, who had the task of subjugating Guatemala from 1523 to 1525. In a letter to Cortés, in which Alvarado provides a narrative of his military campaign, he says, in a statement epitomizing the Spanish imperialist understanding of what they were doing:

> After having sent my messengers to this country, informing them
> of how I was to come to conquer and pacify the provinces that
> might not be willing to place themselves under the dominion of
> His Majesty, I asked of them as his vassals (for as such they had
> offered themselves to your Grace) the favor and assistance of
> passage through their country; that by so doing, they would act
> as good and loyal vassals of His Majesty and that they would be
> greatly favored and supported in all justice by me and the
> Spaniards in my company; and if not, I threatened to make war
> on them as on traitors rising in rebellion against the service of
> our Lord the Emperor and that as such they would be treated,
> and that in addition to this, I would make slaves of all those
> who should be taken alive in the war.[31]

Thus the Indians enter into the language of empire building as "vassals,"
an Other viewed as an imperfect extension of the appropriating Spanish
self and in the service of that self. This fixing of their place as subjects
in the service of Spanish political designs allows for a hierarchy to be established in the economy of humanness. This discursive economy, assisted
by and intertwined with the forms of otherness already in hand as a result
of the Christian self-understandings of the Spanish, pervaded the Spanish
experience in Mesoamerica. For example, Alvarado found "infidels" with
"evil intentions."[32]

> And as I knew them to have such a bad disposition toward the
> service of His Majesty, and to insure the good and peace of this
> land, I burnt them, and sent to burn the town and to destroy it,
> for it is a very strong and dangerous place, that more resembles
> a "robbers" stronghold than a city.[33]

While Alvarado is waging war, a war of subjugation by direct, military means, his textual practice plays a supporting role. For example, there
are no individual names attached to Indians in his account, a depluralizing
practice which allows them no recognizable and coherent culture. In addition, he often switches subject and object perspectives, as he tends first
to characterize the improprieties of what they do (the imperfect subjects),
characteristically inserting their conduct into a frame of meaning within
his practices, and then justifies treating them (the objects) as commodities for a slave market.

Alvarado, also a master of the understatement, leaves us to understand
that with regard to Spanish–Indian relations, "we," the Spanish, "defeated
them." But even some of his contemporaries resisted the discourse that
allowed Alvarado a peace of mind and moral contentment as he went
about his cruelties. The author/priest Bartolemé de las Casas remarked,

The Constitution of the Central American Other

> Let us again speak of the great tyrant captain (Pedro de
> Alvarado) who went into the kingdom of Guatemala, who, as it
> has been said, surpassed all past and equalled all present
> tyrants. . . . He advanced killing, ravaging, burning, robbing
> and destroying all the country wherever he came, under the
> above mentioned pretext, that the Indians should subject them-
> selves to such inhuman, unjust, and cruel men, in the name of
> the unknown King of Spain, of whom they had never heard and
> whom they considered to be much more unjust and cruel than
> his representatives.[34]

Las Casas makes another appearance below. At this point it is useful
to summarize Todorov's observations about the Indians encountered by
the Spanish and then constituted through the opportunities and constraints
imposed by two major forces: the drive toward the universal victory of
Christianity and the new relationship of gold and the production of wealth
to what was important in the Spanish society (and in European society
in general). It was these drives, according to Todorov, that help us understand the Spanish discursive economy: "difference is corrupted into
inequality, equality [corrupted] into identity."[35] This egocentric experience
of alterity is initially pointed out in his assessment of Columbus's relationship with the Indians he meets.

> Either he conceives the Indian (though without using these
> words) as human beings altogether, having the same rights as
> himself; but then he sees them not only as equals but also as
> identical, and his behavior leads to assimilationism, the projec-
> tion of his own values on the others. Or else he starts from the
> difference, but the latter is immediately translated into terms of
> superiority and inferiority (in his case, obviously, it is the
> Indians who are inferior). What is denied is the existence of a
> human substance truly other, something capable of being not
> merely an imperfect state of oneself.[36]

Christianity implanted in Spanish culture a social self-centeredness that
equated everything connected with Spain and its Catholicism as natural,
true, and right. Without getting into an extended analysis of this relationship between Christianity and ethnocentrism, it should suffice to cite as
an example the Spanish *Requerimiento*, which was the injunction, required
by Spanish law, to be read to the Indians whenever Spaniards would first
step on appropriated soil. The text gives a history of humanity centered
on the appearance of Jesus Christ. Christ was the "master of the human
lineage" who bestowed his power on Saint Peter, and in turn the pope,
who, it seems, authorized the Spanish to take possession of the American

continent. In addition to being informed, the Indians are given a choice: become Christians and vassals or "we shall forcibly enter your country . . . make war against you in all ways and manners that we can, and shall subject you to the yoke and obedience of the church. . . ."[37]

In this text, then, spiritual expansion and sovereign power are combined. More important, the universalistic notions of Christianity are incorporated into Spanish colonialist pretensions, producing a cultural intolerance toward things constituted as alien. Complementing the misfortunes the Indians experienced as a result of their perceived distance from Christianity was that which they experienced as a result of their proximity to gold, a proximity in which they were to suffer by comparison. The Spanish discourse on human subjects did not locate the non-Christian in a place of value which would inhibit the conduct flowing from their valuing of gold. Indeed, gold itself, given the meaning and value attached to it by the Spanish, spiritually diminished the Indian. Todorov again:

> Certainly the desire for riches is nothing new, the passion for gold has nothing specifically modern about it. What is new is the subordination of all other values to this one. . . . Money is not only the universal equivalent of all material values, but also the possibility of acquiring all spiritual values.[38]

It is this "homogenization of values by money" that is the new phenomenon and it "heralds the modern mentality, egalitarian and economic."[39] The impoverished reading of the Indian in Spanish discourse is a function, then, of an expanding and already expansive circuit of capital and Christianity. They serve as forces which both constrain the more pluralistic constructions of the Indian and a more reflective self-consciousness that encounters with an other can engender.

Alvarado and las Casas were exemplary voices in this power- and meaning-deploying circuit. In some ways, their voices represent two contending discourses contributing to the constitution of the Indian subject, as evidenced by las Casas's remarks on Alvarado's cruel excesses. But we can be misled if we see the voices only as contending and neglect their complementary roles in the Spanish discursive economy. The former, the voice of the colonizer, seeks to identify the Indian within the reigning system of political homage, as part of that whole with its various conditions and debts; it seeks in other words to reconstitute the Indian-as-subject (albeit a lesser subject) as a nonproblematic entity within a framework of other such politically normalized subjects. And the identities taken on by the Indian, who exists at the periphery of an expanding empire, all relate to a globalizing, politicoeconomic discourse of conquest and subjugation. But the Christian constitution of the Indian also has a subjugating effect. The Other that las Casas recognizes in the Indian is equally constrained and as depluralized as that of the conquistadors. Both are the result of an appropriating discourse that fails to provide a range of possibilities, possibilities which could include an equal, but "not-I," Indian subject. Todorov makes a similar point: "Las Casas loves the Indians. And is a Christian. For him these two traits are linked: he loves the Indians precisely *because* he is a Christian, and his love *illustrates* his faith."[40]

This insight leads Todorov to question whether there is "not already a violence in the conviction that one possesses the truth oneself, whereas this is not the case for others, and that one must furthermore impose the truth on those others."[41] For example, even as las Casas complains of the Spanish enslavement of a particular Indian tribe when "that tribe was equal perhaps even superior to the Spaniards as free men," he adds, in the very next phrase, "except in the matters of Faith and Christianity."[42] It must also not come as a surprise when these two globalizing discourses intersect at the point of the Indian subject, and, thus linked, operate in tandem in the conquest of the Indian bodies and soil. In the construction of the Indian subject, subjugation is thus justified at both the spiritual and material levels.

Contemporary Discourse

In two senses the Indians of Guatemala no longer exist. Although the descendants of the Mayans are still numerous, making up at least 60 percent of the population, their current cultural practices cannot be construed as a legacy from their own cultural past, for they have been shaped by centuries of Ladino domination. Within Guatemala, the "Indian" has been made, not merely contained. What we now take as an Indian ethnic identity has been created both by the original Spanish conquest and by the subsequent contact with Hispanic people. "Ethnicity," as Kay Warren has pointed out, "has been very much the product of the interplay between colonially created cultural identities and broader national systems of ideology, economics, and politics directed by non-Indians."[43]

The second kind of nonexistence for the Indian of Guatemala is produced externally. The depluralization of within-nation attributes by the discourses of the international system and the American foreign-policy discourse leaves no privileged place for the Indian subject, and they fail to appear even as nonvoices, that is to say, as objects. Indeed, within American foreign-policy discourse even Guatemala as a whole unit pales, for the major discursive practice within which we have Guatemala is the geopolitical code. Within this code, Guatemala is primarily a unit within the

The Constitution of the Central American Other

Western hemisphere. This identity locates Guatemala strategically in America's imaginative enactments of its own survival and hegemony struggles.

From the early years after American independence, the discourse at the national level excluded Indians by referring to Guatemala and other units to the south as "Spanish America." As one historian has suggested, we simply did not know "Spanish America" when, under Jefferson, we began to formulate a policy with respect to that part of the world. That it was "Spanish America," however, did constitute a way of knowing, a kind of representational practice that already diminished the multiethnic aspect of the region and took up a practice that affirmed colonial, geopolitical boundaries. "Pan-American" policy, the characterization with which the discourse was inaugurated under Jefferson, was the beginning of the foreign-policy discourse which was to make Central and South America entities which shared more with us, from a geopolitical point of view, than did the nations of Europe. Prefiguring the Monroe Doctrine and Alliance for Progress was Jefferson's avowed policy of keeping the Western Hemisphere free from European intrusion, for security, as it was understood by American leaders in the early nineteenth century, was to be strengthened to the extent that the United States could avoid getting drawn into European-based international conflicts.[44]

The initial discourse within which Guatemala was known was thus based on two metonymies, one ethnic and the other geographic. For us, Guatemala was to be Spanish and part of the Western Hemisphere (understood in a strategic sense). With the use of the former, we affirmed the domination of the Hispanic elements in the population, and with the latter, we identified Guatemala within our own security-policy practices. These two figurations for representing Guatemala remain the prevailing meaning-giving mechanisms with which the foreign-policy discourse constructs Central American nations. Probably more symptomatic than any other current document of this continual reproduction of the authority of the ethnic and geopolitical coding of the region, is what has come to be called the "Kissinger Report" (the above-mentioned *Report of the President's Bipartisan Commission on Central America*).[45] This document more or less reproduces the dominant discourse on Central America that has been shaped since the recognized failures of the Alliance for Progress of the early 1960s.

Certainly there are variations within this discourse on Central America in general and Guatemala in particular, and American scholars and leaders vary widely in their construals of the region. But the variations of orthodox and heterodox views tend to be constrained within what Bourdieu has called the "doxa," that stable aspect of discourse which is naturalized and thus not considered controversial.[46] At one extreme, for example, is a position which is familiar, widespread, and in this case too comical to resist quoting at length. Praising what some would call the new form of colonialism or imperialism — "private investment" — the writer puts it this way:

> From a purely economic viewpoint, foreign private investment is certainly a sound approach to hemisphere development. It channels not only capital but also technical and managerial know-how to the host country, and it also alleviates unemployment and introduces new commodities into the latter's market. In a word, it spreads "Americanism," which may be sneered at by the leftists and pseudoaristocrats, but which is welcome to the consumer masses. It has, however, certain political implications which may make it an onerous burden on relations between the United States and the recipient country. Whenever a Latin American Republic has found it expedient to seize a U.S. company, the shadow of conflict has been cast over its relations with the United States. . . . In plain terms, the U.S. position is that the property rights of its citizens must be protected in a foreign country. Even if the Department of State shows some propensity toward accommodation, Congress usually exerts pressure to proceed firmly against the small brother who has disregarded his big brother's rights.[47]

The only unintelligible part of this statement is the reference to "pseudo-aristocrats." Perhaps this is a displacement of one of the author's private quarrels (anger and envy of an acquaintance with more inherited status and a less extreme neoimperialist view?). Otherwise, the passage recycles the venerable colonialist code in which imperialism has always been a pious social mission in places which are both not fully grown ("little brothers") and morally deficient (the "rights" not recognized and the "expedient" that encourages expropriation). Equally significant is how obtuse this thinking is as regards the political economy of private investment, which, in more acute accounts, is seen to put "commodities" out of the reach of more people than those to whom it makes them available. The above statement is merely one example of what Bakhtin terms a discourse that is "crassly accommodating" to the interests of centralizing power (indeed the kind of crassly accommodating discourse that has come to distinguish the writing in publications of the American Enterprise Institute).[48]

More sensitive to the aftereffects of economic neoimperialism is this statement:

> Recent economic growth in Latin America has tended, in many
> cases, not to promote social equity but to exacerbate the
> inequality of income distribution, not to stimulate fundamental
> change but to reinforce existing structures, not to promote sta-
> bility but to raise expectations and intensify frustration.[49]

While this writer is sensitive to the consequences of the role private
investment has played, his thinking remains within the dominant geopolitical discourse. Latin America for him is still to be seen as a series of
national objects placed under more careful scrutiny for purposes of creating a Western Hemisphere more impervious to "foreign" threats, that is,
those coming from outside the hemisphere. While he does not see an
"immediate threat," to American security, he nevertheless conceives of U.S.
policy as aimed at preventing "instability" so that those places especially
subject to "sudden convulsions and shifts" can be prevented from creating
"future security problems."[50] Here he recapitulates the now-familiar discourse produced by comparative-politics theorists who, part in reaction
to the Hitler phenomenon, have conceived a stability-oriented knowledge
of exotic (non-U.S.) governments. This has involved a multiparty phobia,
a suspicion of anything ideological — which has meant any of the "isms" —
and, in recent years, the notion that instability in what we call the "Third
World" invites superpower confrontations or the spread of communism.
Thus, for example, when military-oriented governments with U.S. back-
ing have managed almost total repression and opened Guatemala to U.S.
investment, it has been construed as a period of "stability" within the under
standing of orthodox analysts.

This latter analyst is operating within the orthodox point of view, and
like other U.S. leaders, bureaucrats, statesmen, and academics who write
for *Foreign Affairs*, his main way of creating the Latin American Other
comes through his reproduction of the already-formed international system
and American foreign-policy discourses. The main problematic of this discourse at present is the strengthening of the Western Hemisphere within
the now-general perception that the Alliance for Progress has failed to
meet its security-oriented objectives. The various writers who are packaged with this analyst in a collection of post–Alliance for Progress essays
place all Latin American nations in the same strategic space as the United
States. Each country is identified as ethnically Spanish and treated as a
unified actor. But perhaps most significantly, all the countries are seen
as developmentally and thus morally inferior, for they are functioning
at a more primitive stage than the United States (as the developmental
narrative would have it).[51]

One of the most fundamental rhetorical dimensions in the U.S. foreign-policy discourse is its state-centric model of agency. This is an aspect of the discourse which renders it unable, as Richard Ashley has noted, to "accord recognition to — it cannot even comprehend — those global collectivist concepts that are irreducible to the logical combination of state-bounded relations.[52] When one adds the moral-superiority code to the state-centric and geopolitical/security ones, the foreign-policy discourse as a whole becomes a vindication for U.S. intervention to seek to control another state's steering mechanism for its own moral benefit as well as for purposes of U.S. strategic and domestic interests.

This interventionist impetus, moreover, operates within the context of a narrative self-understanding. The foreign-policy discourse that emerges from our nation derives much of its force from the meaning ascribed to America's origin, its destiny, and the interim duties that the commitment to such a beginning and destiny implies. It is a narrative built around the myth that America is a nation created out of a search for "freedom" (as opposed to more favorable tax status, better land, etc.). This notion fuels an interventionist, state-centric foreign policy by casting America as a defender of freedom, an actor committed to helping others achieve a similar destiny.

The narrative, combined with some key tropes such as the above-mentioned bureaucratic/managerial imagery which has lent the foreign-policy discourse the identity of the conflict manager, has thus combined a moralistic code with a rational management vindication. There are other narratives imbedded in the American version of the international system and foreign-policy discourses, but what is most apparent and relevant here is the obsessive preoccupation with geopolitical, security-oriented concerns along with the idea that the United States is a privileged actor with borders. All of this is echoed in a recent presidential speech about Central America.

> We must not turn our backs on our friends. We must not permit
> dictators to ram Communism down the throats of innocent
> people in one country after another. U.S. security — the safety of
> American citizens — that's why Central America is so important.
> Either we pay a modest price now so we can prevent a crisis or
> we listen to the do-nothings and risk an explosion of violence
> that will bring real danger to our borders.[53]

With this as background, we can scrutinize the Kissinger Report, one of the most recent and exemplary reproductions of the American foreign policy discourse as it relates to — indeed reconstructs — how Central America is for us. The Kissinger Report is a more acute view of Central America than the first pro–private-investment position reviewed above.

The Constitution of the Central American Other

Among other things, the report recognizes that the Central American Other has a voice and thus is able to articulate a viewpoint on the history and current status of U.S.–Central American relations. At a minimum, this recognition brings the region closer to having a recognizable subjectivity which is not unlike the American subject's self-understanding.

What is most striking about the rhetorical motions of the report at the outset is the depoliticizing, antiideology code, which is emphasized both in the title and introduction. With two linguistic gestures, first evoking the "bipartisan" idea and, second, claiming to experience what is there rather than recapitulating partisan viewpoints, the report begins by pacifying potential critics. Referring, in his cover letter, to "the lessons of this experience," Kissinger suggests that reality itself produced the commission's consensus on America's policy problems in the region. As he puts it, "The best route to consensus on U.S. policy toward Central America is by exposure to the realities of Central America."[54]

The report goes on to speak of the "remarkable consensus" in the commission despite the existence of both Democrats and Republicans as well as various people from government, academia, journalism, etc. As Kissinger would have it, reality itself scripted the commission's report. But what is "reality"? Without going into an extended epistemological discussion, it should suffice to note that all referents about which one speaks are mediated by our discursive practices. The mediation in this case is the system of representation that is part of the developed international system discourse in general and the related American foreign-policy discourse in particular. The reproduced images of Central America in the report were not acquired through discoveries of commissions. Contrary to Kissinger's claim, reality does not venture out to meet those in pursuit of it. Rather, the pursuers function within a discursive practice that imposes meanings on their world, creating what Kissinger referred to as "reality." Norman Bryson, an art historian, put this well in his discussion of art images and their relationship to the social formation in which they are perceived.

> The image is not obliged to go out of its way to "meet" the social formation, it does not have to exert itself with vigour, with determination to link into the society, since it is always already there at its destination; it has never been in a state of disarticulation.[55]

The Kissinger Commission's findings were "always already there at [their] destination." Central America in general and Guatemala in particular are fully formed within the American foreign-policy discourse that the Kissinger Report puts into play. The "bipartisanship" to which the report refers is simply the orthodox and heterodox views about how to deal with this already-formed set of entities. They reside on the surface of that discourse as implications. The doxa, which is the relatively uncontested grammar of international speech and American interests identified within that speech practice, remains intact and does its work as the report celebrates the extraordinary level of agreement.

In addition to its emphasis on its bipartisan participation and representation of a broad range of views, a gesture aimed at delegitimating disagreement with its findings, the report evinces another legitimating device for prompting a proactive American policy, the concept of the "crisis":

> If there is no time to lose, neither is the crisis in Central
> America a matter which the country can afford to approach on a
> partisan basis.
> The people of Central America are neither Republicans nor
> Democrats. The crisis is nonpartisan, and calls for a nonpartisan
> response. As a practical political matter, the best way to a non-
> partisan policy is by a bipartisan route.[56]

The report goes on to display its Republicans, Democrats, private citizens, academics, a governor, a mayor, business people, etc., to make its bipartisan and representative case, the implication being that in diversity lies objectivity and ideological neutrality. In addition, the grammatical structure of the report supports the tone of this narrative model (a narrative in which the same reality impresses itself on people with widely varying perspectives and roles). Authorial responsibility is suppressed through most of the text with the use of the third person, calling into service scientific and cultural codes which mark the text as an objective history or analysis. A confident authority is imbedded in its language, and when the more personally involved "we" is used, the referent frequently shifts from "we the country" to "we the commission." This subtle linkage between the commission's work and its representation of a national voice not only reinforces the legitimacy of the text but also throws into relief the "not us," in this case, Central America. This "not us" is not identical with a "different us," which would more easily locate the "I" in the Other, giving that Other a full recognition as a subject. The "not us" is the identity which, as Todorov has noted, permits it to be located within a discourse which vindicates power by equating difference with relations of superiority and inferiority. The Kissinger Report is thus an exemplary piece of foreign policy in itself. Along with the general tradition of making foreign the Other, who is not us, it reproduces American foreign-policy's objects, and, in failing to reflect on how we are involved in objectifying the Other, it recapitulates the way American foreign-policy discourse makes its objects.

The Constitution of the Central American Other

This is not, however, to suggest that the subjects and objects in the discourse have not undergone some modifications. As noted above, while until recently, the regions' population has been rendered as a silent set of objects, in the quarter century since the invention of the Alliance for Progress, it has achieved the position of a subject as well. The Latin American has begun to speak, and the Kissinger Report reflects the extent to which American foreign-policy discourse has made a place for at least one and at times multiple voices from within the national units. Moreover, the speaking Other, clearly in evidence in the early part of the report, is at times an Other who would resist the identities it has been lent by the speech practices of its powerful, ever-surveillant neighbor. It is the recognition of this recently modified, speaking Other that undoubtedly led to one of the report's methods for reaching conclusions: extensive interviews with a variety of kinds of persons in each of the Central American countries.

However, despite countenancing voices coming from the region, the Central American Other remains an imperfect, not fully finished one in the Kissinger Report. Paying little attention to the kind of ethnically ambiguous cultures in the various countries, the entire culture is depluralized into something that is almost the same and has a destiny to be the same as what is construed as the Euro-American culture to the north. Noting the persistence of this ideological perception well before the bipartisan commission let reality search it out, a Cuban writer noted, "Our entire culture is taken as an apprenticeship, a rough draft of a copy of European bourgeois culture ('an emanation of Europe,' as Bolivar said)."[57]

The Kissinger Report, with its state-centric and strategic orientation, conveniently glosses over cultural diversity in Central America and takes up this "rough draft" thesis. Early in the report it is asserted that we "share cultures, ideas and values" with Central American nations, but, a paragraph later there is a caution against romanticizing the similarities, and some of the differences are stressed, e.g., their "feudal social structure" and the importance of the military in shaping that structure.[58] Here the report reproduces an ambivalence that is part of the foreign-policy discourse inherited from earlier colonial and neocolonial practices. The more recently independent nations have always been regarded in colonial discourses as mimics of the more thoroughly independent major powers. Edward Said has identified this "conflictual economy" in the colonial discourse which incorporates a demand for identity and stasis, a fixed object of knowledge, and, at the same time, a pressure for change and difference.[59]

This ambivalence is powerfully reflected in the Kissinger Report, which displays in its early sections what Homi Bhabha has called "colonial mimicry." This is "the desire for a reformed, recognizable other, as *a subject*

of a difference that is almost the same but not quite."[60] What this constitution of the imperfect, "almost the same but not quite" subject/Other
encourages is an intensified surveillance, of which the Kissinger Report
is an expression. The report as a whole is an exemplar of what Foucault
has called "normalizing power."

Indeed, so strong is the report's push for identity — stopping just short
of the Roman total denial of otherness — that even the exploitation wrought
by private investment in Central America becomes a sign of similarity.
In the section that extolls similarities it says: "We also share economic
interests. Of all U.S. private investment, 62 percent is in Latin America
and the Caribbean."[61]

Not surprisingly, the report goes on to emphasize our strategic interests
in the area and link the knowledge of Central America to that self-understanding. This emphasis was already reflected in Executive Order 12433
which established the commission. President Reagan's charge to the commission was to "study the nature of United States interests in the Central
American region and the threats now posed to those interests" and to
examine the "internal and external threats to its [the region's] security and
stability." Taking up the charge, the commission notes the need to check
"externally supported insurgences," to stop the exploitation by "hostile outside forces" who will turn any revolution they capture into totalitarian
states, threatening the region and robbing the people of their hopes for
liberty."[62] This stimulates critics of the report like Lowenthal to recognize
that the "single-minded" pursuit of the goal of preventing Soviet involvement is "having the effect of undercutting all other aims."[63]

This single-mindedness turns up in a number of sections where Guatemala is specifically mentioned. The ideational hegemony of the strategic,
security-oriented discourse wholly controls the construction of both yester-
day's and today's "Guatemala." In a "historical overview" of the "crisis"
in Central America, the commission emphasizes the positive implications
of the emerging dictatorships between 1930 and 1960. These dictatorships
(in El Salvador, Honduras, Guatemala, and Nicaragua) "restored order"
and encouraged "economic development and social modernization."[64] But
it is in an ostensible act of self-criticism that the commission discloses its
primary interpretive codes with respect to Guatemala:

> In Guatemala, after the United States helped bring about the fall
> of the Arbenz government in 1954, politics became more divi-
> sive, violent and polarized than in neighboring states. But even
> there, there were efforts to combine military and civilian rule, or
> to alternate between them, in various shaky and uneasy blends.[65]

By the report's account, the actions undertaken by the United States

The Constitution of the Central American Other

do not always work, but they are in the spirit of helping. Nowhere is a problematic about intervention-qua-intervention evoked. There is no question raised about incompatibilities between the construction of American strategic interests and the ability of the Other to acquire even those values to which the commission makes positive gestures, e.g., land reform. Where the commission refers to American participation in the overthrow of Arbenz, it is not mentioned that Arbenz was engaged in land reform.

But the strategic discourse offers an escape plan from these contradictions — in of all places — under the section on human rights:

> On the one hand, we seek to promote justice and find it repugnant to support forces that violate — or tolerate violation of — fundamental U.S. values. On the other hand, we are engaged in El Salvador annd Central America because we are serving fundamental U.S. interests that transcend any particular government.[66]

There is an answer! Within the economies of the strategic discourse, human rights are subordinated to U.S. interests as they are construed within the geopolitical figuration which dominates our constructions of the Other. On Guatemala particularly the commission says:

> The existing human rights situation there is unacceptable and the security situation could become critical. Although the insurgency in Guatemala has been contained for the time being at a relatively low level, military assistance could become necessary. Military aid and military sales should be authorized if Guatemala meets the human rights conditions described in this chapter. In terms of U.S. security interests, Guatemala, with its strategic position on the Mexican border, the largest population in the Central America area, the most important economy, is obviously a political country.[67]

Here the report is struggling to reconcile a reform of the human-rights situation with the dominant interest in stability, which the security-oriented, geopolitical thinking inspires. One can discern, therefore, that human-rights concerns interpose very little in the text. For example, Rios Montt receives positive treatment for his control of insurgency. In a section entitled "Insurgency in Guatemala," the commissioners praise the Guatemalan army under Rios Montt for its efforts to provide food and housing to the villages participating in the "Civil Defense Program."[68] Not mentioned was that during the first six months of Rios Montt's regime there were reported at least five hundred murders per month, and by the end of 1982, a conservative estimate placed the killings in excess of ten thousand.[69] Within the discourse that gives us Guatemala, then, the fact that the Guatemalan army's brutality was "morally unacceptable" has little political importance.

Where does this leave "Guatemala"? Guatemala has been created in the commission's reproduction of the American foreign-policy discourse as a troubled subject, "suffering from violence and economic decline."[70] This grammar of absolution is typical throughout the report inasmuch as it never implicates the United States in the experienced conditions in Central America. As one analyst of the report has noted, the commission fails to raise the question "to what extent has the U.S. contributed to the situation."[71] For example, the dehistoricizing one gets from the grammar of "suffering from violence" constitutes a forgetting of the role the United States played in toppling the last civilian government in 1954 as well as its role in helping to supply the implements of violence used thereafter (even though these things are mentioned later in the report). To the extent that human actors are identified as responsible for violence, the report — again dehistoricizing the circumstances that put the Guatemalan military in control — legitimates that military. "With 20 years of experience in counter-insurgency, the Guatemalan army has so far been able to contain the Guerilla threat, despite the lack of outside assistance, and despite shortages of equipment and spare parts."[72]

Maintaining its interest in regime hegemony at any price, the report here identifies the sides as warriors of a legitimate kind (army) and a dubious kind (guerillas). A representational practice which included ethnicities and social-class backgrounds might indicate what historically embedded grievances are involved. But this omission is coherent with a discursive practice preoccupied with surveillance, control, and stability. Despite the implication of this passage, it has been American support of the Guatemalan army which has not only helped in the slaughter of many Guatemalan citizens, guerillas and nonguerillas, but has also decimated much of what might have been a significant political opposition.

In short, the Kissinger Report is an exemplary piece of ideology (bipartisanship and careful, objective looking to the contrary notwithstanding). It encourages a misreading of itself by the way that it manipulates the inside/outside metaphor, representing forces and processes inside Central American nations and those outside. When it speaks of the failures of economic well-being and social inequality, it exonerates American foreign policy by referring only to forces operating inside each of the countries. But when it struggles to justify American intervention in situations of domestic unrest, it, in Anibal Romero's terms, "explicitly identifies the advance of the indigenous revolutionary insurgencies with the 'projection of Soviet and Cuban power in the region.'"[73] The report thus equates ideological migration — the movement of revolution justifying ideational systems — with outside interference. Here the outside part of the dichotomy again exonerates American foreign policy. This inside/outside figuration, when combined with the report's assumption of the moral superiority of the United States (its first stated objective is, "to preserve the moral superiority of the United States"),[74] provides the general rationale for the already-in-place policy of active economic and civilian/military intervention to help the not-yet-perfected Central American Others. But from our perspective, the most significant ideological dimension of the report is embodied in the section entitled "How We Learned." The methodology reported consists of a canvassing of everyone who was consulted — people at different status levels in the United States and Latin America along with experts in both government and academia. Nevertheless, learning is not what took place. What the Kissinger Report does is hark back to the history of the colonial mentality. The President's Bipartisan Commission on Central America failed to understand both its own discursive practice and to attain a grasp of what Central America could be if it were approached in a less-appropriating form of knowledge/practice. The commission reproduced the kind of Central American isthmus that has been produced in the European imagination for centuries. Insofar as it failed to recognize itself, the commission version of the American foreign-policy discourse "discovered" the world produced in its imagination. The report has thus functioned in a manner similar to traditional colonial literature, which, as a literary theorist has shown, fails to understand the world of possible differences and instead "simply codifies and preserves the structure of its own mentality."[75]

Conclusion: Foreign Policy as a Representational Practice

The discussion has ranged over a variety of seemingly different themes, and although "Guatemala" appears in the title, there is at least as much concentration on what Guatemala is not as there is an attempt to deal with it directly. This indirection and seeming evasiveness amounts, indeed, to an incoherence in the context of the usual practices with which Guatemala is thought and analyzed. But there is a coherence to be discerned here. At the same time that the discussion resists absorption into traditional modes of analyzing foreign policy, it attempts to engage a critical mode, one that treats a discourse in terms of the discursive economies in which it participates rather than on the basis of what are ordinarily taken as the referents of its statements. This critical mode, when applied to a national-level discourse like foreign-policy speech, has the effect of denaturalizing it, showing that it is a practice, one way of constructing a world at the expense of others, which would attract other modes of abiding.

More specifically, the burden of this analysis has been to show how a foreign-policy discourse is governed by a historically developed representational practice which is primarily geopolitical and that this has been combined with a way of constituting the Other, which places that other in a lesser moral space. To show how such a discourse works requires the assumption that the world does not issue a summons to speak in a particular way but rather that ways of speaking are implicated in world making. This has led to a demonstration that in taking for granted and thereby using the prevailing modes of speaking, one accommodates to the structures of intelligibility, which emerge from ways of thinking/living that have tolerated violent and objectifying modes of treating other selves.

Mobilizing this kind of demonstration in the domain of relations within the international system, we have witnessed a process in which discovery and learning about the Other is as violent and appropriative today as it was at the inception of contact between Europeans and the Indian inhabitants of Central America. What is the response to this kind of witnessing? The attempt has been to build a possible response into the inquiry itself. The focus on different ways of constructing the Other — in particular Lopez's discursive practice as he used the arctic region to understand the nonarctic — carries an implicit ethical injunction.

It is always tempting to take a more Kantian approach and simply state as a moral imperative that we should treat the Other as an equally worthy self, but to merely issue this kind of injunction as if it were a product of knowledge is to cut off inquiry into how "knowledge" operates. The purpose here, for example, is not to point to the moral failings of the Kissinger Report but to show how it made its subjects, objects, and relationships. Ordinarily, this making is not brought into ethical/moral discourse insofar as it is ideologically mystified and passed off as a nonevaluative "is." Indeed, it is not surprising that the report represented the genre of security-oriented, foreign-policy decision-making discourse rather than a study into the phenomenological mode of anthropological discourse (a genre close to that with which Lopez worked). However, an emphasis of the differences between the two discursive practices has impeached both the historical and current delusion that the Central American Other can be said to have been "discovered." How to evaluate the worth of the different practices is not something mysterious. Already in circulation are various commitments to what constitutes knowledge and what is reasonable treatment of the Other. Here I have tried to demystify a particular venerable practice which, once disclosed, cannot bear scrutiny by those committed to a knowledge practice that resists crass accommodation to both cynical and obtuse forms of domination and exploitation.

THE POLITICAL RHETORIC

OF PHOTOGRAPHY

Introduction: Politicizing Photography

There is an implicit epistemological code hovering around a photograph. Of all modes of representation, it is the one most easily assimilated into the discourses of knowledge and truth, for it is thought to be an unmediated simulacrum, a copy of what we consider the "real." Despite the elements of photographic practice that contribute to the signifying effects or rhetorical force of photographs — angle of vision, framing, distance, lighting, style of developing, etc. — the interpretive culture within which photographs are displayed tends to bracket the practices involved in creating the image and concentrate on the image itself. Indeed, the photograph is usually treated as so unproblematically "real" that the grammar of discussions of photographs tends to approximate the grammar of face-to-face encounters: "this is John" is an intelligible and appropriate utterance whether one is introducing someone to John or showing them a picture of John.

However, there are some photographs that tend to arrest the subconscious process by which we assimilate the copy to the real. As a result, they allow other than the usual or canonical interpretive codes to enter into the interpretive economy of the contemplation of the image. For example, this Diane Arbus photo of a dwarf (figure 4.1) provokes the kind of thinking that ventures beyond the mere fact of a person being represented for some of the same reasons that "freaks" have always been provocative. Given the range of difference one has come to expect of the human species, the freak has an aura of unreality. And as inquiry has shown, the freak provokes contemplation about people's fortunes. Because most people take for granted the range of normality in general and their normality in particular, and because "normality" functions as a moral as well as descriptive category, people tend to be struck with the profound level of misfortune that seems to have been visited on the freak. Moreover, for some people, thinking about the boundaries of normality/abnormality in physical appearance provokes questions about the distribution of other fortunes, such as those effected by the economic system and related structure of social stratification.

Certainly Diane Arbus's photographic practice was guided by musings about fortune and misfortune, for she spoke of feeling privileged by the accident that separated her from the abnormality of freaks.[1] And it is probably no accident that Lewis Hine, best known for depicting child and adult victims of the depredations of a harsh, unequal work structure, chose to photograph these two people, who might also be called "freaks" (figure 4.2), whose lot, in Hine's imagination, was similar to that of the child laborer or poorly paid adult manual laborer (two of his most frequent photographic subjects).

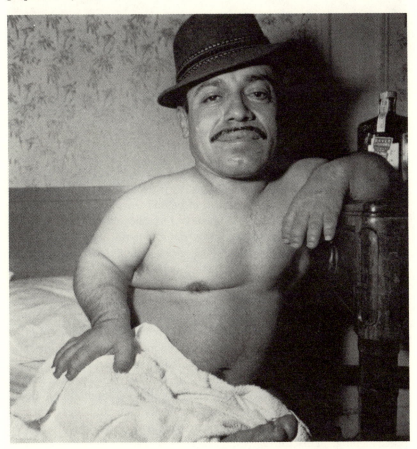

Fig. 4.1. *Mexican dwarf in his hotel room in N.Y.C. 1970.* Photograph by Diane Arbus. Copyright © Estate of Diane Arbus 1970.

The Political Rhetoric of Photography

Fig. 4.2 *Retarded Children, New Jersey, 1924.* Photograph by Lewis Hine. From International Museum of Photography at George Eastman House.

This spillover effect in the imaginative process, from the abnormal to the socially disadvantaged is encouraged by the rhetoric of the photograph itself, whether or not it is a motivation behind the photograph. Because portraiture as a genre tends to be reserved for those in middling-to-high statuses, it is unusual to see a photographic portrait of a "freak." As a result, the viewer, whose interpretive codes are challenged, is inclined to reflect upon status or place within the social order.

But despite the more radicalizing effects we can discern in the Arbus and Hine "freak" photographs, there is much about the photographic genre that lends itself not to the activation of socially implicated and even impertinent questions but to a pacification, a reinforcement of the kinds of interpretive codes that lend an aura of naturalness and permanence to the existing structures. Opinion is therefore divided on how to theorize photography in relation to the social and political order. Since photography's invention in the nineteenth century, scrutiny of its representational qualities has produced both celebrations of its capacity to disclose and demystify and critiques of its tendency to reproduce and reinforce the already-in-place ideological discourses vindicating entrenched systems of power and authority.

Among the more sanguine analysts of photography was Walter Benjamin, who was enthralled by the medium's stop-action and enlargement capabilities, which, in providing opportunities for more careful observation, "make us aware for the first time of the optical unconscious, just as psychoanalysis discloses the instinctual unconscious."[2] More significant than depth of disclosure for Benjamin, however, was photography's ability to represent things in a way that violates ordinary representational practices. Speaking of the early twentieth-century Paris photographs of Eugene Atget, Benjamin pointed to their capacity for the "liberation of the object from the aura."[3] This has the effect of interrupting the usual way of understanding the object. To shatter a traditional viewing practice and hold up for scrutiny what usually goes unnoticed has a tendency, according to Benjamin, to enhance one's political sensibilities.[4] He elaborated on how Atget's photographs achieve this effect:

> Atget always passed by the "grand views and the so-called landmarks"; what gave him pause would be a huge row of bootlasts or Parisian courtyards full of trucks drawn up in rank and file from evening to morning; or those hundreds of thousands of well-worn tables you see, the dirty dishes left standing; or brothel Rue . . . No 5 where the number five appears in giant letters at four different places on the facade. The remarkable thing about these pictures, however, is their emptiness. The Porte d'Acceuil at the fortifications is empty, so too are the triumphal steps, the courtyards, the cafe terraces and, as is proper, the Place du Tertre. They are not lonely, but they lack atmosphere; the city in these pictures is empty in the manner of a flat which has not yet found a new occupant. They are the achievements of surrealist photography which presages a salutary estrangement between man and his environment, thus clearing the ground for the politically-trained eye before which all intimacies serve the illumination of detail.[5]

In contrast with Benjamin, whose optimism was based primarily on his observation of artistic photographs, is Stuart Hall's more contemporary view, developed on the basis of his scrutiny of the news photo. For Hall, news photography abets the more general orientation of the newspaper which reproduces "the core of themes of bourgeois society in terms of *intelligible representations*."[6] For example, reading a news story about the provisional IRA leader Dutch Doherty, entitled "Ulster Wants Doherty Extradicted," Hall notes that the accompanying photograph "carries only a small, head-and-shoulders, 'passport-photo' of the man in question with the simple caption Anthony 'Dutch' Doherty."[7] This, like all news items, presents an ahistorical, instantaneous reality. Thus, "the image loses its motivation. It appears 'naturally' to have selected itself."[8] But the photo

The Political Rhetoric of Photography

is, in effect, ideological. As Hall puts it, "Yet the 'passport photo', with its connotation of 'wanted men', prisoners and the hunted, is not without ideological significance."[9]

This ideological effect of the photograph has been theorized more generally by a number of analysts. For example, Victor Burgin argues that ideology is inherent in the photographic form with its point-of-view perspective and framing, which it inherits from the painting genre:

> The structure of representation — point-of-view and frame — is intimately implicated in the reproduction of ideology (the "frame of mind" of our "point-of-view"). More than any other textual system, the photograph presents itself as "an offer you can't refuse." The characteristics of the photographic apparatus position the subject in such a way that the object photographed serves to conceal the textuality of the photograph itself — substituting passive receptivity for active (critical) reading.[10]

Similarly, Allan Sekula sees the photograph as a mode of representation that tends to technicalize and thereby deny that its form of representation is a practice.[11] He argues that although, in general, "the camera serves to ideologically naturalize the eye of the observer," a photographic art is needed that resists this ideology of its form, for by training the camera on certain things in certain ways, photography can either vindicate a repressive social order or resist it by documenting its more barbaric excesses.[12]

Roland Barthes has also discerned both a naturalizing and a critical dimension in photography. Applying his more general notion of reading, viz. that no text can signify without the complicity of the reader, Barthes explores the reading of photographs, which is governed, he argues, by the set of social codes with which the photograph and viewer interact. Given the relative coherence of those codes, there is a congruence between photographing something and looking at it, and thus there is a tendency for the photograph to be reconciled with the social order.[13] Therefore, to the extent that the codes are ordinary and widely shared, the photograph does not provoke thought. But, according to Barthes, photography can be subversive; it can awaken thought when the images suggest a meaning different from the literal one.[14] This is what makes Arbus's and Hine's "freaks" rhetorically interesting: their above-noted tendency to displace attention from physical characteristics to social ones.

Of course, many of the signifying effects of photographs arise not simply from the rhetorical force of the individual photo. There are photographic arrangements as in the case of the photo album, which presents a sequence of photographs and thus contains a story or narrative. Analyzing Civil War photo albums, Alan Trachtenberg has shown how the sequence of the images tells stories which, for all the horror of death and destruction they display, encourage a belief that maintaining the Union was worth the awful price, or that, despite the war's most grim features, there were courageous acts and brilliant strategies worth celebrating.[15] He finds that the rhetorical force of albums such as George P. Barnard's *Photographic View of Sherman's Campaign* exists not in the accompanying captions but in a narratively oriented, "visual rhetoric" that creates a "lightly structured march of images." The effect of showing Sherman as "an unstoppable force thrusting itself through space, overturning everything in its path, is to memorialize Sherman's power."[16]

Other photographic genres, e.g., the news photograph, are contextualized differently, for the signifying force of the news photograph tends to be a function of the captioning and accompanying journalistic text, not of its place in a photographic sequence. Photography thus speaks and thinks in a variety of ways, and there is no essential answer to how it tends to signify. Its statements, like those in other modes of discourse, must be situated; its signifying force cannot be located wholly formalistically *within* the statement but rather emerges from the general economy of statements, photographic and otherwise, within which it functions. For example, when the early photographs showed close-up scenes of kings, aristocrats, political leaders, and church leaders to the mass public, they had a demystifying effect simply because they showed distant, revered figures in a way that humanized them. Insofar as high position and privilege had been vindicated by the image of a special or spiritual, superhuman quality ascribed to the person of lofty status, the photographs had an authority-challenging impetus. They made privilege appear to be a human contrivance or practice rather than the result of a divine, extrahuman script.

In the modern context, however, photographs of political leaders can have a radically depoliticizing effect just from the very fact that events are being figured on the basis of individual personalities. Journalism in general and photojournalism in particular tend to personalize public events by dwelling on the individuals involved and the personal consequences experienced. This foregrounding of the personal code, accomplished with photographic close-ups of individuals, has the effect, except when accompanied by special rhetorical devices, of silencing the more politicizing codes that could otherwise be evoked.

Therefore, when we interrogate photographs from the point of view of how they speak/think politically, it is necessary to think of them as discursive practices situated within the general economy of societal practices.

The Political Rhetoric of Photography

Given this contextual aspect of their meaning, it can be shown that photographs are not necessarily more politicized and less ideological when they are explicitly called upon in behalf of a political-reform issue. For example, it is at least problematic whether one can regard as more politically radical the photographs of Lewis Hine, which are accorded some of the responsibility for the introduction of child-labor legislation, than the photographs of Alfred Stieglitz and his associates, whose aspirations were avowedly "artistic." Estelle Jussim has posed this question compellingly:

> Are we automatically forced to consider Lewis Hine the more moral and responsible photographer because he bravely climbed the Empire State Building during its construction to photograph noble steel workers grinning among the girders? . . . Can we really differentiate their heroism from the kind of ennoblement which enshrined tractor drivers and women farmers in Soviet posters of the 1930's? Do the seemingly cold abstractions of Stieglitz's cityscapes of this same decade make no human comment or have no human concern simply because we see none of the proletariat?[17]

To begin to sort out the issue of the political rhetoric of photography we must, at a minimum, distance ourselves from a simple view of the political, the view that takes the prevailing discriminations about what constitutes a political issue and looks at the effects of photographs on influencing such issues. To discern the political rhetoric of photography it is necessary, rather, to look at photographic statements on the basis of their tendency to either reproduce dominant forms of discourse, which help circulate the existing system of power, authority, and exchange or to look at them on the basis of their tendency to provoke critical analysis, to denaturalize what is unproblematically accepted and to offer thereby an avenue for politicizing problematics. Taken in this latter sense, photography plays a politically radical role when it opens up forms of questions about power and authority which are closed or silenced within the most frequently circulated and authoritative discursive practices.

For purposes of representing this way of connecting photography to political problematics it is instructive to consider two very different analyses of the photographs of Jacob Riis, who was to the problem of the urban slum what Lewis Hine was to child labor. Riis's *How the Other Half Lives* consisted of pictures of immense human degradation and squalor, and it supplemented his columns, which agitated for public action to help the poor slum dwellers. It is fair to say, as Peter Hales has, that Riis "created a body of work that altered the terms of debate within the medium of photography and had a nearly equal effect on the way Americans saw the city as environment and as metaphor."[18] Riis can reasonably be credited with both inventing the genre of reform photography and situating photography within a generalized rhetoric of reform.[19]

However, despite the significance of urban reform as a political process, it is possible to discern a conservative class-sentiment–reinforcing impetus in Riis's photographic practice. Reviewing Riis's journalistic and photographic corpus, Trachtenberg discloses this dimension in the midst of Riis's political reform rhetoric:

> Accompanied by photographs, his stories and books represented the slum as the antithesis of the home, a breeding ground of menacing ignorance and discontent. By word and picture, Riis portrayed the slum as an offense to all notions of the clean, the sanitary, and the civilized. The portrait appealed to middle-class conscience and to charity-arousing anger against unregulated slumlords, pity for the Italian and Jewish and Chinese and black aliens under their greedy thumb, and satisfaction among the middle classes for their own good fortune. For the social conscience Riis evoked through his spectacles of poverty served also to confirm the high value of the clean, well-equipped, privately owned home as the norm of American life.[20]

At a minimum, the political ambiguity of Riis's photographic rhetoric reveals that the political and ideological dimensions of the image do not yield themselves up easily. Images in general and photography in particular must be read within a politicized reading practice, one which situates the images in order to discern their complicities with prevailing power and authority as well as their challenges. To encourage such a mode of reading, it is useful to begin with an image from which we can have some historical distance.

The Pious and the Political

The virtual photo-realism of this Renaissance group portrait (figure 4.3) tends to arrest reflection and resist the questions about representational practices that arise in connection with paintings. To the extent that we attribute to the painter a commitment to faithful mirror-like reproduction of the scene before him, an attribution encouraged by the painting's clarity and detail, we are disinclined to see the individual images and their relational positions as impositions connected to artistic

The Political Rhetoric of Photography

Fig. 4.3. *Eleanora de Medici, Wife of Duke Vicenzo I Gonzaga, at Prayer with Their Children,* c. 1600, unknown Flemish painter. Museo de Palazzo Ducale, Mantua. By courtesy of the Board of Trustees of the Victoria and Albert Museum.

practice and further disinclined to see the artistic practice as connected to the social formation or broader set of practices which help situate the artistic practice.

But once we get beyond the arresting effects of the first glance at so strikingly "real" a scene and accord recognition to the countless brush strokes and painful sitting hours involved in the crafting of the painting, reflection sets in, evoking irrepressible questions about practices. One of the most immediate queries is provoked by the striking (family) resemblance of the six figures. We are viewing the wife (Eleanora de Medici) and children of a Gonzaga prince. Accepting the "fact" of the family resemblance, we may attribute the extraordinary similarity of visage to generations of inbreeding among princely families cut off by a rigid class system from marriage prospects outside of the family tree.

However, if we pay heed to the fact that we are looking at a painting, we are provided with an alternative hypothesis. The extraordinary degree of family resemblance may be a function of the artistic practice. It could be that what we are viewing is simply the kind of face that the artist was prone to paint (the artist might have labored under the same ability limitations as many who draw contemporary comic strips). Perhaps, then, we are witnessing a homogeneous form of artistic practice rather than a family resemblance.

Another question arises, which also confounds artistic and social practices. The two youngest children are compromising the studied piety of the scene by looking at the artist rather than the altar or whatever object of worship is supposed to be attracting the pious attitudes. Should we say that the children are being impious, or is it more appropriate to surmise that the Gonzaga practices were such as to exempt those so young from the strictures of piety, to expect that the hold of piety should be less strong than the attraction of watching the artist?

This exemption hypothesis is strengthened by a further exemption that seems to have been afforded the youngest subjects. They are exempted from the elaborate and undoubtedly uncomfortable collar worn by their siblings and mother. This latter exemption perhaps spares them the discomfort of helping to demonstrate what was probably a display of wealth and finery which plays a part in motivating the production of the portrait. Moreover, the exemptions afforded the young persons are balanced by the positive role they play in the portrait. Their frontal posture rescues an important feature of the Renaissance portrait. It should be recalled that the painting is undoubtedly for someone (given the political economy of painting at the time), and, like other paintings of the period, it is aimed at the eye of the owner/beholder. The frontal head position of the youngsters can therefore be read as a mannered gesture of recognition of the person for whom the painting was executed.[21]

At the very least, then, the recognition that we are looking at a painting helps us to relate the work to the social formation in which it is situated. In addition, insofar as we can theorize that social formation, we can grasp the ideological import of the painting. Knowing the role that piety played in legitimating high position in Renaissance Italy, we may want to venture the opinion that the ideology of this image/text inheres in the question: why this pose rather than another? Certainly the family did not spend all of its waking hours at prayer; indeed reports of the period suggest an active involvement with commerce. But the selected pose appears designed to imply as much. This is not surprising, given the reasonable assumption that the images produced of great families were probably oriented in part by the impressions those families wished to convey.

The importance of piety among ruling or noble families was one of the

The Political Rhetoric of Photography

major ways of maintaining the legitimacy of their controlling position. Just as in late antiquity when the piety of the emperor was his major claim to rulership, so in Renaissance Italy the piety of the ruling families and princes was a vindication of their position.

Reflective of this is a passage in Count Baldesar Castiglione's *Book of the Courtier*, which was written during the same period that the portrait was executed (and proved so popular in courtly circles it was printed not only in Italian [1528], but also in Spanish [1534], French [1537], English [1561], Latin [1561], and German [1566]). Castiglione echoed the general sentiment of the age when he said that a pious attitude toward God was a sure sign that a commitment to justice characterized the work of the pious prince:

> I should tell how justice also fosters that piety towards God which is the duty of all men, and especially of princes who ought to love Him above every other thing and direct all their actions to Him as to the true end. . . .[22]

In sum, in order to read the practice, both sociopolitical and artistic, involved in the painting, we had to overcome the painting's realism, to recognize that the "real" is always mediated by representational and interpretive practices and thence to recover a context in which we could reasonably situate the work within the particular practices it can (arguably) be said to express.

In the case of photography, resistance to the seductiveness of the real and the subsequent detection of practice and ideology is more difficult. In a sense, the photograph is the quintessential form of ideological statement inasmuch as it is a form of practice that tends to be thought of as a faithful representation. Given the influence of the will to truth in most areas of human existence, photographs derive much of their appeal from what Susan Sontag has referred to as their appearance as "found objects — unpremeditated slices of the world."[23]

To the extent that one can say that "photography" (literally, writing with light) is a genre in which reality is the primary author, there is no disposition to raise the same questions evinced above in connection with the Renaissance painting. For example, even though there is a sense in which the photographic family portrait is an ideological statement about the importance of family solidarity, one that showed a remarkable degree of family resemblance would not present the particular ambiguity identified in the case of the painting, whether the resemblance could be said to be "real" or a function of the way a particular photographer renders faces.[24] Doubtless, the lack of such ambiguities has encouraged the intimate relationship between photography and that which we call "evidence," as that concept is used in almost any disciplinary practice that evokes the validational codes of "empirical truth," "correspondence," "proof," etc. And since the time of its invention in the first half of the nineteenth century, photography has become a standard with which truth in everyday life is judged. As one historian of photography has put it, "The everyday viewer began to assume the photographic image was the norm for truthfulness of representation."[25]

Despite the existence of the occasional individual photograph or photographic study which tends to resist the ordinary, normalizing effects of the photographic mode of representation, the bulk of photography remains naturalizing in its effect. This is primarily because of the historically forged link between photography and evidence or truth, a link which presents a greater barrier against critique or demystification than other forms of writing in which it is more difficult for the writer or the writing to be distanced from the production of meaning and in which the interpretive codes of readers are more diverse and contentious. Photography can be quintessentially ideological then, because insofar as it appears to claim innocence of a productive, meaning-creating practice, it has a long history of interpretive tradition on its side. What is "real" in the case of an image is not invented from moment to moment by viewers. The "real" is forged over a period of time by the social, administrative, political, and other processes through which various interpretive practices become canonical, customary, and so thoroughly entangled with the very act of viewing they cease to be recognized as practices. Such practices run from the trivial one wherein people in societies that produce numerous, two-dimensional images in paintings and photos learn to interpret them in an imagined, three-dimensional space to the more complex sets of rules with which viewers of a snapshot of a person in a seemingly active posture attribute to that figure the beginning, continuation or cessation of an action (the complexities associated with interpreting action from a single instant are well represented in Freud's interpretation of Michelangelo's statue *Moses*).

With a recognition that any realistic image, even the photograph, acquires its meanings in confrontation with viewing practices, it becomes possible to inquire into the ideational force of both the image production and viewing practices. While there are many possible axes of evaluation we could apply, the piety theme, introduced in connection with the Gonzaga family portrait, provides one of the more apt and politically significant ones. The portrait embodies a double piety. The figures' postures and position in front of the altar can be read as an expression of the religious piety of the Gonzaga family, but the representation and recognition of that first kind of piety puts into play a second kind. This is the kind of piety identified by Kenneth Burke, a piety that carries the notion outside of its religious context and regards as pious any form of representation that reinforces incumbent authorities and proprieties.[26] Within this second kind of piety, the Gonzaga portrait performs a pious political function insofar as it helps to reproduce the conditions for vindicating the authority of the princely family it represents. The painting is thus ideological in that the image promotes a form of meaning and value while appearing to merely represent the "real."

To understand the interpretive dynamic encouraged by realist images, it is propitious to move from Renaissance painting to photography, because "Renaissance painters," as Nichols notes, "fabricated textual systems approximating the codes relating to normal perception better than any other strategy until the emergence of photography."[27] What is most significant in this respect is the Renaissance painter's use of a vanishing point, which connects the viewing subject with the image. Inasmuch as the vanishing point creates for us a reciprocal place as viewer, we are locked in or enthralled by what the image displays. Our resistance or possible distancing from the re-presenting of a particular reality is overcome to the extent that we fail to recognize we are created as a subject/viewer as the objects are rendered in a particular way. Failing to reflect on our constructed viewer mode of subjectivity *in* the painting, we are overcome by its sightliness; we fail to see that the painting's reality *for us* is an enactment, reflecting a reality-making process in which we are implicated as users of visualizing codes.

Similarly, the photograph, with its depth of field, not only gives us an image to which we accord a "reality," given the match between photography and normal perceptual codes, but also situates us as a subject/viewer. And insofar as we "see" the real, we are encouraged to fetishize it, particularly in the case of the still photograph. This is the case for several reasons, not the least of which is the role that the photograph has played in social usage. Because it has played a role as a souvenir or keepsake, helping to mark the lives of individuals, family groupings, etc., its referent tends to be taken as the real, whereas, for example, another visual medium, film, "is mainly oriented toward a show-business-like or imagining referent."[28] In addition, the photograph is under the control of the viewer, whose lingering look can preform the fetishizing function, while a medium such as film has a tempo controlled by the film maker, causing it to be more difficult for the viewer to naturalize the images.[29]

Moving from painting to photography and from Renaissance Italy to contemporary America, we can find numerous examples of this pious, ideological function we observed in the Gonzaga portrait. A recent photographically supported story in the weekly newsmagazine *Time* provides an exemplary case of this effect in which the rhetoric of a religious imagery helps to set up a political piety (figure 4.4). The photographic iconography in this obviously crafted set of juxtapositions is unmistakable.[30] The set of photographs is arranged in the form of a cross, which is the beginning of a powerful allegory in which a political reading emerges from a religious one.

If we bracket, for the moment, the legal discourse within which we are initially encouraged to place our viewing and reading, we are seeing a three-layered religious signification: the cross (the pattern of the photos), the Father and the Son (the dean and what is probably a portrait of a venerable authority in back of him), and Jesus and the two thieves (the dean flanked by the two contentious faculty members). This tripartite Christian piety shifts easily into a political piety by dint of both the photographic and written journalistic practices.

The initial politically pious gesture is displayed at the top of the page: the heading "law." One way of stating the position of the critical–legal-studies advocates is to say that they are attacking the boundaries which distinguish the legal discourse from the social, political, and administrative discourses within which it is situated. In so doing they politicize what has ordinarily been regarded as a matter of both a tradition and a kind of expertise necessary to interpret that tradition. Among other things, critical legal studies amounts to the statement that the idea of the "law" is ideological insofar as it is represented as a pristine discourse standing for the legitimated norms by which a society ought to be controlled. The "crits" argue, in effect, that such an epistemological privileging of the legal code is an encouraged misreading, which insulates existing forms of power from criticism; legal norms embody power relations, which ought to be understood in a political context.

Thus, the "law" heading of *Time's* essay establishes the "rarity" of the law against the critical–legal-studies position, and the subheading "of two minds in a bitter academic feud" further depoliticizes the issue.[31] Rather than emphasizing the context of the dispute, this subheading focuses attention on disagreement per se. Indeed, throughout the article, the major theme is the disruption of business as usual at Harvard Law School. The costs of this are elaborated as the casualties are listed: one professor leaving for the University of Chicago and the distraction of many students. Finally, near the end of the piece, the writers seem to valorize the disinterest of the students in the content of the issues. "Despite all the ferment among their teachers, most students have a different focus. 'Everybody just wants to get a job,' says Second-Year Student Sheila Maith. 'I don't think anybody has a commitment to being on one side or the other as

The Political Rhetoric of Photography

Law

Critical Legal Times at Harvard

Of two minds in a bitter academic feud

Along the corridors of Harvard Law School, professors still refer to one another as "colleagues," but the atmosphere of late seems something less than collegial. An intellectual debate has ripened into a feud about the shape of legal education and the legitimacy of the law itself. On one side stand the adherents of Critical Legal Studies, who charge that the American legal system and its supposedly disinterested rules are prime instruments of social injustice. On the other side are more traditional professors who contend that the faculty "crits" are waging "guerrilla warfare" at the law school. For Dean James Vorenberg, striving to stay neutral in the dispute, the result is "a tremendous sense of vibrancy and energy." But sometimes, he acknowledges, "things get out of hand."

Less gently, a dean at a rival school asserts that Harvard is now "an extremely unpleasant and politicized environment," adding that "those who want to work on scholarship don't want to waste a lot of time on internecine war." Indeed, the Cambridge institution has had unaccustomed recruiting trouble. Despite its continued prestige, Harvard has not hired any professor from another law school for a tenured position since 1981, either because candidates have failed to win approval from the divided faculty or because those on whom compromise was finally achieved declined the offers. One professor already at the school, and affiliated with C.L.S., has had the decision on her tenure delayed for two years.

During a debate before alumni on the subject earlier this year, Corporate Law Professor Robert Clark, a leading opponent of the crits, charged that they had purposively created "prolonged, intense, bitter conflict" and engaged in "a ritual slaying of the elders." One wounded elder is Professor Paul Bator, a former U.S. deputy solicitor general. After 26 years at Harvard, he is moving in January to the more congenial precincts of the University of Chicago Law School, a redoubt of legal conservatism. Calling the C.L.S. movement a force for "philistinism" and "mediocrity," Bator believes that the intellectual integrity and academic excellence of Harvard are at stake. "On that," he has declared, "there is no right or left. Only right and wrong."

Critical Legal Studies was born during the late 1960s among a group of student activists and younger faculty at Yale Law School. By 1977 C.L.S. adherents had formed a network that now has about 400 members. Its annual conference today attracts roughly 1,000 participants. Proponents hold positions at some of the nation's most prestigious legal institutions, including Stanford and Georgetown. But with three of the best-known

Dean Vorenberg: man in the middle
Sometimes "things get out of hand."

'Crit' Kennedy

Foe Clark

crits—Duncan Kennedy, Morton Horwitz and Roberto Unger—among those on its 64-member faculty, Harvard has become the leading C.L.S. center. "The battle is fiercer here than elsewhere," says Kennedy, who jokingly refers to himself and the others as "the unholy triumvirate." Less a coherent philosophy than an angle of inquiry, C.L.S. has roots in "legal realism," whose supporters in the 1920s and '30s began to argue that legal precedents could be found to support either side of most cases, and that judicial decisions depended less on the abstract "science" of law than on judges' personal predispositions, beliefs and prejudices.

Proceeding from there to an even broader indictment, the crits have borrowed from philosophical realms outside legal thought, including structuralism, semiotics and the "Frankfurt school" of such neo-Marxist theorists as Jürgen Habermas and Theodor Adorno. They propose that law is no more than a means by which unjust power relations are dressed in the costume of eternal truths. Some of the C.L.S. adherents, like Kennedy, also flaunt a confrontational '60s style of incivility and antic provocation in relations with their colleagues. But at bottom, he is deadly serious. "The legalization of the rules," Kennedy inveighs, "the presentation of the rules as the consequence of a neutral, legal, analytic process, makes things that are rotten and unjust look inevitable, logical and inherently fair."

The battle may be academic, but it is far from meaningless. The institution is in the midst of a curricular reform that, if successful, would likely be imitated elsewhere. As Kennedy notes, "Harvard is the most influential law school on legal education and how the outside world perceives law." It has also been a source of much of the thinking that is being fought over, including the mainstream faculty notion that law can contribute to incremental but progressive change in American society. "So many people on either side of the debate are the personification of the ideas being challenged," says David Douglas, a graduate last spring. "It's more than an intellectual debate for them. It's a critique of their life's work." Third-Year Law Student Dan Gordon puts it more dryly: "It's hard to distinguish the personal animosities from the intellectual arguments."

Despite all the ferment among their teachers, most students have a different focus. "Everybody just wants to get a job," says Second-Year Student Sheila Maith. "I don't think anybody has a commitment to being on one side or the other as much as the faculty does." As for the bulk of the faculty, the "mushy centrist types," as one professor describes himself, they celebrate the clash of new ideas, though sometimes wearily these days. Notes Professor Laurence Tribe: "I especially disagree with the rigidity, orthodoxy and intolerance that both extremes display toward those who are not part of their camp." It may be remembered, however, that the charge of arrogant complacency was once leveled at the entire Harvard faculty. Whatever the excesses and inadequacies of the challengers on the left and right, they have at least changed that. —**By Richard Lacayo.**
Reported by Joelle Attinger/Boston

Fig. 4.4. *Critical Legal Times at Harvard.* Copyright 1985 Time Inc. All rights reserved. Reprinted by permission from TIME. Photographs by Steve Liss.

much as the faculty does.'" And they tie this conclusion up more tightly with a remark from someone from the "center" who provides them with a stinging quote to the effect that both sides are "extremes" which display "rigidity, orthodoxy and intolerance."[32]

It is evident that the rhetoric of both the individual photos and their juxtapositions reinforce the rhetorical force of the article's celebration of a no-nonsense approach to managing the controversy. The centering of the dean helps privilege the managing of conflicts over having them, and the management trope is doubled with the emphasis on the dean's (capable) hands, which are prominent at the bottom of the photo. Lest there be any doubt about the privileging of the management over the contentiousness code, the second caption under "Dean Vorenberg: man in the middle," whose legitimacy is supported by tradition (the portrait in the background), is, "Sometimes things get out of hand."[33]

What is "out of hand"? It is controversy, represented not only by the written text but also by the two thieves, characterized as an open mouth (a captious Professor Kennedy) and an angry stare (a sullen, embittered Professor Clark). What is said here with the photographically doubled text is that venerable institutions ought not to be disrupted. Some controversy is condoned, for the article ends up with a line about how the "feud" has had the effect of opposing the "arrogant complacency" with which the Harvard Law faculty had once been charged.[34] But the main signification is bound up with a pious approach to the institution. With its symbolic displacement, the photographic allegory encourages a reverence for conflict management and a firm resistance to politicization.

Resistance to politicizing is also effected photographically with the close-up photographic style, which gives us only the heads in two cases and only half a body in the other. What this kind of camera work does is "enhance the power of the expressive dimension," which displaces news stories away from a political point and focuses attention instead on some aspect of the persons involved.[35] In this case, the photographic close-up of the dean and the two law professors emphasizes the personalities and emotional dimensions of the controversy rather than the political dimension, which goes to the heart of the relationship between law and political process.

What remains if we are to contextualize the article as we did the Renaissance painting is its relationship to the social formation in which it is situated. *Time* is a magazine designed not for the presentation of critical thought but for the rapid dissemination of what is thought of as news, packaged in a way that provides perfunctory readers an undemanding text. In 1929, its founders, Henry Luce and Britton Hadden, selected the name with the recognition that no publication had yet adapted itself to the pace of a working society whose perfunctory reading habits required weekly summaries of news.[36] More important, *Time*'s style represented a significant change in the structure of publishing, which took place along with the development of the consumer society in the twentieth century. As Gisela Freund points out:

> As America increasingly became a society of consumers, the powerful economic incentive of advertising forced changes in the publisher's role. From the time advertising became their major source of profit, publishers were no longer interested in their reader as reader, but in the reader as consumer.[37]

Thus, the centrist piety of the *Time* essay derives not so much from the conservative tradition it has had since it was so marked by the views of its founder and publisher, the notoriously conservative Henry Luce, but more from the controls exerted within a social formation which has commodified the newsmagazine. The pressure this commodification exerts is not directed primarily toward particular ideologies embodying the interests and values resident, consciously or not, within certain sectors of the society; rather, the pressure is toward holding interested readers and toward avoiding offending those with any recognizable ideological orientation.

Certainly the normal or ordinary images, which represent existing authoritative institutions, are not neutral, but because they are naturalized and thus not read as promoting a point of view, they are received as noncontroversial. When keeping one's readers and advertisers imposes itself on a magazine as the major objective, the continual support or reinscription of the status quo is the likely result.

Time's photographically enhanced celebration of the status quo in the piece on critical legal studies at Harvard, like the Renaissance painting, is therefore better understood as a genre of image production intimately related to its context of authority, association, and exchange than as a particular editorial point of view. And in this case, part of the ideational work of the photographic images is accomplished with accompanying captions, which, along with the juxtapositions of the images, lend a kind of signification that might be absent if the images were presented alone.

Photography and "The Criminal"

There are other ways in which photography has played a role in either politicizing or depoliticizing legal discourses. These are connected to photography's epistemic authority. In general, the emergence of photographic representation as a criterion of evidence and truth has been accompanied by the development of disciplinary/knowledge agencies whose activities support forms of social and political regulation. And the two practices — the social and photographic — have developed an intimate, mutually supportive relationship. Toward the end of the nineteenth century, photographic practices, given their prestige with respect to modes of representation thought to reflect reality, increasingly assumed a role in helping to reinforce the prevailing systems of power, authority, and exchange. This reinforcing role is connected to the naturalizing force implicit in ordinary photographs. To the extent that a pictorial representation of an event, a person, or group of persons is thought to represent the "real," those who have the power to contextualize those representations with captions or strategic placement and distribution of the pictures, are those with a stake in avoiding forms of representation likely to provoke contention. Indeed, the mark of what is called a "realistic" representation is that it is uncontentious: it tends to discourage active, combative interpretive activity, unless it resists ordinary interpretation by dint of its unusual juxtapositions or placement.

Perhaps the most striking examples of photography's naturalizing effect has been its role in policing and law enforcement, where its functioning has been markedly ideological. For example, in the development of the nineteenth-century practice of identifying those called "criminal types," can be read a political process of producing legitimate and illegitimate identities, connected to a more general intensification of social and administrative surveillance.[38] The discourse representing this production of the criminal type can thus be read within a politicized understanding, for the reality of what constitutes the criminal is one kind of reality among a variety of possibilities. For example, what separates activities considered "commercial" from those considered "criminal" is the tendency of a system of power to create and approve certain activities by certain categories of persons and to create and discourage others. But rather than representing itself as contentious and strategic, the official criminal code and various supplementary, criminalizing codes are situated in a variety of discourses which tend to naturalize them; they mystify a human, power-related practice by characterizing law enforcement as a scientifically neutral form of implementation, enacted upon an unambiguous reality.

The Political Rhetoric of Photography

Among the discourses that have helped to depoliticize law enforcement is that supplied by eugenics. Francis Galton, who pioneered it, established eugenics as a science which purported to discern the relationship between a person's innate qualities and their place within the system of social stratification. As one analyst puts it, "To eugenics the pauper, the unemployed, the criminal, the insane and the inveterately ill were considered not as social categories but entirely as natural ones."[39] The eugenics point of view quietly gained in prestige into the twentieth century, and it was in this connection that photography played a supportive role. Galton and his successors — criminal anthropologists and other social thinkers like Havelock Ellis — promoted the view that there are distinct criminal types and that these types have physically visible manifestations. Galton created composite photographic portraits to represent criminal types, a contrivance he saw not as partisan or ideological but as a scientific mode of representation aimed at overcoming the limits of disaggregated modes of everyday perception. Ellis used photographs to support his claim, in *The Criminal*, that criminal types have definite physical characteristics, which are inherited. (This example [figure 4.5] is supported by text that emphasizes the tendency of criminals to have protruding ears, which Ellis regarded as unambiguous testimony to the inheritance of criminal proclivities.)[40]

This eugenic view of the criminal, for which photography has played a supportive role, has waned in modern law-enforcement circles, but it is not entirely discredited. (Indeed, James Q. Wilson and Richard Hernstein's recent *Crime and Human Nature* revives the thinking behind the old eugenic approach.)[41] But while the eugenic notion is no longer as prestigious as it was in the early half of this century, there remains a residue of its thinking in the everyday understandings which tend to link crime with certain types of persons. Given that the opportunity structure distributes advantageous, legal means of economic gain for some and not others and that power and authority are behind the ennobling of some activities and the discrediting of others, certain persons (often in the same gender, ethnic group, class, etc.) end up disproportionately in criminalized and other deviant categories. For example, recent immigrants to the United States, who lack social and other supports for legitimate forms of remunerable activity turn, not surprisingly, to illegitimate ones. But the modes of representation of those called "criminals" simply show types of persons, and therefore films, television dramas, illustrated magazine stories, and other visually oriented media continue to reinforce a depoliticized, eugenically oriented understanding of crime.

Photography's role in encouraging this kind of thinking remains pervasive. Consider, for example, the signifying practice in this advertisement

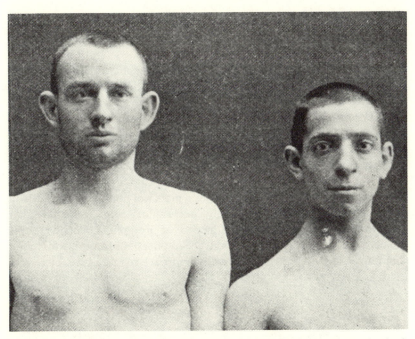

Fig. 4.5. *Outstanding Ears (Elmira)*. Reprinted from Havelock Ellis, *The Criminal*, 4th ed. rev. (London: Walter Scott, Ltd., 1913), p. 70.

by the Software Publishers Association (figure 4.6). Here, the ahistoricity of the photographic mode of representation as well as the thinking behind this particular example does not lend itself to a politically sophisticated understanding of criminality as a boundary-drawing practice of a society. Neither the photograph itself nor the place in which it is situated contains codes that would encourage a problematizing of the criminal. Criminality is naturalized here, for the suggestion is that it is a matter of seeing. We supposedly know how a criminal looks, and in this case the visual coding of the criminal is produced by the absence of the "criminal type."

There is no evidence here that the software publishers (or the commercial artist who created the ad) accept the old Galton/Ellis eugenic model, viz. that the sightliness of the criminal is owed to inherited criminality-producing characteristics. But the view is informed by a tradition, beginning in the nineteenth century, which represents a shift from an interest in questions about crime to an interest in criminals. This tradition, which depoliticizes crime by searching for the criminal type instead of illuminating the process that produces both crime and the knowledge about criminals, is reaffirmed and strongly encoded in the recent Wilson-Hernstein study. Their preoccupation with the same question originally posed in the nineteenth century is clear, "We will be concerned more with criminality than with crime."[42]

Drawing on this ideological/naturalizing way of posing the question of criminal danger, the Software Publishers Association statement focuses our attention on the criminal. But unlike the straightforward scientific style of the Wilson-Hernstein study, the photographic rhetoric is ironic, developing its rhetorical force with the play of presence and absence. Who is the absent, real criminal type? Given that we are being shown what is normally not a criminal, all of the codes have to be read as absent. These codes are ethnic/racial, gender, class, and psychological. "She does not look like a common criminal," because she is *not* a man, *not* nonwhite, *not* a Mediterranean, black or, more generally, nonAnglo/Aryan, *not* blue collar or lower class, and, finally, *not* a morose or brooding personality type.

There is much one could say about the implications for political understanding of reinforcing this criminality approach to crime and the stereo-

a common criminal.

She doesn't look like a common criminal. But she just copied software illegally. It's not a common crime. It's a Federal offense.

The unauthorized duplication of copyrighted software is a violation of United States and Canadian Copyright Laws, and is punishable in civil and criminal court by fines and imprisonment.

This common criminal wouldn't dream of stealing money from someone's wallet. She's got her principles. But she doesn't consider that making an illegal copy of a program is just like stealing money from the people who created that program. And she doesn't consider that everyone will pay for her crime—by paying higher prices.

If you know people who make illegal copies of software, tell them they're breaking the law. Help stop this crime before it becomes any more common.

The unauthorized copying of software is a crime.

Fig. 4.6. *A common criminal.* Advertisement courtesy of Software Publishers Association.

types of the common criminal that supplement it. Certainly the signifying practice in the announcement supplements a form of social control based on class, racial, and ethnic biases. But there is a less obvious political dimension represented in the picture and text, which emerges in the primary appeal of the announcement. The implied reader is a businessperson who might have occasion to either violate copyright laws or supervise others who do ("lower level" employees, to which the gender code is an implicit reference); "he" (we assume by the figuration of absence) is being encouraged to engage in social control.

Thus, this picture of a friendly, cheerful, well-dressed middle-class office worker and the scripted request "to help stop this crime before it becomes any more common," participate in what D. A. Miller has termed "a general economy of policing power."[43] Note that there is no suggestion that a policing authority be called in. There is no need to arrest this cheerful-looking woman; she is not a direct threat to public safety. The "help" that is requested is not help in turning a violator over to the police. The suggestion is, rather, that policing ought to go on in other sectors of the society, while people like this woman ought to experience more gentle forms of social control — e.g., reminders from supervisors who have been apprised of the economic consequences of stealing software.

In short, the photographically oriented announcement participates in a form of authority/power that deploys harsher forms of law-enforcement activities in certain neighborhoods or sectors of the society and with certain class and ethnic/racial targets in mind. Miller has detected the same practice in the nineteenth-century detective novel, which participated in reinforcing a form of policing power that had just emerged. In the novels of Dickens, Eliot, Trollope, Balzac, Stendhal, and Zola, Miller noticed in the way the stories of investigation unfold the implicit suggestion that policing activity ought to be confined to certain classes of people, to "a delinquent milieu."[44]

Similarly in the announcement, the business office is not the milieu for policing authority. If social control is to take place here it should take the form of interpersonal relations as they exist within the hierarchy of the business firm. Why anything more harsh for someone who has "got her principles" and "wouldn't dream of stealing money from someone's wallet"? The signifying practice we see here supports and extends an aspect of policing power not represented in the typical, depoliticizing views of crime and criminality. It helps to re-create politics-as-usual by consolidating two distinct social terrains, that within which harsh, uninhibited forms of law enforcement are practiced and that within which certain classes are granted a reprieve from these forms.

Can photography do anything but reinforce a depoliticized view of crime? Is a genre dependent on visual coding destined only to fetishize what is taken as the real in general and what has been quarantined off as the criminal in particular? Here is an example of a photographic enactment that situates the issue of the criminal in such a way that the effect is radically denaturalizing. The first thing to note about Salvador Dali's photo collage, *The Phenomenon of Ecstasy* (figure 4.7), is the collage effect. Because, as Krauss points out, "photography normally functions as a declaration of the seamlessness of reality itself," the fragmentation in the Dali photo collage is disruptive, intervening in the process through which the viewer's interpretive codes accord a representational quality to photographs.[45] Moreover, the flattening effect of the collage, with its absence of a single focal point which would generate a depth of field, displaces the viewer from the kind of perceptual standpoint associated with ordinary perception.

Within this denaturalizing photographic practice, we observe strips of ears taken from a nineteenth-century catalogue organized around a eugenic approach to the criminal type. How does the photo collage speak of the criminal? Dali, like others in the surrealist movement, sought to disrupt the authoritative hold of the real exercised by the existing rationalistic/logical discourses. To show that the real is inseparable from the imaginative enactments through which it is engendered, Dali developed a critical approach modeled on the paranoiac mode of obsessive perception. Given that the paranoid systematically and obsessively multiplies phenomena (seeing almost everything as an example of the thing most feared), Dali's paranoiac-critical method involved a form of hyperrealism, the kind of incessant doubling of images peculiar to or at least characteristic of the paranoid's perceptual orientation.[46]

But rather than expanding anxiety, the paranoiac-critical method served for Dali to extract objects and persons from their ordinary surroundings in order to show that the real is a contrivance or a practice that is so authoritative it has come into language as the only possibility. To resist this hold of the real as it exists within prevailing rationalistic discourses, Dali doubles and redoubles his images. Krauss has elaborated the effect of this doubling:

> Nothing creates this sense of the linguistic hold on the real more
> than the photographic strategy of doubling. For it is doubling
> that produces the formal rhythm of spacing – the two-step that
> banishes simultaneity. And it is doubling that elicits the notion
> that to an original has been added its copy. The double is the
> simulacrum, the second, the representative of the original. It

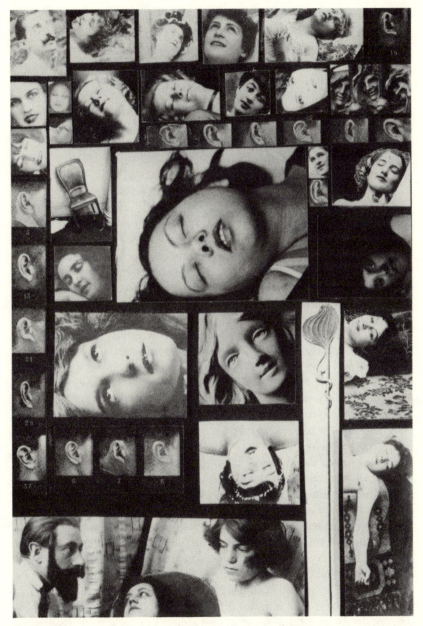

Fig. 4.7. *The Phenomenon of Ecstasy, 1933.* Photo collage by Salvador Dali. Copyright ARS, NY/SPADEM 1987.

> comes after the first, and in this following it can only exist as a
> figure, or image. But in being seen in conjunction with the
> original, the double destroys the pure singularity of the first.
> Through duplication, it opens the original to the effect of differ-
> ence, or deferral, of one-thing-after-another.[47]

Among other things, Dali's photo collage says that the eugenic model
of criminality is one fantasy among others. It is conjured up in one's imagination, and to take it as a privileged reality is to uncritically accept the
authoritative hold of rationalistic discourses on the reality of such a
fetishized notion of criminality.

However, one need not necessarily turn to surrealist methods to create
a politicized mode of photographic rhetoric on the idea of crime and the
criminal. Lee Friedlander has evoked a radicalizing vision related to these
issues with relatively ordinary pictures in his photographic study of life
and work in the factory valleys of Ohio and Pennsylvania.[48] To understand
the rhetorical force of his camera work, it is necessary to emphasize two
especially significant dimensions of the rhetorics which vindicate a society's
creation and administration of a "carceral apparatus."[49] One is connected
with the above-noted, modern emphasis on knowledge of the criminal.
Insofar as criminology has become a science there has been a tendency
to look for generalizations which support a representation of the criminal
as a type, and photography, as we have seen, has played a role along
with other modes of discourse in focusing attention on the criminal as
a type of person and away from the economies of crime, i.e., away from
the historical and structural conditions involved in the constitution of the
positively and negatively valued activities recruited into noncrime and
crime categories respectively. What this criminological emphasis has
amounted to is a depluralizing (as well as a depoliticizing) of notions of
crime and criminals. And this depluralizing has helped to legitimate the
deployment of a policing type of law enforcement in certain places. It is
clear, as was discussed above in connection with figure 4.6, policing does not
belong in the business office applied to well-dressed, business secretaries.

In addition to the criminologically oriented discourse's depluralizing of
the types of persons imagined to engage in crime-related activities — creating the image that people get what they deserve with respect to the attention of law enforcement — is the second dimension, which is the belief in
the propriety of the boundaries of the crime/policing/incarcerating discourses. To the extent that we imagine a society's carceral system as limited
to its crime prevention, law enforcement, and prison system, while accepting the propriety of policing's targets, we fail to discern the incarcerating
effects of other social institutions and processes, which represent themselves within other discursive economies. Like Foucault then who liberates

the idea of "the carceral" from the specific penal institutions (and applies it to education, medicine, social work, etc.), Friedlander has created a rhetoric — photographically — that shows incarcerating and subjugating effects of factory work involving persons working with/under machines.[50]

Two aspects of incarceration/subjugation are represented with the photographic rhetoric. The first is a counterrhetoric, which speaks against the depluralizing effects of the work place. Friedlander shows us different kinds of persons whose clothing, hairstyles, tattoos, sports-team logos, etc., display the diversity of their private lives and imaginations, a diversity that appears constrained and expressively ineffectual with the confining, separating, and homogenizing factory space, where the workers can scarcely exchange even nonverbal forms of communication. At the very least, the rhetorical force of the photographs makes it difficult for the viewer to be comfortable with a depluralizing utterance such as "factory workers."

The second and more powerful rhetorical dimension of the photographs connects the homogenizing effects of the factory setting with the carceral theme. Here are people who appear to be surrounded, pinioned, or captured by the machines at which they work. These images make it difficult to resist a politicized, class analysis of the subjugating effects of factory work, which creates a monotonous, imprisoning, and homogenizing environment for a culturally diverse set of persons. The photographic representation is constructed both through the image of factory work as incarceration and through the contrast between the tendency of persons to express their personalities through their clothes, hairstyles, and allegiances and the depluralizing factory setting.

Thus, whereas photography has made a substantial contribution to naturalizing existing approaches to crime and criminality, we have here a photographic practice that defamiliarizes work-place practices in such a way that we get a politicized reversal, a glimpse of an incarcerating socioeconomic practice that enforces an ugly, subjugating uniformity. And we see the naturalized hold of the simple category factory worker loosened. The photographic representation in Friedlander's study resists the subjugating practices of the work place by showing both the diversity of the subject and the poverty of the ordinary, work-related discourse within which factory work is usually represented.

Photography and the Politics of Meaning

There are norms besides those explicit ones, such as the criminal codes, with which photography interacts in politically relevant ways. These are more subtle, meaning-engendering norms involved in the

The Political Rhetoric of Photography

production and reception of images. One of the primary effects of these norms is through the already-in-place proprieties, which govern the kinds of images one living in a given age and a particular social formation expects. When there is no directing caption accompanying the image, the existing codes with which images are consumed and placed are given free play. To the extent that a given image accords with the familiar and already known, it is naturalized and read as an unproblematic representation, and insofar as the preponderance of images accord with the pertinent codes in a social formation, the codes themselves, which perform a kind of captioning without leaving a mark on or near the image, do the ideational work. Indeed, an image is taken as "real" to the extent that the interpretive codes with which it is received function unnoticed.

With an appreciation of this more implicit form of meaning production — the operation of the existing, familiar interpretive practices on an image — we can understand the effects of images which do not sit comfortably within the corpus of naturalized opinions or "doxa" of the society in which they are presented.[51] Such images, which challenge the existing set of codes rather than recycle and reinforce them, are impertinent or politicizing inasmuch as they pose questions to what is regarded as appropriate and authoritative.

Just as we saw a form of piety functioning within both the painted and photographic image, we can find examples of impiety in both. For example, an art historian has illustrated the way that paintings can violate the existing doxa by representing within the same frame discursive practices thought to be disparate. Referring to Géricault's portraits of the mad (figure 4.8), he states that they are

> from the first a contradiction, if the historic purpose of the portrait genre is to record a precise social position, a particular instance of rank in the hierarchy of power: the portrait of the insane is therefore an impossible object, a categorical scandal, since the mad are exactly those who have been displaced from every level of the hierarchy, who cannot be painted; Géricault fuses the categories together, of privilege and placelessness, society and asylum, physical presence and juridical absence.[52]

The impious effects, like the pious effects in the examples above, emerge from the relationship between the image and the social formation in which it is situated.

Photography has produced its categorical scandals as well — for example, August Sander's seemingly ambitious but politically humble project of photographing the people of the twentieth century. Portraits such as this (figure 4.9) violate the portrait genre in the same way that Géricault's portraits do. But it was this comprehensive ambition of Sander's that made these photographs a problem for the Third Reich. Novelist Richard Powell puts it well. "Sander's gallery of anarchists, minorities, and transients crossed the view of the German people the Nazis were trying to foster." It was not only what he showed but how he showed it, for he "compounded his sin by presenting these dregs alongside the industrious and propertied without editing or commentary."[53] Despite the effect he achieved, Sander

Fig. 4.8. *Portrait of a Kleptomaniac.* Painting by Jean Louis André Théodore Géricault. From Museum Voor Schone Kunsten.

eschewed a politicizing framework for his efforts, noting, "It is not my intention either to criticize or to describe these people but to create a piece of history with my pictures."[54]

Nevertheless, the Nazis understood well certain aspects of the politics of representational practices, and in 1938 they destroyed the plates and all the copies they could find of the first installment of his opus, *Faces*

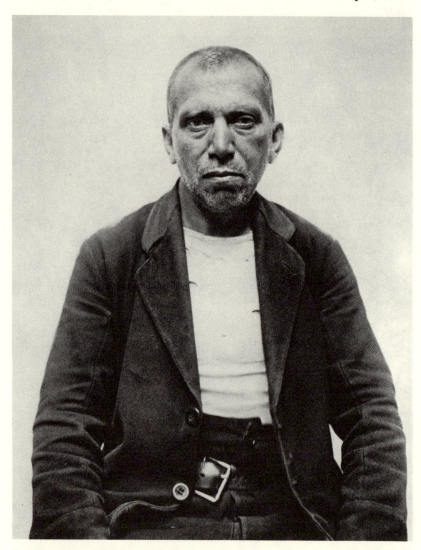

Fig. 4.9. *Inmate of an Asylum, 1926*. Photograph by August Sander. By courtesy of Schirmer/ Mosel Verlag Munich.

of Our Time. Sander's photographic practice could be read as impious or politically radical, however, only in a limited sense. Like Géricault's portraiture, Sander's photographic portraits spoke against a preexisting tradition. His selection of the less beautiful and socially honored aspects of humanity contrasted with the tradition of depicting nobility and attractiveness in photographic portraits. And with the coming to power of the Nazis, whose program explicitly sanctioned the depicting of Germany through only certain types of persons, the sheer variability of Sander's portraits was bound to be read as a subversive political statement.

But there is a sense in which Sander's project manifested a pious, conservative ideological impetus. Ironically, the types that Sander was interested in portraying coincided with existing class and occupational divisions. Whereas he violated the representational practice of the Nazis by the sheer comprehensiveness of his work, which subverted the narrowing of the legitimate types the Nazis wished to portray, at another level, he reproduced the mentality behind the Nazi program. By laboring within the conventional social and occupational categories, his camera work tended to naturalize social practices. Moreover, this kind of naturalization, which turns human classificatory practices into something that appears naturally produced, is more extreme in a visual than a verbal mode. The rhetoric of the camera, which represents persons on the basis of their appearance, has the effect of tying human classificatory practices to something physically based and visually obvious. The systematic aspects of the camera work — angle of vision, degree of close-up, pose, and facial expressions — produce the impression that the subjects themselves are responsible for all of the appearance of sameness within classifications.

In addition to the ideology of the photographic form, which militates in a naturalizing direction with a suggestion that people are naturally selected into their social roles, is the traditional narrative structure of Sander's album *Faces of Our Time.* Sander created what one historian of photography has called "the first properly discursive photo-book in the history of the medium . . . a complex work, combining a taxonomy, a history and a point of view."[55] While this observation is contestable, particularly in light of the implicit narratives one can discern in American Civil War albums, it is certainly the case that a principle of order and a notion of history provide the rhetorical force of Sander's photo book. "Country people, artisans, urban workers, merchants, artists and writers show themselves to Sander in an orderly, consistent way in poses appropriate to their station, rank or class."[56] And the temporal progression, implicit in the structure of the photo book, is stated in Sander's introduction. His overall purpose of showing "man" in the twentieth century was to provide a view of humanity tied first to the earth (the country people representing the past) and then to move "forward," reaching what he called "the highest peak of civilization."[57] The book thus begins with peasants, moves through middle-class subjects, and ends with painters, composers, artists, and writers.

Nevertheless, while Sander's ideology of form and narrative evidence an observance of traditional categories and social ordering, other aspects of his photographic work, the depth in the photos themselves, have a more impious or subversive, political level of signification. The facial expressions of each "type" of person seem to reflect the effects of an inegalitarian society as it registers itself differently on the countenances belonging to persons in different classes. Thus we see the haughty self-confidence of the composer, Hindemith, and the studied insouciance of the son of a wealthy industrialist (figures 4.10 and 4.11). By contrast we observe the diffidence, bordering on insecurity and fear, in the visage of the young pipe fitter from Cologne (figure 4.12). These contrasts constitute a rhetoric on behalf of Sander's avowed hope for a better society in a future under socialism.

There is a modern photographer whose portraits also constitute a categorical scandal, and the politicizing signification in his camera work is relatively unambiguous. Richard Avedon, who is best known as a fashion photographer, has executed a series of portraits he has called *In the American West.*[58] The portraits effect a startling reversal of the photographic rhetoric with which we have come to apprehend the West. Although each portrait is captioned, giving the residence and vocation of each subject (figures 4.13, 4.14, and 4.15), the most powerful signification of the images emerges from what Barthes has called the "codes of connotation" which are neither "natural" nor "artificial" but "historical." Barthes's point is that the image alone cannot provoke these codes; they are, rather, part of a historical "stock of signs" or "rudiments of a code" which the viewer brings to the image.[59]

In the case of the West, this stock of signs was produced initially by the kinds of representations which accompanied and helped legitimate the westward expansion of white Europeans on the North American continent. For these Americans, the West was depicted primarily as land and open space, and, to the extent that the West's earlier inhabitants were represented at all, they were characterized in the dominant historical accounts as impediments to the use of the land and space.[60]

This scripted conceptualization of the West has been continually supported by photography. As Trachtenberg has pointed out, the early photographers "mapped landscapes" and helped perpetuate a landscape view of the West. The rhetoric of this photographic imagery helped promote public willingness to support a policy of conquest, settlement, and

Fig. 4.10. *The Composer Paul Hindemith, Cologne, 1926.* Photograph by August Sander. By courtesy of Schirmer/Mosel Verlag Munich.

exploitation.[61] The predominant photographic representation of the West remains landscape oriented. Among the most skillfully executed, artistic, and influential are the photos of Ansel Adams, who gives us a view of the West as mountains, sky, and open space with only the barest hint that it is inhabited (see figure 4.16). Clearly Adams's photographic practice is meant to celebrate wilderness in general and western wilderness in par-

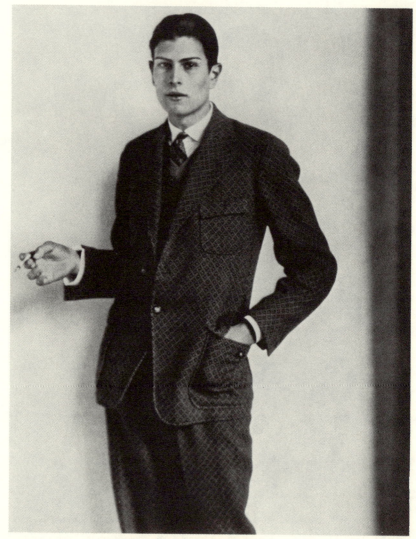

Fig. 4.11. *The Son of the Cologne Brewer Friedrich Winter, 1926*. Photograph by August Sander. By courtesy of Schirmer/Mosel Verlag Munich.

ticular. But for purposes of understanding Avedon's reversal and its implications, Adams's practice can also be treated in terms of the silences it helps to administer.[62]

Insofar as we are encouraged to have the West as landscape/wilderness and space, we are rendered inattentive to the West as something else — people. As is the case throughout the United States, where people dwell

Fig. 4.12. *Fitter, Cologne, 1929.* Photograph by August Sander. By courtesy of Schirmer/ Mosel Verlag Munich.

there also dwell the effects of inequality: poverty, misery, unpleasant working conditions, and failure, all of which exist alongside wealth, joy, and success. To recover this dimension of the West, a dimension congenial to a more politicizing apprehension of the region, one has to defamiliarize it, to represent it in a way that challenges the dominant representational practice.

The Political Rhetoric of Photography

Fig. 4.13. *Unidentified migrant worker, Eagle Pass, Texas, 12/10/70.* Photograph by Richard Avedon. Copyright © 1985 by Richard Avedon Inc. All rights reserved.

This is precisely what Avedon has done. The disruptive power of his human figures takes place in the context of an interpretive tradition to which photography has contributed, one which has depopulated the West and thus deproblematized the West's human situation. Avedon's photographs repopulate the West and, at the same time, introduce a highly

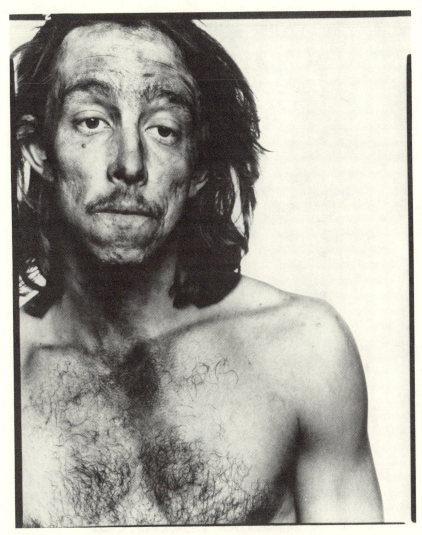

Fig. 4.14. *Nicholas Burum, coal miner, Somerset, Colorado, 12/17/79.* Photograph by Richard Avedon. Copyright © 1985 by Richard Avedon Inc. All rights reserved.

charged political problematic, the human costs associated with working in the West's less pleasant and less remunerative work sites.

Avedon's photographic reversal serves at once as a commentary on the West from the point of view of how it can be read through its less felicitous inhabitants and as a commentary on the pastoralization of the West to

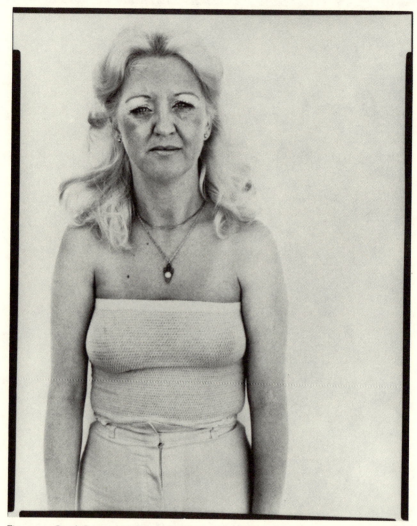

Fig. 4.15. *Carol Crittendon, bartender, Butte, Montana, 7/1/81.* Photograph by Richard Avedon. Copyright © 1985 by Richard Avedon Inc. All rights reserved.

which traditional photography has contributed. In the context of the inter- pretive tradition, then, his photographs must be read not only as the presentation of a more oppressed and unfortunate part of our western population but also as an overcoming of the silences created and admin- istered by a practice as broad as public-land acquisition and use policy

The Political Rhetoric of Photography

Fig. 4.16. *Winter Sunrise, The Sierra Nevada, from Lone Pine, California, 1943.* Photograph by Ansel Adams. Courtesy of the Trustees of the Ansel Adams Publishing Rights Trust.

and as narrow as the photographic practices which have provided a representational vindication of that policy.

Interestingly, it is undoubtedly Avedon's particular form of photographic practice as a fashion photographer as much as it is his political sensitivity that has produced the politicizing implications of his photographs. It would have been difficult for a landscape photographer to reverse the implied rhetorical force or kind of signification of the photographic practice which has brought us the West. Even those who have been particularly sensitive to the social, economic, and political plight of the Indians have tended to reproduce a West in which the person is dominated by the landscape.

For example, Laura Gilpin, a photographer whose book *The Enduring Navaho* undeniably testifies to her devotion to the dignity and survival of the Navahos, presents a pastoral image of the Southwest (figure 4.17). Avedon, perhaps because he is neither western born nor a devotee of western landscape, brought to his photographic study a different genre of photographic attention. The fashion photographer's close-up view of

The Political Rhetoric of Photography

the person and whiting out of the background is designed to direct the viewer's attention to the appearance of the fashion model in a particular outfit. But what is a narrowing of the gaze within the genre of fashion photography has provoked a broadened, political insight when the genre is mixed. The interdiscursive play of fashion photography with a photography of social commentary has resulted in a powerfully political form of representation. Avedon's repopulating of the West has not only pointed to a form of oppression, which has lurked in the shadows of the western landscape, but has also produced an implicit critique of a long history of representational practice.

Conclusion: Rich and Poor

This analysis began with a contemplation of two photographs — Arbus and Hine's "freak" portraits — which, given the impertinence of their statements within normal photographic practice, provoke thought about the economies of social identities in general and the problem of economic and social equality in particular. To conclude, it is useful, therefore, to consider a photographic study with a signifying practice which speaks more directly to this issue. The study combines text and image in a novel way. In contrast with the journalistic photographic practice, which guides interpretation with captions designed to impose the news angle (and all that angle implies about the situation of the medium) on the meaning of the accompanying images, Jim Goldberg's pictures, offered under the rubric *Rich and Poor* are accompanied by retrospective statements of the photographed subjects, who were asked to comment on their own portraits.

There are many who simply demonstrate a socially concerned photography by photographing down-and-out people; but Goldberg's work is different from what Allan Sekula has called the "find-a-bum school of concerned photography."[63] The rhetoric of his pictures as well as that emerging from his juxtapositions in the album provoke thinking beyond the mere existence of certain social types. Goldberg displays a marked attention to language, both the language of the photograph and those discursive practices which situate what his camera shows — the understandings of self and Other that make authoritative the system of social stratification and encourage people to naturalize their place within that system.

Goldberg's photographic practice provides critiques of current ideological thinking at various levels. First, his violation of the ordinary mode for captioning helps disclose one of the mechanisms, the controlling caption, implicated in producing the photographic rhetoric. Whether or not we wish to privilege the perspective of the photographed subject, the

Fig. 4.17. *The Prairie,* 1917 platinum print by Laura Gilpin. Copyright 1981, Amon Carter Museum, Fort Worth, Texas.

novelty of Goldberg's method makes us aware that photographic rhetoric is a practice intimately tied to its discursive accompaniments. Second, Goldberg's juxtaposition of rich and poor, placing the two types one after the other and occasionally including the two within the same picture, makes a statement about how to understand inequality. At a more manifest level, Goldberg's photographs partake of a typical political genre, the photographic exposé. By giving us a picture of life behind the walls of "transient hotels: dark and slanted floors, smelling of piss, alcohol, and cheap food, bare light bulbs,"[64] and behind the walls of the sedate mansions of the wealthy, he helps us overcome the institutionalized structures through which we ordinarily achieve our images of how people live — the media, architecture, city planning, etc. This has a politicizing effect inasmuch as it impacts on our moral and political sensibilities, which are already in circulation and thus susceptible to being activated but are usually protected from arousal. At a minimum, the photographs and accompanying text provoke questions about the authority and power behind a way of life that produces such a contrast in levels of well-being.

But Goldberg's photographic study is politicizing at a more subtle level. The juxtaposition he has created — his connection of poor and rich — challenges one of America's discursive legitimations of inequality. This is the tendency to explain a person's economic success or failure with resort to questions that arise out of an individualistic ideology: questions such as "why is X rich?" or "why is Y poor?" This kind of question encourages a narratively oriented discourse which focuses on the choices made by people at various stages in their lives or on the events that have influenced them at various times. A more politically acute mode of questioning is produced within an awareness of the social formation as a whole. Within a structural rather than individual narrative discourse, we can recognize that some are poor because others are rich. We live in a social formation that allows extreme variation in well-being. Goldberg's juxtaposition thus challenges the individualistic, narrative model and encourages a more politicized, structural one for understanding inequality.

Perhaps more powerful, however, is the signification we can discern when we look at the photographs in combination with the biographical codes. The separation of the camera work from the text, which Goldberg surrenders to his subjects, diminishes the authorial/intentional code and focuses our reading on how life behind the walls of transient hotels and wealthy homes reflects the way American society translates economic inequality into lived experience. Given the structural imperatives of a system of inequality, many of the dominance relations can be witnessed within the homes of the wealthy. Sylvia Stone and Vickie Figueroa, assisted by Goldberg's camera work, tell us, at one level, of the gap between one's young hopes and older age experiences, a reality across classes (figures 4.18 and 4.19). But at another level we see/read the surcharge that the class structure places upon dashed hopes.

Vickie Figueroa does not discuss the class structure in theoretical abstractions, but her simple declarative statements make it easy to read. Goldberg captures many of the nuances of ownership of the space in which the two women stand. Apart from the foregrounding and backgrounding of "Mrs. Stone" and Vickie Figueroa respectively, the placement of the hands—Sylvia Stone's resting on *her* counter and Vickie Figueroa's behind her—make clear whose kitchen we are seeing. The social-dominance structure outside the kitchen is reproduced in the economy of gestures within it.

In figure 4.20, we see a variety of social codes, the major one being another dimension of social dominance. The central, dignified placement of Edgar Goldstine and the marginal one of Regina Goldstine—she is even off the carpet—in a servile standing position reproduces their self-understandings. Mr. Goldstine's commentary on his wife is in the language of a job-performance rating from a superior, while Mrs. Goldstine's is that of a servant/faithful, worshipping the power of the boss. Indeed power and control is what speaks at the highest volume in the pictures of the rich.

In many scenes, the power and control are not accompanied by the pattern we get in some of Goldberg's in-home, class and status juxtapositions. In figure 4.21, for example, we see how the wealthy operate within

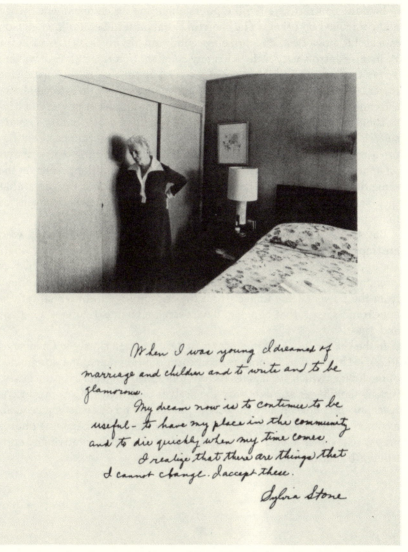

When I was young I dreamed of
marriage and children and to write and to be
glamorous.
    My dream now is to continue to be
useful — to have my place in the community
and to die quickly when my time comes.
    I realize that there are things that
I cannot change. I accept these.

                                    Sylvia Stone

Fig. 4.18. Untitled. Photograph by Jim Goldberg. From *Rich and Poor* by Jim Goldberg. Copyright © 1985 by Jim Goldberg. Reprinted by permission of Random House, Inc.

a self-understanding which naturalizes their position. Both the postures and the statement convey the assumption that privilege is a natural phenomenon. And in figure 4.22 is the undiluted power that goes with wealth. This man experiences his power psychologically and reproduces it by creating the environment within which he sits/kneels for the photograph.

The Political Rhetoric of Photography

In stark contrast, we see the poor inhabiting an environment owned and controlled by others. The cheerful floral pattern behind Joe Peterson mocks his powerless and hopeless condition (figure 4.23). And Anne Williams controls very little of her environment (figure 4.24). Can we find a way to turn this family scene into a joke about the pretensions of the lower class (figure 4.25)? Compare this, which among other things shows the child alone, a hostage to the brutalizing conditions of poverty (a brutalizing which his father displaces ideologically by attributing David's suffering to his fragility [figure 4.26]), with this *New Yorker* cartoon (figure 4.27). The cartoon is pacifying rather than disturbing, for it shows an underclass family in blissful ignorance of their condition, while, at the same time, reassuring the higher classes (e.g., *New Yorker* readers) that their self-understanding is closer to their "reality." In general, it tells us that class difference is, if anything, a source of amusement.

But, finally, it is not just the poor, the Lindas, Larrys, and Davids, who are trapped, imprisoned within a class structure. Class structures as a whole are imprisoning, and Goldberg's camera, trained on the rich, serves as a reminder to them that they are under surveillance. Wealth is no reprieve from the power of the image, from the economies within which certain appearances, e.g., that of aging, have decreased value (figures 4.28, 4.29, and 4.30).

In the last analysis, the dominance pattern between classes in Goldberg's study are bisected by a more general form of dominance, the dominance of the image, which subjugates the photographed subjects in both classes. Just as Goldberg's subjects saw themselves and then helped produce a revealing discourse on who they are in particular and on society in general, a contemplation of one of our most pervasive kinds of image, the photograph, tells us who we are in general and what is authoritative and controlling in particular.

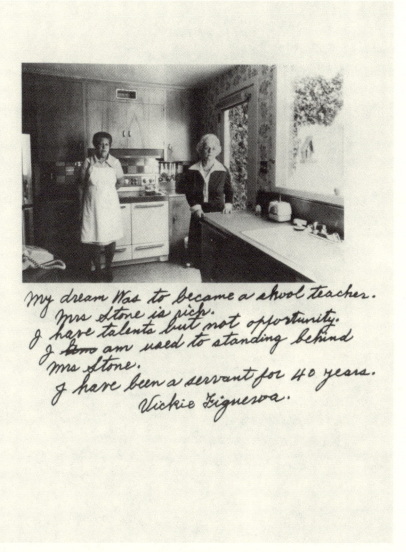

My dream was to became a shool teacher.
Mrs Stone is rich.
I have talents but not opportunity.
I ~~have~~ am used to standing behind
Mrs Stone.
I have been a servant for 40 years.
Vickie Figueroa.

Fig. 4.19. Untitled. Photograph by Jim Goldberg. From *Rich and Poor* by Jim Goldberg. Copyright © 1985 by Jim Goldberg. Reprinted by permission of Random House, Inc.

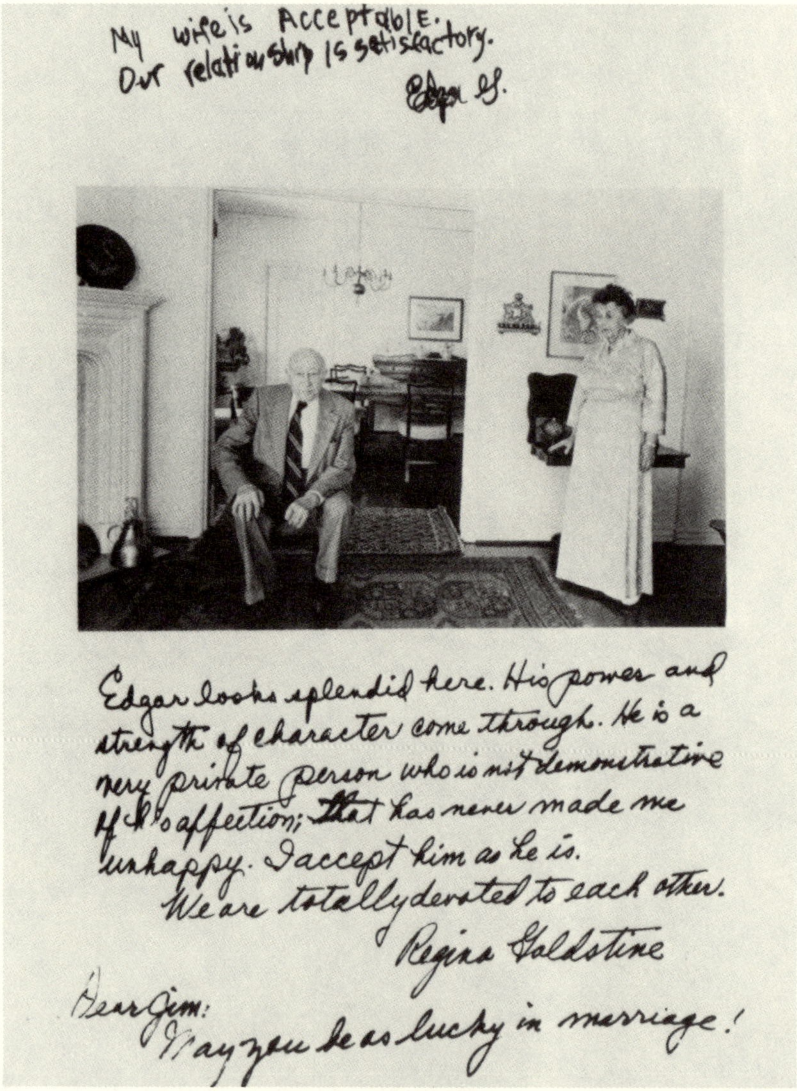

The Political Rhetoric of Photography

My wife is Acceptable.
Our relationship is satisfactory.
Edgar G.

Edgar looks splendid here. His power and
strength of character come through. He is a
very private person who is not demonstrative
of his affection; that has never made me
unhappy. I accept him as he is.
We are totally devoted to each other.
Regina Goldstine
Dear Jim:
May you be as lucky in marriage!

Fig. 4.20. Untitled. Photograph by Jim Goldberg. From *Rich and Poor* by Jim Goldberg. Copyright © 1985 by Jim Goldberg. Reprinted by permission of Random House, Inc.

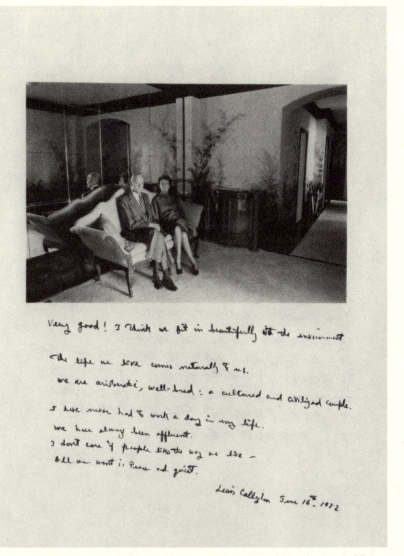

Fig. 4.21. Untitled. Photograph by Jim Goldberg. From *Rich and Poor* by Jim Goldberg. Copyright © 1985 by Jim Goldberg. Reprinted by permission of Random House, Inc.

The Political Rhetoric of Photography

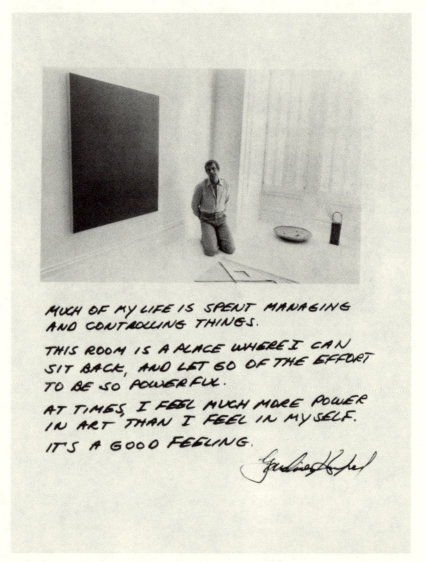

Fig. 4.22. Untitled. Photograph by Jim Goldberg. From *Rich and Poor* by Jim Goldberg. Copyright © 1985 by Jim Goldberg. Reprinted by permission of Random House, Inc.

Fig. 4.23. Untitled. Photograph by Jim Goldberg. From *Rich and Poor* by Jim Goldberg. Copyright © 1985 by Jim Goldberg. Reprinted by permission of Random House, Inc.

The Political Rhetoric of Photography

I AM A 29 yEAR old FemALe who Loves plANts ANd ANIAMALs who cAme to SAN FRANOISCO from A quiet towN IN OREgoN 3½ yEAKs Ago. I DON'T LIKE It HERE!

THE CITy hAs made me dISliKe myself now I get depressed eAsiLy, whIch mAkes me sleep Alot ANd wAtch A lot of hoRRoK MoVIES. I guess the picture shows me in A 50-50 mood ANd iN A slmplQ WAy of livINg. NO MONEy MEANs LIVING IN tHE PITS.

anne williams

Fig. 4.24. Untitled. Photograph by Jim Goldberg. From *Rich and Poor* by Jim Goldberg. Copyright © 1985 by Jim Goldberg. Reprinted by permission of Random House, Inc.

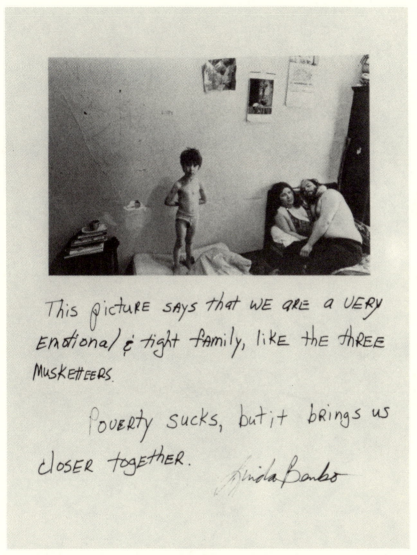

This picture says that WE are a very Emotional & tight family, like the three Musketeers.

Poverty sucks, but it brings us closer together. *Linda Banbo*

Fig. 4.25. Untitled. Photograph by Jim Goldberg. From *Rich and Poor* by Jim Goldberg. Copyright © 1985 by Jim Goldberg. Reprinted by permission of Random House, Inc.

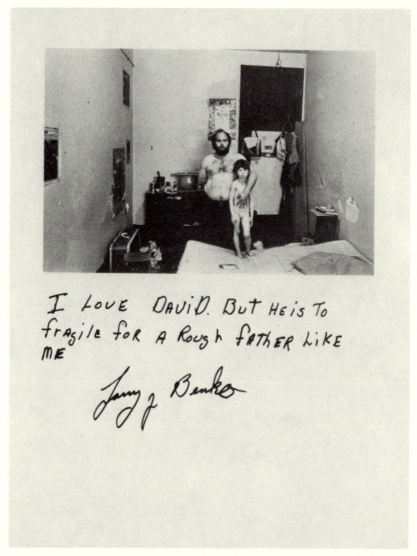

Fig. 4.26. Untitled. Photograph by Jim Goldberg. From *Rich and Poor* by Jim Goldberg. Copyright © 1985 by Jim Goldberg. Reprinted by permission of Random House, Inc.

*"How about Hardee's, Dunkin' Donuts, Holiday Inn,
H & R Block? How did they get started?"*

Fig. 4.27. Drawing by Booth. © 1985 The New Yorker Magazine, Inc.

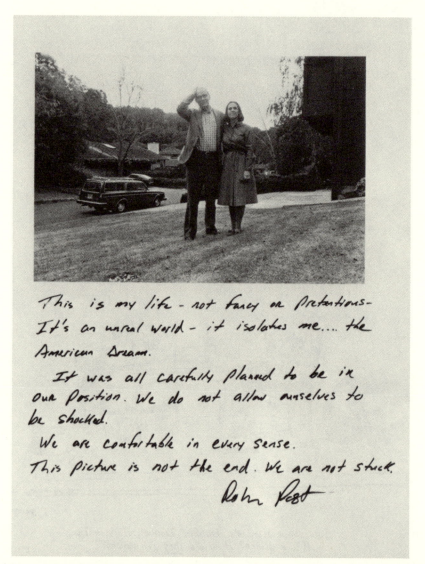

This is my life - not fancy or Pretentious - It's an unreal world - it isolates me..... the American Dream.

It was all carefully planned to be in our Position. We do not allow ourselves to be shocked.

We are comfortable in every sense.

This picture is not the end. We are not stuck.

Rohn Post

Fig. 4.28. Untitled. Photograph by Jim Goldberg. From *Rich and Poor* by Jim Goldberg. Copyright © 1985 by Jim Goldberg. Reprinted by permission of Random House, Inc.

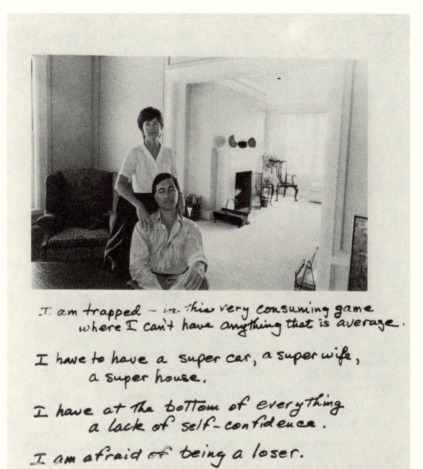

Fig. 4.29. Untitled. Photograph by Jim Goldberg. From *Rich and Poor* by Jim Goldberg. Copyright © 1985 by Jim Goldberg. Reprinted by permission of Random House, Inc.

The Political Rhetoric of Photography

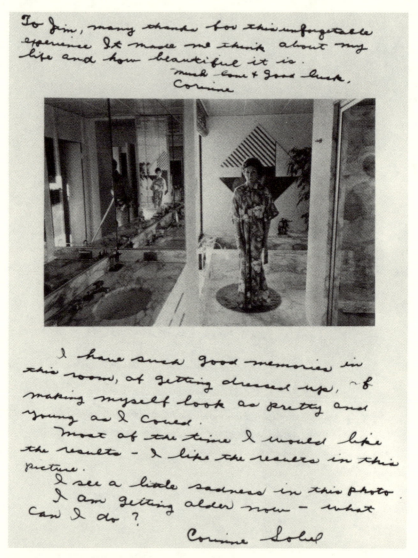

Fig. 4.30. Untitled. Photograph by Jim Goldberg. From *Rich and Poor* by Jim Goldberg. Copyright © 1985 by Jim Goldberg. Reprinted by permission of Random House, Inc.

NOTES

INDEX

NOTES

Preface

1. Gustave Flaubert, *Bouvard and Pécuchet*, trans. A. J. Krailsheimer (Baltimore: Penguin, 1976), p. 129.

2. Ibid.

3. An argument for the ubiquity of representation and the absence of a definitive presence is presented in Jacques Derrida, "Sending: On Representation," trans. Peter and Mary Ann Caws, *Social Research* 49 (1982): 294–326.

1. The Problem of Ideology

1. Peter Brown, *The Making of Late Antiquity* (Cambridge: Harvard University Press, 1978), p. 12.

2. Ibid., p. 13.

3. Michel Foucault, "About the Concept of the 'Dangerous Individual' in 19th Century Legal Psychiatry," *International Journal of Law and Psychiatry* 1 (1978): 3.

4. A. J. Gurevich, *Categories of Medieval Culture*, trans. G. L. Campbell (London: Routledge and Kegan Paul, 1985), p. 295.

5. Ibid., p. 296.

6. Theodor W. Adorno, "Cultural Criticism and Society," in *Prisms*, trans. Samuel and Shierry Weber (Cambridge: MIT Press, 1981), p. 29.

7. Paul de Man, "The Epistemology of Metaphor," in *Language and Politics*, ed. Michael Shapiro (New York: NYU Press, 1984), pp. 193–214.

8. Ibid., p. 204.

9. Sabina Lovibond, *Realism and Imagination in Ethics* (Minneapolis: University of Minnesota Press, 1983), p. 37.

10. For this argument see de Man, "The Epistemology of Metaphor," in *Language and Politics*, p. 214.

11. This point receives extended treatment in Michael J. Shapiro, *Language and Political Understanding* (New Haven: Yale University Press, 1981), chapter 3.

12. Fredric Jameson, *The Political Unconscious* (Ithaca, N.Y.: Cornell University Press, 1981), pp. 59–60.

13. Michel Foucault, *The History of Sexuality*, trans. Robert Hurley (New York: Pantheon, 1978), p. 25.

14. Ibid., p. 48.

15. Michel Foucault, *The Archeology of Knowledge*, trans. A. M. Sheridan Smith (New York: Pantheon, 1972), p. 120.

16. Foucault, *The History of Sexuality*, p. 43.

17. Christian Metz, *Psychoanalysis and Cinema*, trans. Celia Britton, Annwyl Williams, Ben Brewster, and Alfred Guzzetti (London: MacMillan, 1982), p. 11.

18. Ludwig Wittgenstein, *On Certainty*, ed. G. E. M. Anscombe and G. H. von Wright, trans. D. Paul and G. E. M. Anscombe (Oxford: Blackwell, 1969), p. 493.

19. Michael Foucault, "The Order of Discourse," in *Language and Politics*, p. 127.

20. Martin Heidegger, *The Piety of Thinking* (Bloomington: Indiana University Press, 1976), p. 29.

21. Martin Heidegger, *Nietzsche 2: The Eternal Recurrence of the Same*, trans. David Farrell Krell (San Francisco: Harper and Row, 1984), p. 27.

22. This position was first elaborated in Jürgen Habermas, *Knowledge and Human Interests*, trans. Jeremy J. Shapiro (Boston: Beacon, 1971), pp. 301–17.

23. Hans-Georg Gadamer, "On the Scope and Function of Hermeneutical Reflection," in *Philosophical Hermeneutics*, trans. David E. Linge (Berkeley: University of California Press, 1977), pp. 18–43.

24. Clifford Geertz, "Deep Play: Notes on the Balinese Cockfight," in *The Interpretation of Cultures* (New York: Basic Books, 1973), pp. 412–53, and *Negara* (Princeton: Princeton University Press, 1980).

25. Geertz, *Negara*, p. 122.

26. Clifford Geertz, "Blurred Genres: The Refiguration of Social Thought," *The American Scholar* 49 (spring 1980): 165–79.

27. Geertz, *Negara*, p. 13.

28. Ibid., p. 121.

29. Ibid.

30. For an analysis of Geertz's discursive strategy see James Clifford, "On Ethnographic Authority," *Representations*, no. 1 (spring 1983): 118–46.

31. Clifford Geertz, "The Politics of Meaning," in Geertz, *The Interpretation of Cultures*, p. 311.

32. Michel Foucault, "Two Lectures," in *Power/Knowledge*, ed. Colin Gordon, trans. Colin Gordon, Leo Marshall, John Mepham, Kate Soper (New York: Pantheon, 1980), pp. 78–108.

33. Ibid., p. 93.

34. The interplay of archeological and genealogical analyses is explicated by Foucault in his "The Order of Discourse," in *Language and Politics*.

35. Foucault, "Two Lectures," in *Power/Knowledge*, pp. 102 and 133.

36. Foucault, "Two Lectures," in *Power/Knowledge*.

37. Gerald Raulet, "Structuralism and Post-Structuralism: An Interview with Michel Foucault," *Telos* 55 (spring 1983): 202.

38. Benita Parry, *Conrad and Imperialism* (London: MacMillan, 1983), pp. 8–9.

39. Roland Barthes, *Mythologies*, trans. Anette Lavers (New York: Hill and Wang, 1972), p. 129.

40. Ibid., p. 116.

41. Louis Althusser and Etienne Balibar, *Reading "Capital,"* trans. Ben Brewster (London: NLB, 1970), pp. 25–26.

42. Louis Althusser, *For Marx*, trans. Ben Brewster (New York: Pantheon), p. 68.

43. Althusser and Balibar, *Reading "Capital,"* p. 26.

44. Louis Althusser, "Ideology and Ideological State Apparatuses," in *Lenin and Philosophy*, trans. Ben Brewster (New York: Monthly Review Press, 1971), p. 162.

45. Ibid., p. 170.

46. Pierre Bourdieu, *Outline of a Theory of Practice*, trans. Richard Nice (Cambridge: Cambridge University Press, 1977), p. 168.

47. Ibid., p. 170.

48. Martin Seliger, *Ideology and Politics* (New York: Free Press, 1976).

49. Althusser, *For Marx*, pp. 232–35.

50. Adorno, "Cultural Criticism and Society," in *Prisms*, p. 21.

51. Thomas Mann, *Joseph in Egypt* 3, trans. H. T. Lowe-Porter (New York: Alfred A. Knopf, 1938), p. 3. For an analysis of the rhetorical effects of grammar, see Roman Jakobson, "Concluding Statement: Linguistics and Poetics," in *Style in Language*, ed. Thomas Sebeok (Cambridge: MIT Press, 1960), pp. 350–77.

52. On the relationship of narrative to ideology see Jameson, *The Political Unconscious*, and Hayden White, "The Value of Narrativity in the Representation of Reality," *Critical Inquiry* 7 (autumn 1980): 5–28.

53. Joseph Gusfield, *The Culture of Public Problems* (Chicago: University of Chicago Press, 1981).

54. This discussion of dimensions of ideology benefits from the insights of John B. Thompson in his *Studies in the Theory of Ideology* (Berkeley: University of California Press, 1984).

55. *Njal's Saga*, trans. Magnus Magnusson and Hermann Palsson (Baltimore: Penguin, 1960).

56. Jean Baudrillard, "Fetishism and Ideology," in *For a Critique of the Political Economy of the Sign*, trans. Charles Levin (St. Louis: Telos Press, 1981), p. 98.

57. Jameson, *The Political Unconscious*, pp. 53–54.

58. Fredric Jameson, "Class and Allegory in Contemporary Mass Culture: *Dog Day Afternoon* as a Political Film," *College English* 38 (April 1977): 847.

59. Theodore W. Adorno, "On the Fetish-Character in Music and the Regression of Listening," in *The Essential Frankfurt School Reader*, ed. Andrew Arato and Eike Gebhardt (New York: Continuum, 1982), p. 273.

60. Jameson, "Class and Allegory in Contemporary Mass Culture," 854.

61. See Dennis Brailsford, *Sport and Society: Elizabeth to Anne* (London: Routledge and Kegan Paul, 1969), pp. 85–99.

62. Ibid., pp. 101–3.

63. Parry, *Conrad and Imperialism*, p. 1.

64. Ibid., p. 22.

65. Ibid., p. 21.

66. Ibid., p. 22.

67. Ibid.

68. Ibid., p. 38.

69. Ibid.

70. Michel Foucault, *Discipline and Punish: The Birth of the Prison*, trans. Alan Sheridan (New York: Pantheon, 1977), p. 272.

71. D. A. Miller, "The Novel and the Police," *Glyph* 8 (1981): 140.

72. Jay Folberg and Alison Taylor, *Mediation* (San Francisco: Jossey-Bass, 1984), p. 9.

73. Ibid., p. 7.

74. Jean Baudrillard, "The Ideological Genesis of Needs," in *For a Critique of the Political Economy of the Sign*, pp. 63–87.

75. Ibid., p. 67.

76. For a brief discussion of this role of the confessional by Foucault see Raulet, "Structuralism and Post-Structuralism: An Interview with Michel Foucault."

77. This discussion of Wilson's analyses is a slight revision of two earlier analyses. I analyze *The Investigators* (New York: Basic Books, 1978) in my "Literary Production as a Politicizing Practice," in *Language and Politics*, pp. 215–53, and this is repeated along with the addition of the analysis of "Thinking about Crime," in my "The Rhetoric of Social Science: The Political Responsibilities of the Scholar," in *The Rhetoric of the Human Sciences: Language and Argument in Scholarship and Public Affairs*, 2 ed., ed. John Nelson, Allan Megill, and Donald N. McCloskey (Madison: University of Wisconsin Press, 1987), pp. 522–50.

78. Shapiro, "Literary Production as a Politicizing Practice," in *Language and Politics*, p. 246.

79. Foucault, *Discipline and Punish*, p. 272.

80. *The Shorter Oxford English Dictionary on Historical Principles* (Oxford: The Clarendon Press, 1933), s.v. "task."

81. James Q. Wilson, "Thinking about Crime," *Atlantic Monthly*, September 1983, pp. 86–87.

82. Ibid., p. 79.

83. Martin Heidegger, "The Thing," in *Poetry, Language, Thought*, trans. Albert Hofstadter (New York: Harper and Row, 1971), p. 170.

84. See Shapiro, *Language and Political Understanding*, chapter 7.

85. These observations are informed by Alan Garfinkel's discussion in *Forms of Expression* (New Haven: Yale University Press, 1981), p. 85.

86. Wilson, "Thinking about Crime," p. 82.

87. Gillian Beer, *Darwin's Plots* (London: Routledge and Kegan Paul, 1983), p. 53.

88. See Benjamin Lee Whorf's discussion of Hopi grammar, "Time, Space, and Language," in *Culture in Crisis*, ed. Laura Thompson (New York: Russell and Russell, 1973), pp. 152–72.

89. Beer, *Darwin's Place*, p. 57.

90. Ibid., p. 69.

91. Jameson, *The Political Unconscious*, p. 40.

92. Claude Lévi-Strauss, *The Savage Mind* (Chicago: University of Chicago Press, 1966), p. 32.

93. Foucault, *Discipline and Punish*, pp. 293–308.

94. Paul Veyne, *Writing History*, trans. Mina Moore-Rinvolucri (Middletown, Conn.: Wesleyan University Press, 1984), p. 20.

95. Donald Meyer, *The Positive Thinkers* (New York: Pantheon, 1980).

96. Kenneth Burke, *Permanence and Change* (Los Altos, Calif.: Hermes, 1954), p. 74.

97. Ibid., p. 90.

98. Ibid., p. 119.

99. Jameson, "Class and Allegory in Contemporary Mass Culture," 852.
100. Ibid.
101. Foucault, *Discipline and Punish*, pp. 231–56 passim.
102. Misia Landau, "Human Evolution as Narrative," *American Scientist* 72 (May/June 1984): 262–68.

2. Reading Biography

1. Kenneth Burke, *Permanence and Change* (Los Altos, Calif.: Hermes, 1954), pp. 71–79.
2. Malcolm X, *The Autobiography of Malcolm X*, with Alex Haley (New York: Random House, 1964).
3. John William Ward, "Who Was Benjamin Franklin?" *The American Scholar* 32 (autumn 1963): 544.
4. Ibid.
5. Ibid.
6. Benjamin Franklin, *The Autobiography* (New York: Washington Square Press, 1940), p. 13.
7. Ibid., p. 17.
8. Herman Melville, *Israel Potter* (London: Jonathan Cape, 1925).
9. Alexander Keyssar, *Melville's "Israel Potter": Reflections on the American Dream* (Cambridge: Harvard University Press, 1969), p. 1.
10. Melville, *Israel Potter*, p. 92.
11. Alexander Keyssar, *Melville's "Israel Potter": Reflections on the American Dream*, p. 25.
12. For a discussion of the "ideology of sacrifice," see William Connolly, *Appearance and Reality in Politics* (Cambridge: Cambridge University Press, 1981), chapter 3.
13. Sigmund Freud, "Creative Writers and Day-Dreaming," in *Collected Papers* (London: Hogarth Press, 1959), p. 153.
14. Samuel Schoenbaum, *Shakespeare's Lives* (Oxford: Clarendon Press, 1970), p. ix.
15. For an approach that highlights the poststructuralist treatment of displacement see Mark Krupnick, ed., *Displacement: Derrida and After* (Bloomington: Indiana University Press, 1983).
16. Neil Herz, "Freud and the Sandman," in *Textual Strategies*, ed. Josué V. Harari (Ithaca, N.Y.: Cornell University Press, 1979), pp. 296–321.
17. Friedrich Nietzsche, *Ecce Homo*, trans. Anthony M. Ludovici (New York: Russell and Russell, 1964), p. 1.
18. Martin Heidegger, *Nietzsche 2: The Eternal Recurrence of the Same*, trans. David Farrell Krell (San Francisco: Harper and Row, 1984), p. 9.
19. Nietzsche, *Ecce Homo*, p. 5.
20. Harold Garfinkel, "Passing and the Managed Achievement of Sex Status in an 'Intersexed' Person," in *Studies in Ethnomethodology* (Englewood Cliffs, N.J.: Prentice-Hall, 1967), pp. 116–85.

186

Notes to Pages 66–75

21. Quoted in Erich Auerbach, *Mimesis*, trans. William R. Trask (Princeton: Princeton University Press, 1968), p. 9.

22. Ibid., p. 10.

23. Ibid., p. 18.

24. Ibid., p. 8.

25. Ibid., p. 13.

26. Ibid., p. 15.

27. James Clifford, "On Ethnographic Authority," *Representations*, no. 1 (spring 1983): 126–27.

28. Henry Adams, *The Education of Henry Adams* (Boston: Houghton Mifflin, 1961), p. 434.

29. Ibid., p. 483.

30. Huntington Williams, *Rousseau and Romantic Autobiography* (New York: Oxford University Press, 1983), p. 123.

31. See, for example, book 12 in Jean-Jacques Rousseau, *The Confessions*, trans. J. M. Cohen (New York: Penguin, 1953), where he refers to his reaction to an anonymous pamphlet describing him in uncomplimentary ways.

32. Nietzsche, *Ecce Homo*, p. 102.

33. Sigmund Freud, *Leonardo da Vinci: A Study in Psychosexuality*, trans. A. A. Brill (New York: Random House, 1947).

34. Ibid., p. 56.

35. Ibid., pp. 111–12.

36. Ibid., p. 56.

37. Ibid., p. 120.

38. William McKinley Runyan, *Life Histories and Psychobiography* (New York: Oxford University Press, 1982), p. 36.

39. The "at what price" imagery is taken from Michel Foucault's interview: Gerald Raulet, "Structuralism and Post-Structuralism: An Interview with Michel Foucault," *Telos* 55 (spring 1983): 195–211.

40. Runyan, *Life Histories and Psychobiography*, p. 52.

41. For a discussion of how motives should be regarded as typical vocabularies rather than as mental causes of behavior, see C. W. Mills, "Situated Actions and Vocabularies of Motive," *American Sociological Review* 5 (December 1940): 904–13.

42. I elaborate this point in Michael J. Shapiro, "Literary Production as a Politicizing Practice," *Political Theory* 12 (August 1984): 387–422.

43. For a more extended treatment of Handke's writing from a political perspective see Michael J. Shapiro, "Toward a Politicized Subject: Peter Handke and Language," *Boundary* 2, 8 (Winter/Spring, 1985): 393–418.

44. Peter Handke, "Changes during the Course of a Day," in *The Inner World of the Outer World of the Inner World,*" trans. Michael Roloff (New York: Seabury, 1974), pp. 101–7.

45. Louis Althusser, "Ideology and Ideological State Apparatuses," in *Lenin and Philosophy*, trans. Ben Brewster (New York: Monthly Review Press, 1971), p. 170.

46. Ibid., pp. 172–73.

47. Peter Handke, *A Sorrow beyond Dreams* in *Three by Peter Handke*, trans. Michael Roloff (New York: Avon, 1977), pp. 261–62.

48. Ibid., p. 245.

49. Ibid., p. 247.

50. Ibid., p. 286.

51. For a good analysis of this dimension of Handke's writing—his parodic realism—in the context of approaches to realism, see David H. Miles, "Reality and the Two Realisms: Mimesis in Auerbach, Lukács and Handke," *Monatshefte* 61 (winter 1979): 371-78.

52. Doris Kearns, *Lyndon Johnson and the American Dream* (New York: Harper and Row, 1976).

53. Ibid., p. 54.

54. Ibid., p. 421.

55. Ibid., p. 422.

56. This critique of the narrowness of the conventional political discourse is found in Michel Foucault, *The History of Sexuality*, trans. Robert Hurley (New York: Pantheon, 1978).

57. See Roderick P. Hart, "Political Linguistics and Rhetorical Insight: A Macroscopic Tracing" (paper delivered at the annual convention of the International Communication Association, Honolulu, Hawaii, May 1985).

58. See Fredric Jameson, *The Political Unconscious* (Ithaca, N.Y.: Cornell University Press, 1981), p. 79, for a treatment of the ideology of form.

59. Norman Mailer, *The Executioner's Song* (New York: Warner Books, 1979).

60. Michel Foucault, *Discipline and Punish: The Birth of the Prison*, trans. Alan Sheridan (New York: Pantheon, 1977), p. 272.

61. M. M. Bakhtin, "Discourse and the Novel," in *The Dialogic Imagination*, trans. Caryl Emerson and Michael Holquist (Austin: University of Texas Press, 1981), p. 271.

62. Ibid., pp. 271-72.

63. Ibid., pp. 272-73.

64. Ibid., p. 262.

65. See Jean-Paul Sartre, *L'Idiot de la famille*, 3 vols. (Paris: Editions Gallimard, 1971). All quotations, with the exception of one, which is specified, are from the English translation (which covers only part of vol. 1 at this point): *The Family Idiot*, trans. Carol Cosman (Chicago: University of Chicago Press, 1981). And see Michel Foucault, ed., *I, Pierre Riviere, Having Slaughtered My Mother, My Sister, and My Brother . . . : A Case of Parricide in the Nineteenth Century*, trans. Frank Jellinek (New York: Pantheon, 1975), and Michel Foucault, ed., *Herculine Barbin*, trans. Richard McDougall (New York: Pantheon, 1980).

66. Sartre, *The Family Idiot*, p. ix.

67. Jean-Paul Sartre, *Search for a Method*, trans. Hazel E. Barnes (New York: Vintage, 1963).

68. Ibid., p. 61.

69. Ibid., pp. 42-43.

70. Sartre, *L'Idiot de la famille*, p. 783: "Words wreak havoc when they become able to name what had been lived namelessly."

71. Sartre, *The Family Idiot*, p. 439.

72. Sartre, *Search for a Method*, p. 141.

73. Bakhtin, "Discourse in the Novel," in *The Dialogic Imagination*, p. 199.
74. Sartre, *The Family Idiot*, p. 39.
75. Ibid., p. 439.
76. Ibid., p. 70.
77. Ibid., p. 66.
78. Ibid., pp. 24–25.
79. Ibid., p. 30.
80. Foucault, ed., *Herculine Barbin*.
81. Foucault's discussion of normalizing power is well developed in his *Discipline and Punish: The Birth of the Prison;* see *The History of Sexuality* for his treatment of the king-centric or sovereignty-oriented nature of the conventional idea of political discourse.
82. Foucault, ed., *Herculine Barbin*, pp. xi–xii.
83. Ibid.
84. Foucault, ed., *I, Pierre Riviere, Having Slaughtered My Mother, My Sister, and My Brother . . .* , p. viii.
85. Ibid., p. xi.
86. Michel Foucault, "Afterword: The Subject and Power," in *Michel Foucault: Beyond Structuralism and Hermeneutics*, ed. Hubert Dreyfus and Paul Rabinow (Chicago: University of Chicago Press, 1982), p. 216.
87. Foucault, ed., *I, Pierre Riviere, Having Slaughtered My Mother, My Sister, and My Brother . . .* , p. 108.
88. Ibid., pp. xi–xii.

3. The Constitution of the Central American Other

1. Tzvetan Todorov, *The Conquest of America*, trans. Richard Howard (New York: Harper and Row, 1984).
2. *New York Times*, 18 December 1985, p. A–15.
3. This distinction between colonial and class relations is made by Rodolpho Staverhagen, "Classes, Colonialism and Acculturation," in *Masses in Latin America*, ed. Irving Louis Horowitz (New York: Oxford University Press, 1970), pp. 235–88.
4. Kenneth Burke, *The Philosophy of Literary Form* (Berkeley: University of California Press, 1973), p. 26.
5. *London Times*, 19 January 1986, p. 39.
6. Michel Foucault, "Questions on Geography," in *Power/Knowledge*, ed. Colin Gorden, trans. Colin Gorden, Leo Marshall, John Mepham, and Kate Soper (New York: Pantheon, 1980), p. 77.
7. Donald K. Emmerson, " 'Southeast Asia': What's in a Name," *Journal of Southeast Asia Studies* 15 (March 1984): 1–21.
8. Todorov, *The Conquest of America*.
9. Foucault, "Questions on Geography," in *Power/Knowledge*, p. 77.
10. *Time*, 17 December 1984, p. 22.
11. Rosalind Krauss, "Photography's Discursive Spaces: Landscape/View," *Art Journal* 42 (winter 1982): 311–19.
12. Ibid., 311.

13. Ibid.

14. Barry M. Blechman and Stephen S. Kaplan, *Force without War* (Washington, D.C.: Brookings Institution, 1978), p. 4.

15. Ibid., p. 31.

16. Ibid., p. 48.

17. Jacques Lacan, "Agency of the Letter in the Unconscious," in *Ecrits*, trans. Alan Sheridan (New York: W. W. Norton), p. 152.

18. Paul Veyne, "The Inventory of Differences," trans. Elizabeth Kingdom, *Economy and Society* 11 (May 1982): p. 177.

19. Ibid.

20. Michel Foucault, *The History of Sexuality*, trans. Robert Hurley (New York: Pantheon, 1978), pp. 25–37.

21. George Bataille, *Lascaux; or the Birth of Art*, trans. Austryn Wainhouse (Lausanne, Switzerland: Skira, 1955), pp. 125–26.

22. Elaine Scarry, "Injury and the Structure of War," *Representations*, no. 10 (spring 1985): 1–51.

23. Barry Lopez, *Arctic Dreams: Imagination and Desire in a Northern Landscape* (New York: Scribners, 1986), p. 13.

24. Ibid., p. 12.

25. Ibid.

26. Ibid., pp. 137–38.

27. Ibid., p. 201.

28. Bradley S. Klein, "Strategic Discourse and Its Alternatives" (paper delivered at the twenty-seventh annual convention of the International Studies Association, Anaheim, Calif., March 1986).

29. Todorov, *The Conquest of America*, p. 5. By present estimates, during the two hundred years following Columbus's "discovery" of the New World, the Spanish colonizers were responsible, directly or indirectly, for the destruction of 70 million Indians (Todorov, p. 133).

30. Ibid., p. 5.

31. Sedley Mackie, ed., *An Account of the Conquest of Guatemala in 1524 by Pedro Alvarado* (Boston: Milford House, 1972), pp. 53–54.

32. Ibid., p. 60.

33. Ibid., p. 63.

34. Ibid., pp. 125–26.

35. Todorov, *The Conquest of America*, p. 146.

36. Ibid., p. 42.

37. Ibid., p. 147.

38. Ibid., p. 142.

39. Ibid., p. 143.

40. Ibid., p. 168.

41. Ibid.

42. Bartolomé de las Casas, *History of the Indies*, trans. and ed. Andree Collard (New York: Harper and Row, 1971).

43. Kay B. Warren, *The Symbolism of Subordination: Indian Identity in a Guatemalan Town* (Austin: University of Texas Press, 1978), p. 5.

44. Arthur Preston Whitaker, *The United States and the Independence of Latin America, 1800–1830* (Baltimore: Johns Hopkins University Press, 1941).

45. Henry Kissinger, *The Report of the President's Bipartisan Commission on Central America* (New York: Macmillan, 1984).

46. Pierre Bourdieu, *Outline of a Theory of Practice*, trans. Richard Nice (Cambridge: Cambridge University Press, 1977), p. 168.

47. Edmund Gaspar, *United States–Latin America: A Special Relationship?* (Washington, D.C.: American Enterprise Institute, 1978), p. 49.

48. M. M. Bakhtin, "Discourse and the Novel," in *The Dialogical Imagination*, trans. Caryl Emerson and Michael Holquist (Austin: University of Texas Press, 1981), p. 282.

49. Abraham Lowenthal, "Alliance Rhetoric versus Latin American Reality," in *Latin America and the United States in the 1970's*, ed. Richard Gray (Ithaca, Ill.: Peacock, 1979), p. 118.

50. Ibid.

51. For an analysis of the way the Other is denied coeval status by the use of temporal tropes, see Johannes Fabian, *Time and the Other* (New York: Columbia University Press, 1983).

52. Richard Ashley, "The Poverty of Neorealism," *International Organization* 38 (spring 1984): 239.

53. Ronald Reagan speech reported in *The Honolulu Advertiser*, 1 July 1983.

54. Kissinger, *Report*, p. 1.

55. Norman Bryson, *Vision and Painting: The Logic of the Gaze* (New Haven: Yale University Press, 1983), p. 152.

56. Kissinger, *Report*, p. 5.

57. Roberto Fernandez Retamar, "Caliban: Notes towards a Discussion of Culture in Our America," trans. Lynn Garafola, David Arthur McMurray, and Robert Marquez. *Massachusetts Review* 15 (winter–spring 1974): 10.

58. Kissinger, *Report*, p. 9.

59. Edward Said, *Orientalism* (New York: Vintage, 1979), p. 13.

60. Homi Bhabha, "Of Mimicry and Man: The Ambivalence of Colonial Discourse," *October* 28 (spring 1984): 126.

61. Kissinger, *Report*, p. 8.

62. Ibid., p. 4.

63. Abraham Lowenthal, "The United States and Central America: Reflections on the Kissinger Commission Report," in *The Central American Crisis*, ed. Kenneth M. Coleman and George C. Herring (Delaware: Scholarly Resources, Inc., 1985), p. 206.

64. Kissinger, *Report*, p. 24.

65. Ibid., p. 25.

66. Ibid., p. 123.

67. Ibid.

68. Ibid., p. 119.

69. Richard Alan White, *The Morass: United States Intervention in Central America* (New York: Harper and Row, 1984), pp. 104–5.

70. Kissinger, *Report*, p. 35.

71. Anibal Romero, "The Kissinger Report and the Restoration of U.S. Hegemony," *Journal of International Studies* 13 (summer 1984): 117.

72. Ibid.,35–36.

73. Ibid., 123.

74. Kissinger, *Report*, p. 45.

75. Abdul R. JanMohamed, "The Economy of Manichean Allegory: The Function of Racial Difference in Colonialist Literature," *Critical Inquiry* 12 (autumn 1985): 64.

4. The Political Rhetoric of Photography

1. See Diane Arbus's statement quoted in Leslie Fiedler, *Freaks* (New York: Simon and Schuster, 1978), p. 318.

2. Walter Benjamin, "A Short History of Photography," trans. Stanley Mitchell, *Screen* 13 (spring 1972): 7.

3. Ibid., 20.

4. For an extended discussion of this point, see Walter Benjamin, "The Work of Art in the Age of Mechanical Reproduction," in *Illuminations*, ed. Hannah Arendt, trans. H. Zohn (New York: Schocken, 1969), pp. 217–51.

5. Walter Benjamin, "A Short History of Photography," 21.

6. Stuart Hall, "The Determinants of News Photographs," in *The Manufacture of News: Social Problems, Deviance, and the Mass Media,* ed. Stanley Cohen and Jock Youngs (London: Constable, 1973), p. 181.

7. Ibid., p. 189.

8. Ibid.

9. Ibid.

10. Victor Burgin, " 'Looking at Photographs,' " *Tracks* 3 (fall 1977): 139.

11. Allan Sekula, "Dismantling Modernism, Reinventing Documentary (Notes of the Politics of Representation)," *Massachusetts Review* 19 (winter 1978): 860.

12. Ibid., 862.

13. Roland Barthes, *Camera Lucida: Reflections on Photography,* trans. Richard Howard (New York: Hill and Wang, 1981), p. 28.

14. Ibid., p. 38.

15. Allan Trachtenberg, "Albums of War: On Reading Civil War Photographs," *Representations,* no. 9 (winter 1985): 1–32.

16. Ibid., 24.

17. Estelle Jussim, "Icons or Ideology: Stieglitz and Hines," *Massachusetts Review* 19 (winter 1978): 682.

18. Peter Hales, *Silver Cities: The Photography of American Urbanization 1839–1915* (Philadelphia: Temple University Press, 1984), p. 163.

19. Ibid., p. 164.

20. Alan Trachtenberg, *The Incorporation of America* (New York: Hill and Wang, 1982), p. 127.

21. This aspect of Renaissance painting is elaborated in John Berger, *Ways of Seeing* (London: Penguin, 1972).

22. Count Baldesar Castiglione, *The Book of the Courtier,* trans. Leonard Eckstein Opdycke (New York: Horace Liveright, 1901), p. 267.

23. Susan Sontag, *On Photography* (New York: Farrar, Straus and Giroux, 1973), p. 69.

24. The role of the photograph in the expression of family solidarity is discussed in Pierre Bourdieu, *Un Art moyen,* cited in Rosalind Krauss, "Photography and the Simulacral," *October* 31 (winter 1984): 56.

25. Donald English, *Political Uses of Photography in the Third French Republic 1871–1914* (Ann Arbor, Mich.: UMI Research Press, 1984), p. 12.

26. Kenneth Burke, *Permanence & Change* (Los Altos, Calif.: Hermes, 1954), pp. 71–79.

27. Bill Nichols, *Ideology and the Image* (Bloomington: Indiana University Press, 1981), p. 52.

28. Christian Metz, "Photography and Fetish," *October* 34 (fall 1985): 82.

29. Ibid., 81.

30. *Time,* 18 November 1985, p. 87. I am indebted to Professor David Trubek of the Institute for Legal Studies, University of Wisconsin, Madison, for calling the photographic iconography to my attention.

31. "Rarity" is a concept of Michel Foucault developed most elaborately in his *Archeology of Knowledge,* trans. A. M. Sheridan Smith (New York: Pantheon, 1972), pp. 118–25.

32. *Time,* 18 November 1985, p. 87.

33. Ibid.

34. Ibid.

35. Hall, "The Determinants of News Photographs," in *The Manufacture of News,* p. 178.

36. Gisela Freund, *Photography & Society,* trans. David Godine (Boston: David Godine, 1980), p. 143.

37. Ibid., p. 142.

38. This is the general argument in Michel Foucault, *Discipline and Punish: The Birth of the Prison,* trans. Alan Sheridan (New York: Pantheon, 1977).

39. David Green, "Veins of Ressemblance: Photography and Eugenics," *Oxford Art Review* 7 (1985): 9.

40. Havelock Ellis, *The Criminal* (Boston: Longwood, 1977).

41. James Q. Wilson and Richard Hernstein, *Crime and Human Nature* (New York: Simon and Schuster, 1985).

42. Ibid., p. 23.

43. D. A. Miller, "The Novel and the Police," in *Glyph* 8 (1981): 128.

44. Ibid., p. 129.

45. Rosalind Krauss, "Photography in the Service of Surrealism," in *L'Amour fou,* ed. Rosalind Krauss and Jane Livingston (New York: Abbeville, 1985), p. 28.

46. For Dali's description of this method see André Parinaud, *The Unspeakable*

Confessions of Salvador Dali, trans. Harold J. Salemson (New York: Quill, 1981), pp. 140–44.

47. Krauss, "Photography in the Service of Surrealism," in *L'Amour fou,* p. 28.

48. Lee Friedlander, *Factory Valleys* (New York: Callaway, 1982).

49. This is Michel Foucault's expression in *Discipline and Punish.*

50. Permission to reproduce Friedlander's photographs could not be obtained. See his individual portraits in *Factory Valleys* (New York: Callaway, 1982).

51. This way of using the concept of the doxa is from Pierre Bourdieu, *Outline of a Theory of Practice,* trans. Richard Nice (Cambridge: Cambridge University Press, 1977), p. 168.

52. Norman Bryson, *Vision and Painting* (New Haven: Yale University Press, 1983), p. 42.

53. Richard Powell, *Three Farmers on Their Way to a Dance* (New York: Morrow, 1985), p. 42.

54. August Sander, *Men without Masks: Faces of Germany, 1910–1938* (Greenwich, Conn.: New York Graphic Society, 1973).

55. Ian Jeffrey, *Photography: A Concise History* (New York: Oxford University Press, 1981), p. 135.

56. Ibid., p. 137.

57. Sander, *Men without Masks,* introduction, p. 12.

58. Richard Avedon's *In the American West* is now published (New York: Abrams, 1985). My discussion is based on a prepublication subset of his photographic study printed in *Texas Monthly,* September 1985, pp. 148–67. I am grateful to Professor Folke Lindahl of the James Madison College, Michigan State University, for calling the photographs to my attention.

59. Roland Barthes, "The Photographic Message," in *The Responsibility of Forms* (Hill and Wang, 1985), p. 10.

60. This point is made by Alan Trachtenberg in his discussion of the influence of Frederick Jackson Turner in *The Incorporation of America* (New York: Hill and Wang, 1982), pp. 28–29.

61. Ibid., p. 20.

62. This notion of administering silences belongs to Michel Foucault. See especially his *History of Sexuality,* trans. Robert Hurley (New York: Pantheon, 1978).

63. Sekula, "Dismantling Modernism, Reinventing Documentary (Notes on the Politics of Representation)," 867.

64. Jim Goldberg, *Rich and Poor* (New York: Random House, 1986), afterword. I am indebted to a student/friend Jayadeva Uyangoda, who made helpful suggestions for interpreting the Goldberg photographs.

INDEX

Abraham, biography of, 66
Adams, Ansel, 155-56
Adams, Henry, 68, 69, 71
Adorno, Theodor, 25, 27; on fragmenting of totality, 30; on nonideological thinking, 6, 14; operational terms of, 31; on prevailing language, 6; on regression of listening, 30
Agency/agents: of divine power, 3-4; identities/models of, 3-4, 5; knowledge, 18
Allegory, 139
Alliance for Progress, 112, 114, 118
Althusser, Louis: on *Capital*, 22; on misrecognition, 23, 24, 31, 74; on problematic, 22; on science v. ideology, 22, 24; on symptomatic reading, 22-23
Alvarado, Pedro de, 107-8, 110
American Enterprise Institute, 113
Anti-Christ, 63
Arbenz regime, 100, 119, 120
Arbus, Diane, 124-25, 128, 162
Archeological analysis, 18, 28
Arevalo, Marco Vinicio Cereza, 90
Ashley, Richard, 115
Atget, Eugene, 127
Attitude, 29
Attunement, 8, 15
Auerbach, Erich, 66-67
Austin, John, 13
Authority: in biography, 72-73, 79; biography challenges, 79; discourse reinforces, 10, 11; epistemic, 141; in ethnography, 67-68; first-person, 67-68; judgment based on, 13; in language, 48, 73, 117; language challenges, 73, 74-75; mediation recreates, 42; photography challenges, 129; photography reinforces, 137-40, 141; piety reinforces, 136; rationalities derive cogency from, 37; of referent, 26-27; of state, 26-27; text claims, 67; writing reinscribes, 42
Autobiography/autobiographical codes, 65; of Adams, 68, 69; biography

compared to, 60, 61; Foucault publishes, 80, 84-88; of Franklin, 57-58; Freud on all writing as, 60, 61; of Malcolm X, 56; Nietzsche, 63-64, 69; piety in, 57; of Rousseau, 68-69; textualists on, 61
The Autobiography of Malcolm X, 56
Avedon, Richard, 154, 156, 158-62
Aztecs, 92-93

Bakhtin, M. M., 81, 113; on language, 79, 80
Balinese society, 16-17, 26
Barbin, Herculine, 80, 84, 85-86
Barnard, George P., 129
Barthes, Roland, 28, 31; on codes of connotation, 154; on mythical speech, 21-22; on reading photographs, 128
Bataille, George, 102
Baudrilard, Jean, 27-28, 40
Beckett, Samuel, 54
Beer, Gillian, 48, 49
Beliefs, 24, 105-6
Benjamin, Walter, 126-27
Bhabha, Homi, 118-19
Bhopal, India, 95-96, 97
Bible, biography in, 66-67
Biography/biographical codes: authority and power in, 72-73, 79; authority challenged by, 79; autobiography compared to, 60, 61; biblical, 66-67; boundaries of, 60-65; debunked, 58-59; demythologized, 57; depoliticizing in, 76-77; displacement in, 70, 71; epistemological, 80; as ethical/valuational, 65-67, 83; as first-person, 68-69; fixation on heroes of, 70, 71; force metaphor in, 68, 69, 75; Foucault uses, 83, 85, 86; of Franklin, 56, 57, 58-59; Freud's of da Vinci, 69-71; Garfinkel's, 64-65; grammar of, 68-69; Handke's, 73, 74-75; of heroes, 55, 58, 62, 66, 70, 71; of Lyndon Johnson, 75-77, 78; and knowledge of, 67, 68-71; in knowledge texts, 63; misread, 71;

Index

Index

COMPOSED BY B. VADER DESIGN/PRODUCTION, FORT COLLINS, COLORADO
MANUFACTURED BY THOMSON-SHORE, INC., DEXTER, MICHIGAN
TEXT AND DISPLAY LINES ARE SET IN PALATINO

Library of Congress Cataloging-in-Publication Data
Shapiro, Michael J.
The politics of representation.
(Rhetoric of the human sciences)
Includes bibliographical references and index.
1. Communication—Political aspects. 2. Rhetoric.
I. Title. II. Series.
P95.8.S54   1988   303.2   87-40373
ISBN 0-299-11630-1

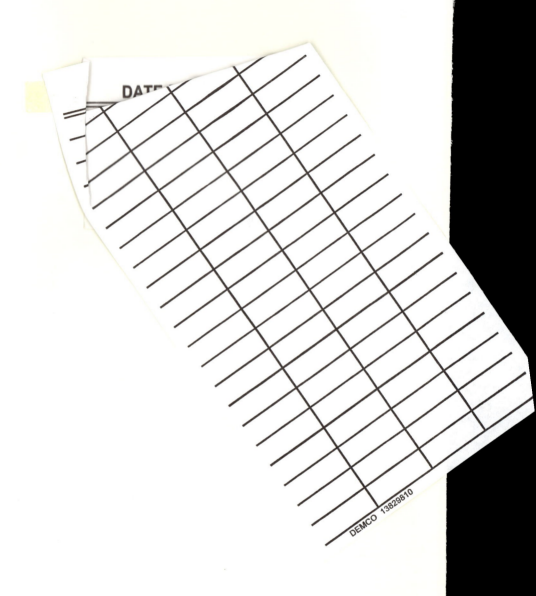

DATE

DEMCO 13829810